Literary culture in c‹

MANCHESTER
UNIVERSITY PRESS

Everyone who can read and write should consider himself a potential author of books. You never know what you can do until you have tried. We should all look upon the writing of books for our own people as a vitally important form of national service, which in fact it is. You will also get some fees ... Remember that we are mainly trying merely to share with our own folks some of the good things that we have received by our education, and to show them how necessary it is that they should read. (Rev. C. G. Baeta, *Hints to Authors of Vernacular Books*)

The presence and circulation of a representation (taught by preachers, educators, and popularizers as the key to socioeconomic advancement) tells us nothing about what it is for its users. (Michel de Certeau, *The Practice of Everyday Life*)

Literary culture in colonial Ghana

'How to play the game of life'

Stephanie Newell

Manchester University Press

Published by Manchester University Press
Oxford Road, Manchester M13 9NR, UK
www.manchesteruniversitypress.co.uk

British Library Cataloguing-in-Publication Data
A catalogue record for this book is available from the British Library

ISBN 0 7190 6273 X *hardback*
       0 7190 6274 8 *paperback*

First published 2002

10 09 08 07 06 05 04 03 02   10 9 8 7 6 5 4 3 2 1

Typeset by
D R Bungay Associates, Burghfield, Bewrks
Printed in Great Britain
by Bell & Bain Ltd, Glasgow

Contents

Tables and plates

Tables

Plates

Acknowledgements

Richard Rathbone kindly and expertly 'chopped' the first draft of this book and spotted several historical inaccuracies: any factual errors that have crept into the final manuscript are my own. Immense gratitude also goes to Karin Barber who commented on an earlier draft: along with other members of the ESRC-funded 'Social Histories of Reading in Africa' research group, she provided constant stimulation on the subject of African readerships.

I am particularly indebted to Stephan Miescher, Misty Bastian, Anita Kern and Paul Richards for their perceptive comments on individual chapters, and to Dee Mortensen at Indiana University Press, who stimulated a necessary reorganisation of the final manuscript. Intellectual input also came from Kari Dako and Lyn Innes, and intriguing stories of early libraries in Ghana from Evelyn Evans.

Librarians provided a great deal of material for this book. In Ghana, archivists at the National Archives in Accra and Cape Coast brought forth a constant stream of relevant documents. In Britain, invaluable assistance came from Sarah Irons at the African Studies Centre in Cambridge, the staff at Rhodes House Library in Oxford, the staff at the British Library in London, and the wonderfully enterprising Terry Barringer who worked for many years at Cambridge University Library. John Pinfold and Sheila Allcock provided much-needed texts, conversation and hospitality in Oxford, as did David and Margareta Kimble in Chagford. Jan Newell was an enthusiastic indexer.

Especial thanks go to Margaret Hawke and Andy Forgan for rescuing me from the sound of fire alarms and drilling during the noisy 'summer shutdown' in Cambridge. Peter Leadbeater's sense of fun and Dorian Addison's humour also helped me through the writing process. The research for this book was made pleasurable by the one and only 'Auntie', Mrs Emily Asiedu, whose home in Accra provided tranquillity, novels, stimulating company and delicious food.

The project was funded by the Smuts Memorial Fund at the University of Cambridge, with additional contributions from Robinson

College, the African Studies Centre and the Judith E. Wilson Fund in Cambridge. Research was made possible by a three-year Smuts Memorial Fellowship at the African Studies Centre and Robinson College, Cambridge.

Permission to republish a version of chapter 1 came from the editor of Interventions: chapter 1 appeared as 'Paracolonial networks: some speculations on local readerships in colonial West Africa', *Interventions*, 3 (3) 2001.

Abbreviations

Introduction: the formation of readerships

What happens *before* the act of reading even starts? Readers need to stand somewhere before they pick up a book and the nature of that 'somewhere' ... significantly influences the ways in which they interpret (and consequently evaluate) texts. (Rabinowitz, *Before Reading*)

In 1935 the Methodist Book Depot launched an essay competition in the Gold Coast,[1] inviting commentaries on the topic, 'My Favourite Book – and Why'. More than two hundred entries were submitted to the Depot and the following gems of literary interpretation emerged: *Alice in Wonderland* is praised in one essay for the way in which Alice 'became obedient when she was reduced to a small strip of a girl';[2] the novel 'provides me with much food for thoughts [*sic*]', the writer continues, for Alice 'was so sarcastic and somewhat self-conceited at the start and so submissive and civil towards the end'.[3] Another essayist praises a book called *Advice to Youngmen* (probably a simplified version of William Cobbett's *Advice to Young Men* of 1830): the reader should consult this book so 'that he may know how to play the game of life'.[4] The Christian *Mothercraft Manual* elicits a powerful response from one young woman: 'For fear of forgetting some good parts in it', she writes, 'I am treating it as my bosom friend.'[5]

These essays contain a unique record of reader responses to the literature that was circulating around colonial West Africa at a particular moment in the mid-1930s, and they raise intriguing questions about the cultural practices, aesthetic values, social formations and institutional contexts which helped to shape African readers' responses to literature in the colonial period. The moral lessons gleaned from books such as *Alice in Wonderland* and *Advice to Youngmen* raise questions about the ways in which literacy was taught in West African mission schools, and the manner in which the colonial classroom forged new subjectivities among readers. How did English literature help to shape elite and non-elite readers' social and economic aspirations in colonial society? Who owned books in colonial Ghana, and which titles held the greatest appeal, at different times, to

different categories of African reader? When it came to interpreting literary texts, how resilient were local oral and rhetorical conventions? When
one develops an interest in locally published West African texts and local
attitudes towards literacy, it is impossible to avoid these questions, which
are centred upon the category of readers.

Literary culture in colonial Ghana delves into 'the nature of that "somewhere"'[6] from which African readers commenced their journey through
books in the period before independence, appropriating the tools of literacy to carve out new cultural and economic spaces for themselves. The
book aims to provide a history of reading culture in Ghana which concen-
trates, in the first five chapters, on the changing nature of the missionary
and colonial classroom in the early twentieth century, attending to the
teaching of literacy, the medium of instruction in schools and alterations
to the literature syllabus, as well as to the responses of African readers to
the reading matter in circulation around colonial schools. Focusing as
much upon local reading practices and attitudes towards literacy as upon
the early creative writers who were active in the Gold Coast between the
turn of the century and the 1940s, *Literary culture in colonial Ghana* opens
a window into a set of African 'literacy practices' which were carefully
appropriated and recrafted from the colonial culture.[7] Constantly relating
texts to their readerships and the social formations within which readers
moved, the book reaches beyond the national borders of what is now
Ghana and explores the literary networks that stretched along the entire
west coast of Africa, discussing the reasons why best-selling Victorian novelists such as Marie Corelli proved to be so popular among elite Creoles in
Freetown and *also* among non-elite, newly educated 'youngmen' in the
Gold Coast, and the reasons why Charles Dickens and John Ruskin were
the favourites of colonial educators and *also* of ambitious, but socially powerless, young African men.

At one level, this is a study of the book as an 'agent of change' and
transformation, but such a concept of literacy cannot be divorced from the
particularities and dynamics of local readerships and the social contexts of
literacy. Colonial literacy must always be situated within the complex
social, economic and political relationships which determined the way in
which it was regarded locally. Following in the footsteps of 'new literacy'
theorists such as Brian Street (1984), my aim in this book is not simply to
assess the 'impact of literacy' in colonial West Africa, although I am keen
to emphasise the significance of books as material objects circulating in the
empirical world.[8] Colonial reading culture cannot, however, be regarded

as an autonomous practice which was thrown like a punch at Ghanaian society, knocking existing interpretive practices out of action. Rather, in the century prior to Ghanaian independence, colonial literacy was dropped like a pebble into a pool of existing literacies and narrative conventions, sending ripples through the multiplicity of reading practices which operated already in local cultures.

African readers carried complex bundles of assumptions into the interpretive process, and yet the voices and values of these locals – whose lives were caught up in the dramatically changing environment of colonial West Africa – have almost disappeared into the thick soup of history. Active several generations ago, these readers ascribed meanings to terms such as 'literacy' and 'literary' which cannot simply be extrapolated from evidence about contemporary readers. *Literary culture in colonial Ghana* explores how the literary networks that grew up alongside colonialism in 'British West Africa' reveal the dynamic way in which local readers appropriated and utilised English-language texts for their own immediate ends, using literature to express their own social and economic aspirations within the rapidly changing and highly charged atmosphere of colonial society.

This is a study of a *vital* reading culture, providing a prehistory of West African literature in the twentieth century. Through books and newspapers, African readers in the colonial period engaged in debates about education, literature and literacy. Focusing upon Ghana in particular, I seek to retrieve some fragments from the past, interweaving textual analyses of local novels and plays with an exploration of the broader educational, cultural and intellectual contexts within which the earliest West African readers operated. Local literary production is investigated alongside the influence of foreign novels, movies and plays. In chapters 1 and 2, Ghanaian literary and debating societies are studied in detail for the first time, and the neologism 'paracolonial' is developed to describe the attitudes, aspirations and activities of non-elite readers who were neither the direct products of British colonialism nor the products of purely pre-colonial formations. Literary and debating clubs were composed of aspirant intellectuals who attended meetings for study and debate, and chapters 1 and 2 explore the issues and ideologies that were articulated through club membership. The majority of club members were unmarried young men, migrants to urban centres who met in order to escape the boredom and loneliness of evenings in a strange place. In the social space opened up by these meetings, young scholars shared ideas with one another. In their discussions of Dickens and Shakespeare, and in their assessments of

European fiction, they actively constituted their own literacy, seeking power from their readings and embedding English literature in local discourses about gender, education, self-help and morality. Chapter 2 suggests that gender is a vital consideration in the assessment of Ghana's literary and social clubs: more than simple networks of urban sociability, clubs were arenas for the negotiation of new masculine identities.

Before opening the first page of a text, African readers had already taken up culturally nuanced positions in relation to the material. Whether it was a vernacular Bible or a 'reduced' English classic, a school primer or a local popular novel, readers modified the material as well as being influenced by it, bringing into the text a great deal of cultural baggage which cannot be abandoned by the wayside if the local significance of literacy is to be assessed accurately. As the epigraph to this chapter makes clear, it is necessary to ask 'What happens *before* the act of reading even starts?'[9] Albeit riddled with difficulties of retrieval, an exploration of the reading contexts and pretexts which underpin early Ghanaian texts will, I hope, bring to light the complex, often competing local concepts that were attached to the word 'literacy' by different interest groups in British West Africa. To enter printed material through reading is to bridge the great divide between print and voice set in place in the 1980s by anthropologists such as Jack Goody (1987) and Walter J. Ong (1982), and upheld in more sophisticated forms by contemporary cultural historians.[10] According to these scholars, what is written becomes somehow 'fixed' and what is oral remains forever 'fluid'.

Literary culture in colonial Ghana postpones such conclusions and studies the impact of readers upon texts, as well as of texts upon readers. Throughout the book, specific reading material is linked to local attitudes towards literacy and to cultural representations of literacy. In so doing, it becomes easier to appreciate that neither oral nor written forms are necessarily *fixed* or *neutral*: readers dislodge texts from their supposed moorings and fill them with vibrant new narratives about themselves and their futures.[11]

Continuing the project to situate literacy, chapters 3, 4, 5 and 6 examine why the Gold Coast vernaculars failed to inspire local authors to write fiction, and the ways in which mission schools helped to shape literary expectations amongst African readers. These chapters explore precisely what the mission-schooled African was able to read and write, particularly during the period of educational reform in the 1920s and 1930s, and the ways in which Christian beliefs and teaching techniques influenced local interpretations of literary texts.

Missionaries and schoolteachers produced enormous quantities of 'good' literature for Africans in the colonial period. Ideas about the African's capacity to be a *good reader* formed the axis around which discussions of 'civilisation', 'progress' and decolonisation rotated, and chapters 3 and 4 chart the social and intellectual effects of these assumptions in West Africa. The common belief was, as one educationist put it, 'Reading is one of the fundamentals of education, and education is the backbone of civilisation... Reading truly maketh a full man.'[12] Attention was focused to a remarkable degree by all parties upon the activities of the newly literate man and, with increasing fervour as the twentieth century progressed, upon his shadowy semi-literate and 'illiterate' brother.

By the 1920s, however, African readers had fully inserted themselves into colonial literacy and asserted their own set of literary values to such an extent that government officials and educationists became increasingly concerned about the circulation of 'immoral' and 'seditious' literature around British West Africa. Chapters 3 and 4 describe the ways in which the colonial administration attempted to counter the influx of 'bad' literature to the Gold Coast. In an effort to consolidate the ideology of indirect rule and instill in young Africans a sense of pride in their 'traditional' heritage, in the late 1920s the government introduced vernacular languages to the first three standards of primary school. The production of printed literature in African languages was, however, stymied for several years by orthographic arguments among educationists, many of whom rejected the new phonetic script for Akan languages. In the midst of this confusion, as chapter 3 reveals, groups of young Africans started to carve out vernacular spaces for themselves, writing and staging local language plays. Such spontaneous vernacular agency among newly literate readers quietly challenged colonial representations of reading and established the foundations for post-colonial drama in Ghanaian languages.

The reading matter in circulation around missionary schools and the emergence of a local print culture between the 1880s and 1940s gave rise to African spaces within colonial, institutional literacies in Ghana: these African spaces invoked and refracted particular European and missionary conceptions of reading, but fell outside the Eurocentric association of reading with the interiority, truth, silence and the private sphere. A new set of associations emerges in colonial Ghana, in which the activity of reading is linked with noise, argument, public debate and the 'ethical' agency of the reader. The public–private dichotomy – one of the most persistent western constructions of the post-enlightenment era – breaks down in this dynamic process: the West African readerships described in this book make up 'reading publics' whose sense of the text is simultaneously personal and social, and whose use of books breaks down any simple image of the solitary private reader or the intensely subjective text. Books in colonial Ghana were regarded by readers as relevant to their personal, domestic lives and *also* as instruments to excite public debates about individual morality. The sense of public and private amongst African readers was not caught in the net of an 'either–or' dichotomy. Rather the public and private combined in a 'both-and' situation, where readers interpreted texts and generated meanings which related both to their own personal lives and also to society at large.

Moving away from the institutional pressures upon Ghanaian readers to the local effects of colonial literacy, the second part of the book discusses the creative writings of 'colonial subjects' and the ways in which the works of local authors resonate with the literacies explored in the first part of the book. These chapters consider the ways in which Ghana's earliest authors deployed their English literacy in order to 'become public', in order to carve out textual territories in which they could rewrite colonial policy and imagine ideal African leaders. What connects these early authors together is the way in which they stretched and pulled English literacy into new shapes to suit Ghana's tradition of active, participatory interpretation of texts. Rather than simply reflecting the region's educational history, early creative writers in Ghana transformed colonial literary values and put them to new uses.

Narratives were central to moral and political debates in colonial West Africa. The chapters on J. E. Casely Hayford and Kobina Sekyi reveal that from the start, elite political activity in the region was saturated with storylines and moral messages, thoroughly mediated by the written word. The *politics* of writing and interpretation will be examined in these chapters, for as Ray Jenkins (1985) argues, Ghanaian intellectual history is characterised by periods of systematic and intense literary activity and periods of relative silence. Highly educated Africans tended to respond to political crises by producing works of history, for they were acutely aware of the need to produce a past capable of carrying the educated elite into power-sharing relationship with the colonialists and chiefs.[13] Additionally, through the use of fictional narratives, Sekyi and Casely Hayford and other members of the coastal elite reworked their 'traditional' heritages, making the past absorb their social and political ideals. Until February 1948, when

government policemen triggered violent mass protests and eventual constitutional reforms in Ghana by shooting at and killing African ex-servicemen during a protest near Christiansborg Castle, the pressure for
decolonisation was characterised by this 'literary activism', carried out
through the local printing presses rather than by physical confrontations
with the colonial authorities.

What emerges from this study is a strong sense that, through the
activity of reading, 'colonised' readers produced distinctive cultural,
meanings for themselves and, in the process, generated a set of specifically West African interpretive practices. Literacy created a meeting point
for readers and genres, where issues and ideals could be explored in the
public space opened up by the book. *Literary culture in colonial Ghana*
concludes with an overview of Ghanaian reading culture in the colonial
period, arguing that people's attitudes towards the function of fiction,
their values and expectations, form a distinctive literary aesthetic: the
readers, writers, club members and debaters appearing in this book indicate the emergence of a coherent set of African aesthetic values in colonial Ghana. Indeed, the colonial government's efforts to eliminate
verbosity and prevent the development of locally styled English seem to
have come up against this solid wall of local standards. Local readers
instilled into the English language local aesthetic principles and assertions of status which outlasted and contested the government's utilitarian attitude towards the teaching of English.

British colonialism did not have a single, unitary impact in West Africa,
and it is risky to generalise about the region's educated elites and their political histories at any stage of colonial development. The incorporation of
Nigeria, Sierra Leone, the Gambia and the Gold Coast into the Empire
occurred at different moments in the imperial understanding of Africa and
generated different colonial formations in each country.[14] Even within individual West African countries, colonialism did not spread across and submerge entire regions like a steadily expanding flood. Rather, as Jean Allman
and Victoria Tashjian argue for Ghana, its influence was 'disaggregated –
episodic and uneven, gendered and generational'.[15] Given the incoherent
character of British colonialism in Ghana, the dominant forces of the period
must be opened up to the intimate and mundane chronologies of birth,
gender, education, marriage and death.[16]

Literary culture in colonial Ghana aims to 'rediscover the ordinary' in
amongst the epic, staging-post events of West African history:[17] it does not
focus exclusively upon the modernising elites of 'British West Africa' and

their different, particular constructions of the past and the future. The book is not a comprehensive cultural history: rather, it focuses upon the neglected, low-rank class of African readers in Ghana, who emerged in force in the 1920s and 1930s and have been variously labelled 'middlemen' and cultural 'intermediaries' by the few scholars to have studied them in detail.[18] Ghanaian literary history is viewed through the prism of this culture-producing group, whose production of a reading culture has been neglected in histories of the region. It is necessary to culturally contextualise terms such as reading and literacy if one wishes to avoid labelling writing as a neutral force and African readers as the passive recipients of texts and concepts controlled from above. The chapters that follow seek to understand the multifarious ways in which literate men and women who hovered on the outskirts of the elite, but were not yet a part of it, interpreted Christian and colonial texts and appropriated metropolitan culture to suit their own particular aims and objectives in colonial society.

Bookshops, bibliophiles and libraries in the Gold Coast

In Bill Ashcroft's recent book, *Postcolonial Transformation* (2001), readers in all areas of the world are described as a 'function' of the text.[19] Other literary theorists also tend to emphasise monolithic categories such as '*the* reader' or '*the* colonial subject', neglecting the material, historical and social dimensions of books and reading in different communities. In an attempt to correct such a bias, the remainder of this introduction chases an elusive paper trail, piecing together the contents of elite, non-elite, private and public libraries before moving on, in subsequent chapters, to develop a full-blown conceptual framework for reading in colonial Ghana.

In the mid-eighteenth century the Reverend Thomas Thompson, from the Society for the Propagation of the Gospel in Foreign Parts, arrived in the Gold Coast: during his short stay on the Coast, he distributed devotional texts, started a school for the people of Cape Coast and sent three young Africans – including the famous Philip Quaque – to London for training.[20] From these humble beginnings grew the educational wings of the missionary movement, powered by the evangelical zeal of European Christians who raised funds for schools, printing presses, literature and personnel for West African missions. Denominational 'book depots' arrived in the region, selling imported devotional literature and printing vernacular translations of the scriptures. The first Ewe grammars and primers were produced in the

1850s at the Bremen Mission, which had operated in the East of the country since 1847. In the late 1870s, after sixty years' activity on the Gold Coast, the Basel Mission set up a Book and Tract Depository at the Christiansborg Middle School, offering books at reduced prices. A small printing press was established at Akropong, and in 1896 the Basel Mission opened a separate Book and Bible Depot in Accra, selling books in English, Ga and Twi.[21] 'It is our aim to bring good Christian literature to the natives on the coast, and to exclude the trade in books not suitable for the minds and hearts of our people', wrote C. Buyers, the first manager of the Mission's Book and Bible Depot.[22] Similarly, after fifty years' educational work on the Gold Coast, in 1882 the Wesleyan Methodist Mission set up its own bookshop and press: its first Fante publication appeared in 1885, and by 1892 annual sales from the Book Depot amounted to £1,000.[23] Perhaps the most significant aspect of missionary endeavour was the introduction of local printing presses through which local authors found an outlet for their writing, including Christian newspapers, vernacular publications, 'how to' pamphlets and, finally, full-length novels and plays.

Table 1 The provision of primary and secondary education, 1901–50

Year	Government and grant-aided institutions	Non-grant-aided institutions	Total number of institutions	Enrolment in grant-aided institutions	Enrolment in non-grant-aided institutions	Total enrolment
1901	135	120	255	12,018	Not avail.	–
1911	160	217	377	18,680	Not avail.	–
1920	218	309	527	28,622	13,717	42,339
1925	236	300	536	32,839	Not avail.	–
1930	344	253	597	42,445	11,696	54,151
1935	389	283	672	45,305	17,170	62,475
1940	472	476	948	62,946	28,101	91,047
1945	503	Not avail.	–	74,183	69,129	143,312
1950	1,621	1,378	2,999	209,303	71,717	281,020

Computed from Gold Coast, *Reports of the Education Department* (Accra: Government Printer, 1901–50); Gold Coast, *Report of the Education Department 1937–1941* (Accra: Government Printer, 1942), pp. 29–30, and A. W. Cardinall, *The Gold Coast 1931* (Accra: Government Printer, 1932), pp. 194–200.

Source: Philip Foster, *Education and Social Change in Ghana* (London: Routledge [1965] 1998: 113)

Christian booksellers and publishers in West Africa were intimately
bound up with economic growth and rising levels of literacy in particular areas. Hence, in considering the rapid increase in enrolments to primary and secondary schools between 1911 and 1920, detailed in Table 1,
the impact of the cocoa boom in southern Ghana cannot be underesti-
mated, for it gave commoners access to unprecedented amounts of dis-
posable wealth, which many families used to educate their children in
local mission schools.

Each mission's bookshop was located in the thick of its own schools
and churches, pulling customers from its pupils and converts (see Plate I).
For many decades until at least the 1890s the missionary book stores dominated the influx of literature to the Gold Coast, supplying biblical and
informational literature alongside 'edifying works of general reading'.[24]
'Our one and only aim', declared L. S. Pickard, the Book Steward of the
Wesleyan Book Depot, 'is to make available to the African unlimited supplies of good literature, social and religious, in English and the vernacular'.[25] The bookshops provided material for the African reading clubs and

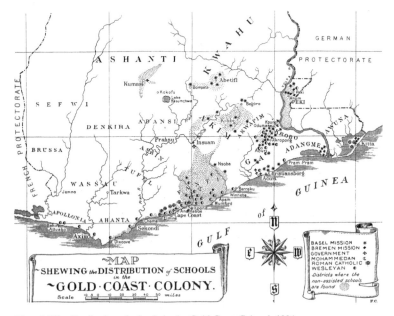

Plate I 'The distribution of schools in the Gold Coast Colony', 1904

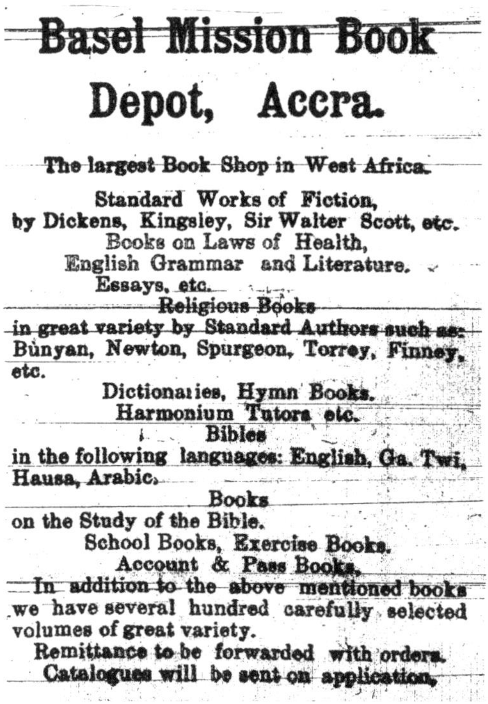

Plate II Advertisement
for the Basel Mission
Book Depot, Accra, 1912

**Basel Mission Book
Depot, Accra.**

The largest Book Shop in West Africa.
Standard Works of Fiction,
by Dickens, Kingsley, Sir Walter Scott, etc.
Books on Laws of Health,
English Grammar and Literature.
Essays, etc.
Religious Books
in great variety by Standard Authors such as
Bunyan, Newton, Spurgeon, Torrey, Finney,
etc.
Dictionaries, Hymn Books.
Harmonium Tutors, etc.
Bibles
in the following languages: English, Ga, Twi,
Hausa, Arabic.
Books
on the Study of the Bible.
School Books, Exercise Books.
Account & Pass Books,
In addition to the above mentioned books
we have several hundred carefully selected
volumes of great variety.
Remittance to be forwarded with orders.
Catalogues will be sent on application,

small private libraries which sprang up in the affluent, urban areas along the southern half of the Gold Coast in the 1870s. Until the colonial government standardised the curriculum in mid-1920s and introduced uniformity to the Standard VII examination, the missions also controlled the school syllabus, hand-picking 'good' reading matter for use in their classrooms and setting their own examination papers.[26]

Missionary bookshops remained the dominant mode of bookselling in the Gold Coast for many years, and they perfected at an early stage the art of mail-order advertising. Constantly keeping up with the times, they sold school textbooks and examination crammers as well as local language pamphlets and translations of the Bible (see Plate II). Reflecting changes in government educational policy, the bookshops also started to stock government publications such as *The Rights and Duties of a Citizen* and *Practical Woodwork Guide for Teachers* after 1925, when citizenship and various crafts and trades were prescribed on the syllabus.[27] Profits from the sales of lucrative lines, such as school textbooks, allowed the booksellers to subsidise religious material for West African readers.

While missionary *booksellers* remained competitive and robust, stocking imported textbooks alongside low-cost devotional material, missionary *publishers* struggled continually to secure readers for the useful, morally upright pamphlets produced on their presses. Many of their publications in the 1910s and 1920s were considered dull. 'I do not remember deriving any very great pleasure from the English reading material presented to us in the primary school' commented Dr Daniel A. Chapman, African headmaster of Achimota School.[28] In addition, after a long period of market dominance, in the 1920s missionary publishers started to experience increased competition from the entry of publishers such as Oxford University Press and Longmans, Green and Co., into the sphere of educational publishing for the colonies: Longmans, for example, produced large numbers of 'simplified' and 'reduced' versions of English novels in the 1920s, designed especially for colonial schoolchildren; and in the 1930s Oxford University Press entered the market with low-cost literature for colonial schools.

While the literate percentage of Ghana's population remained small until the 1950s (see Table 2), the growing attendance at primary schools and consolidation of the education system in the 1920s boosted the popular demand for reading matter, a demand which the missionaries were continually attempting to guide and fulfil.

Table 2
Percentage of population with six or more years of education in 1948

Area	Standard III (i.e. six years of primary education) and above
The Colony	5.80
Northern Territories	0.21
Asante	3.90
Accra district	12.00
Accra town	17.80
Cape Coast district	4.50
Cape Coast town	24.90
Kumasi district	4.70
Kumasi town	0.50

Source: extracted from Foster ([1965] 1998: 119)

Throughout the 1930s, 'graded library lists' were published regularly in the Christian journal, *Books for Africa*; at the same time, missionary booksellers published regular advertisements of 'Good Books to Read' in the African-owned press, promoting such titles as *Hester Ann Rogers (Story of a Persecuted Methodist Saint)*, *The Unitary Faith* and *What it Means to be a Christian*.[29] Missionaries looked on in consternation as improvements in international transport and communications systems in the 1930s made it possible for locally situated readers to obtain an ever-widening array of literature by mail order. While many missionaries were anxious not to see the arrival of 'immoral' books which, they believed, would retard the steady social and moral development of Africa's new readers, foreign publishers benefited from the expanded global market: in increasing numbers, they started to advertise their products in colonial newspapers, drawing upon readerships that had, hitherto, been carefully patrolled by the missionary booksellers (see Plate III).

In addition to increased competition from secular publishers, the Great Depression, which took hold of West Africa at the end of 1930, seriously

Plate III Advertisement for a free book, *The Key to the Development of the Inner Forces*, sent out to the colonies from a depot in Brussels, 1925

THE MAGNETIC GIRL.

How She Compels Others To Obey Her Will.

Simple Method that Anyone Can Use to Develop Hypnotic and Telepathic Powers, To Influence People and Heal Themselves and Others Through Suggestion.

"To Uplift and Benefit Mankind," says Rev James Stanley Wentz.

Wonderful Book Describing Strange Power and a Character Delineation Free to All Who Write.

"The wonderful power of Personal Influence, Magnetism, Fascination, Mind Control, call it what you will, can surely be acquired by everyone no matter how unattractive or unsuccessful," says Mr. Elmer Ellsworth Knowles, author of the new book entitled: "The Key to the Development of the Inner Forces." The book lays bare many astounding facts concerning the practices of the Eastern Yogis, and explains a unique system for the Development of Personal Magnetism, Hypnotic and Telepatic Powers and the curing of disease and habits without drugs.

Miss Josephine Davis, the popular stage favourite whose portrait appears herewith declares that Prof. Knowles' book opens the door to success, health and happiness to every mortal, no matter what his or her position in life.

Josephine Davis.

The book which is being distributed broadcast free of charge, is full of photographic reproductions showing how these unseen forces are being used all over the world, and how thousands upon thousands have developed powers which they little dreamed they possessed. The free distribution of 100,000 copies is being conducted by a large Brussels institution, and a copy will be sent post free to anyone interested.

In addition to supplying the books free, each person who writes at once will also receive a character delineation of from 400 to 500 words as prepared by Prof. Knowles.

If you wish a copy of Prof. Knowles' book and a Character Delineation simply copy the following verse in your own handwriting:

"I want power of mind,
Force and strength is my look,
Please read my character,
And send me your book."

Also send your full name and address, plainly printed (state whether Mr., Mrs., or Miss), and address your letter to:

National Institute of Sciences (Dept. 1057). No 18, rue de Londres, Brussels, Belgium. If you wish you may enclose 6d. (stamps of your own country) to pay postage, etc. Be sure to put sufficient postage on your letter. Postage to Belgium is 2½d.

affected book sales in the Gold Coast. Amid riots and discontent, figures from the Methodist Book Depot offer a stark commentary on the impact of the slump upon literary consumption: in 1929, book sales in the Gold Coast amounted to a grand total of £2,000, but by the end of 1933, the Depot achieved a turnover of only £300.[30] The economic crisis also affected education. 'So important a bearing has this crisis on Education', wrote the Director of Education in his report for 1930–31, 'that it is placed first among the outstanding events of the year.'[31] Under pressure from the missionaries, whose resources were dwindling, the government lowered the minimum salary scales for teachers at this time. Faced with a radical drop in exports and a 50 per cent decline in the value of cocoa between 1926 and 1931, the government also reduced the total expenditure on education, withheld newly qualified teachers from jobs and, between 1931 and 1934, halted recruitment to the teacher-training programme at Achimota. In the 'trough year' of 1931, the country faced a 60 per cent drop in the value of trade, and by 1933 the government had set up an employment bureau to deal with the high numbers of unemployed teachers, clerks and workers retrenched from government offices and trading combines. The education of girls was particularly affected by the Great Depression, as parents withdrew their daughters from school and set them to work in more practical, profitable activities.

The Great Depression, combined with competition from large trading companies and British booksellers in the lucrative textbook market, gave rise to an aggressive advertising campaign by the leading missionary booksellers in a bid to recapture their readerships. In the late 1920s and throughout the 1930s, the Methodist Book Depot placed regular advertisements in the Gold Coast press, declaring 'We can obtain any book for you' and 'orders posted direct to you' (see Plates IV, V, VI and VII). In a single month in 1929, the Depot's adverts for *The Life of Aggrey* led to the sale of a

Plate IV Regular advertisement for the Methodist Book Depot appearing in the *Times of West Africa*, 1932

thousand copies at the stiff price of 7/6d, mostly through mail orders.[32] Pragmatically, the managers of the Book Depot had realised that staying above water in troubled times involved foregoing the loss-making religious material in favour of 'any book' from English and African publishers. Despite this partial compromise of missionary goals, their advertisements were praised in London for securing the market and maintaining sales against all the odds.[33]

Plate V Methodist Book Depot advertisement for *Khama the Conqueror* in the *Times of West Africa*, 1932

The outbreak of war in 1939 and consequent restrictions to shipping adversely affected the metropolitan publishing companies, who were unable easily to export regular supplies of books to West Africa from Britain. This provided a boost to the missionary publishers: as the Achimota College Librarian noted in his report for 1939–40, 'Most of the publications issued during the year were printed for the local Book Depots, who acted as publishers and distributors'.[34] Indeed, business rallied during the war, and by 1950 the Methodist Book Depot could boast a market share of 60 per cent of textbook sales in Ghana and distribution figures of 500,000 for textbooks.[35]

With one or two notable exceptions, few African entrepreneurs engaged in the book trade between the 1880s and 1940s. Prior to 1945 and the period of decolonisation, the main independent, African-owned bookshop in 'British West Africa' was that established by T. J. Sawyerr in Freetown, Sierra Leone. Until the Great Depression stifled this business in the early 1930s, the Sawyerr family provided a mail-order service throughout West Africa, advertising new titles in the Gambia, Nigeria, Sierra Leone and the Gold Coast, selling calendars, almanacks and stationery alongside a range of other wares. Whilst Sawyerr's was not the only example of African enterprise in the book trade, it was probably the only

Plate VI Regular column published by the 'Book Steward', the Methodist Book Depot, Cape Coast, in the *African Morning Post*, 1938

Methodist Book Depots.

NOTE. — This space is occupied every week by an article expressing the principles and opinions of the Depot Organisation.

READING   GOOD BOOKS
By The Book Steward
Even when we reckon up all the bad influence that they may have caused, it is still true that in the struggle of the human race toward better things, books have played a very important part.

When men first learned to put their thoughts down in perma. nent form for other men to read and ponder over a great step forward in human history was taken.

How vast the sum of that great record of men's thoughts, and imaginings, and convictions have grown to be in our day! How splendid in number and quality are the great books of our time! But books are for reading and study, and not merely to be put upon shelves. How great would be our neglect and folly. if we were to let them lie there and miss the help, and uplift, and direction that they might bring to us.

To get the habit of reading good books is indeed to walk along a way of life that has rest, and refreshment and inspiration. The opportunity is given to all through the Depot Organisation. To neglect good books is to re. fuse to enter into a most splendid human heritage.

METHODIST BOOK DEPOTS
ACCRA · SWEDRU · SEKONDI
CAPE COAST · TARKWA · KUMASI

HAVE YOU READ

Dr J. B. Danquah's

New Book on,

"LIBERTY OF THE

SUBJECT" ?

IT takes you behind the scenes in the present co- coa movement, and ana- lyses the psychological motives that moved the farmers in a mass to sa- crifice everything to fight the enemy in their midst.

"The emblem of the Gold Coast", states Dr. Dan- quah, "is the Elephant, and the Elephant never forgets".

A BOOK TO READ TO ENJOY AND TO KEEP.

"LIBERTY OF THE SUBJECT"

Price. 1/-, on by. Post. 1/2

Obtainable from

THE METHODIST BOOK DEPOT,

ACCRA · CAPE COAST & BRANCHES,

and from

DUA & CO, LTD., KNUTS- FORD. AVENUE. ACCRA.

Plate VII Methodist Book Depot advertisement for *Liberty of the Subject* by J. B. Danquah in the *African Morning Post*, 1938

instance of book-selling from a permanent base, for the family occupied
their own premises in Freetown. Other African booksellers peddled their
wares along busy trade routes: in the 1930s and 1940s, Christian booksellers
– probably employed as colporteurs by the various missions – were noticed
plying their publications along the railways in the south,[36] and popular
novelists such as J. Benibengor Blay hawked their secular publications
around offices and schools in the 1940s, seeking out customers rather than
trusting readers to visit their premises.[37]

The key feature of the book trade – missionary, secular, European and
African – in colonial West Africa was that book-selling outlets sprang up
wherever Africans were engaged in literary activities: thus many schools,
offices, churches and newspapers had small booksellers on their premises.
Advertisements appeared in the African-owned press as early as 1863 indicating that newspaper offices in West Africa held stocks of imported 'highly
interesting tales' and low-cost 'self improvement' literature (see Plate VIII).
In the 1880s, while advertising for new recruits, secondary schools such as
the Basel Missionary Society Grammar School at Christiansborg, proudly
announced the existence of their bookshops.[38] In addition, as the twentieth
century progressed, increasing numbers of advertisements appeared in the
West African press for sensational books on sex and marriage. Items such as
this furnish vital clues as to the range of titles that were available by mail
order to literate Africans. Taken together, they provide evidence that,
despite the missionaries' best efforts, by no means all local book purchases
were made through Christian book depots.

Despite the large quantity of scholarly material on the history of education and the rise of literacy in Ghana, few studies describe the precise
titles that were available to African readers in the colonial period. When
browsing the shelves of bookshops, school libraries or private collections
of books, which books would have appealed the most to local readers?
What were the contents of the average intellectual's library? How did the
African intellectual's tastes differ from those of the primary-schooled
'scholar'?[39] Why were certain books preferred at particular times, and
which books displaced them in popularity?

Few literate Africans would have been wealthy enough to purchase substantial libraries of their own, and it is therefore difficult to chart their reading preferences over time. Evidence exists, however, that readers borrowed
books from one another: for example, while researching his historical and
ethnographical books at the turn of the twentieth century, J. E. Casely
Hayford borrowed West African history books from professional gentlemen

in Cape Coast, reading foreign authors such as Brodie Cruickshank and local authors such as J. M. Sarbah to inform his ideas.[40] Similarly, the Reverend Asante of Abetifi purchased any books relating to the Gold Coast, including the *Gold Coast Handbook* (1928) and J. B. Danquah's *Akan Laws and Customs* (1928) through to Noel Smith's *The Presbyterian Church of Ghana, 1835–1960*.[41] These local 'gentlemen's libraries' provided a rich resource for many decades: in 1934, during her tour of Africa, Margaret Wrong noted that 'There are some few men of education and means, notably in West Africa, whose English libraries are equal to or better than many private libraries in Europe'.[42] Meanwhile, in Accra in the 1930s, much to the delight of the numerous literary and debating clubs in town, Bishop Aglionby allowed his parishioners to borrow from his small personal library, and in 1935 he donated £1,000 to the government for the construction of a large lending library in Accra.[43]

While Casely Hayford and his peers probably returned their bookloans, flaws in the informal library system are revealed in 1939 when, annoyed at the non-return of books from his collection, Kobina Sekyi sent out a memorandum pleading for the return of fifteen or so titles, including Sir James Frazer's *The Golden Bough*, Ovid's *Love Poems*, *The Rubaiyat of Omar Khayam*, Voltaire's *Candide and Other Romances*, King James I's *Newes from Scotland*, and Hannay's *Symbolism in Relation to Christianity*.[44] Despite Sekyi's annoyance, perhaps these errant borrowers deserve our thanks, for the titles listed here furnish clues as to the contents of the Gold Coast intellectual's personal library in the late 1930s. It is interesting to note that whereas Casely Hayford and his peers borrowed African-authored works of West African history and ethnology in the late nineteenth century, no such text is listed in Sekyi's memorandum. Rather, he has lent out a miscellany of titles, linked perhaps by their non-English bias but otherwise manifesting the eclectic tastes and wide-ranging interests of their highly educated owner. No hint of Sekyi's ardent cultural nationalism can be deduced from the reading material listed here.

Unlike the fragments reported above, the full details of an intellectual's private collection have been preserved in one extraordinary instance: J. E. K. Aggrey's library of nearly 2,500 volumes was inherited by Achimota College upon his death in 1927, and each title was listed in the *Achimota Library Catalogue* (1935). Aggrey's colleague at Achimota, Charles Kingsley Williams, described the collection as 'very finely bound, and covering a very wide range of subjects, with English literature and society, especially Negro sociology, predominating'.[45] Booker T. Washington and W. E.

B. DuBois were well represented in this latter section. Alongside books on West African history, the history section of Aggrey's library included Carlyle's work on the French Revolution and Gibbon's *Decline and Fall of the Roman Empire*, as well as histories of England, America, Greece and Egypt. In the literature section, we discover that a clear favourite with Aggrey was Honoré Balzac, whose *Comédie humaine* dominates the collection; in addition, he owned nineteen Dickens novels, all of Disraeli's publications, several volumes by Victor Hugo, numerous novels by Thackeray, Shakespeare's complete works and several collections of poetry by Bulwer-Lytton. Clearly, Aggrey's reading preferences were solidly nineteenth-century, European and non-Modernist.

Beyond the highly educated elite with their large personal libraries, a different category of African reader, predominantly male and growing larger with each passing decade, carefully purchased and preserved small collections of books. Asserting their 'modern', educated status, lowly African teachers, clerks and catechists purchased 'western' items for their houses, including gramophones, desks and glass-fronted cases. 'Full of paper, books, notebooks, school books, old magazines and journals', an individual's personal library of anthropological, historical and theological books would be displayed in the glass-fronted case.[46]

A careful eye was kept on these scholars' libraries by the missionary authorities, who were conscious of what the Book Steward at the Methodist Mission described as 'the ever present danger of large firms like the United Africa Company and Syrian firms gaining a monopoly with a great increase in prices. . . but no supplies of general or Christian literature'.[47] Regular articles in the *Gold Coast Teacher's Journal* and *Books for Africa* in the 1930s emphasised the types of novel considered appropriate, especially for the mission-trained teacher. Unsurprisingly, not a single British popular novelist is listed in these booklists. Ideally, the African teacher's library should include several Christian titles, ranging from the Bible to devotional, theological and informational pamphlets. Titles such as the *Arabian Nights* and *The Merchant of Venice*, as well as *Robinson Crusoe*, *Gulliver's Travels* and *King Solomon's Mines* should also be present in the teacher's library, 'all in simplified English'; the teacher should also acquire titles from the 'New Method Readers' series, edited by Michael West, including *Dr Jekyll and Mr Hyde*, *Kidnapped* and *Coral Island*.[48]

This reading matter clearly reflects the official perception of him – the addressee is always male in these articles – as marooned in a remote rural

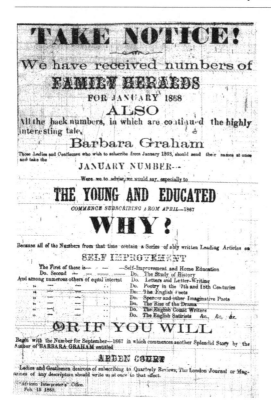

Plate VIII 'Take Notice!' Advertisement for books held at the offices of the *African Interpreter and Advocate*, 1868

school where he will be vulnerable to the morally regressive influence of a 'pagan' community. In addition, the titles on these booklists implicitly alter the reader's masculinity, promoting what Miescher diagnoses as 'a late Victorian ideal of "manliness"', including the qualities of 'robustness, perseverance and stoicism'.[49]

In addition to piecing together the fragments of personal collections, there are several other means by which we can ascertain the changing contents of educated Africans' bookshelves in the colonial period. Firstly, it is clear from the levels of quotation in newspaper articles, letters, editorials and books, that literate West Africans knew certain texts by heart. Chunks of Dickens, the Bible, Shakespeare and Bacon are ubiquitous, quoted regularly in the columns of the press throughout the period, supplemented at different times with references to popular writers such as Marie Corelli or Dale Carnegie. Indeed, the great intellectual and politician, Casely

Hayford, included regular citations from the Bible, Plato and Shakespeare in his work, smoothly incorporating these influential sources into his writing. Chapter 1 expands this theme, tracing the ways in which these local quoters found original uses for the English 'great masters'.

Secondly, perhaps the richest record of changing literary tastes in the Gold Coast is provided by the press. Detailed reports on the activities of literary and debating clubs in the 1870s and 1880s reveal the preferences of educated Africans in this period. Thus, in 1877 a Cape Coast newspaper reveals the beginnings of a literary movement which prevailed in Ghana until the government initiated mass-literacy campaigns after the Second World War. A journalist describes how:

A library is to be procured where young men can meet and lecture and essay and discuss on various subjects ... Let all come forward and help, let all prefer an enlightened mind to a bright coin in an ignorant pocket, and liberally subscribe towards purchasing the necessary books wherein we may peer into subjects that will readily interest and inform at the same time.[50]

Five years later, reports in the *Gold Coast Times* reveal the success of this enterprise, for the Reading Room is now stocked with 'a careful selection of useful works and scientific subjects', and the members are described as 'persons of respectability' and intellectual integrity who would not commit plagiarism or 'literary larceny' in writing their speeches and essays.[51] Sadly, no booklist exists with details of the 'useful' and 'scientific' titles purchased by club members: judging by the soirées and debates held in the club-room, however, it is probable that the library stocked books ranging from Sophocles' *Antigone* to *The Complete Works of Shakespeare* as well as books relating to West African history and culture. These 'literary clubs' became, within fifty years, an influential social movement amongst clerks, schoolteachers, catechists and other white-collar workers in Ghana. Newly educated young men emerged from the primary school system in the 1920s and formed literary and debating clubs, often with libraries of their own in which imported printed literature occupied a central position. As increasing numbers of primary-schooled Africans set up clubs in the 1920s and 1930s, so the literary tastes of Ghana's new readerships are documented in the press of the period.

Thirdly, with the development of school libraries in the 1920s and 1930s, and the rise of public libraries in the 1940s, it becomes possible to study the librarians' reports, booklists and records of loans for evidence of what people borrowed and their changing literary tastes. In 1930, for example, the Librarian of Achimota College noted that a box of fiction had arrived mid-term, 'mostly of the Sherlock Holmes or Sabatini type, and two days later all but one or two of those 34 books had been taken out'.[52] Student demand for particular titles is also reflected in the *Achimota Library Catalogue*, published in 1935: whilst the catalogue fails to record the number of times each book has been borrowed, the popularity of novelists such as Conrad, Kipling, Sabatini, Dickens and Conan Doyle is manifested by the sheer quantity of their titles. According to reports from Achimota School, 1929 and 1930 witnessed a 'marked increase in the number of books taken out from the Fiction section' of the Library;[53] during the early 1930s, boys in the senior forms 'chose works of Thackeray or Kipling. Others preferred writers like Ballantyre, Henty, Marryat, and Talbot Baines Reed.'[54] By 1935, Achimota College Library stocked plentiful supplies of Marie Corelli, Hall Caine and Sabatini alongside Dickens, Thackeray and Scott in its collection of several thousand books, and rapidly increasing numbers of 'book boxes' containing these novels were distributed, without postal charges to the user, from Achimota Library to schools and teachers all over the country.[55] With the Italo–Ethiopian crisis of 1936 and the outbreak of war in 1939, the College Librarian recorded a marked increase in readers of 'the illustrated weekly papers and [the war] made the library more popular than ever'.[56]

This urgent demand for contemporary, easy-to-read fiction and newspapers was not confined to the students of Achimota College. In 1932, the principal of Wesley College in Kumasi registered a change in students' leisure-reading desires from Marie Corelli and Hall Caine to 'Sabatini and Austin Freeman – indeed, any reputable, and perhaps disreputable, detective stories'.[57] Other well-stocked libraries in Ghana prior to 1945 included the collections of the major boys' secondary schools – Adisadel and Mfantsipim schools at Cape Coast, and the Presbyterian Training College at Akropong – and the collection at the elite Rodger Club in Accra, from which European and African readers borrowed works of English literature. As with the boys' secondary schools, however, readers at the Rodger Club were almost exclusively male, a point that will be developed in chapter 2: as 'Marjorie Mensah' pointed out in the *Times of West Africa*, 'although I have made a point to be in the [Rodger Club] Library at least three times a week, I have never met one lady there in quest of a book!'[58]

In Accra in the 1920s, the Gold Coast Education Department had a library for teachers at its headquarters, and within a short space of time, small book deposits were established at each regional office of the Education Department, mostly stocked with titles relating to teaching theory and method. By the mid-1940s, qualified librarians and educationists had started to arrive in the Gold Coast from Britain, holding very different ideas about the value of reading from missionary and colonial educationists. The post-war period brought with it new ideological tensions over African literacy. Whilst the government employed young professionals from Britain to set mass literacy and adult literacy campaigns in motion and to establish a modern library system, complete with branch libraries, children's libraries and mobile libraries, little was done to change the old guard of colonial officials in the Education Department. The resulting tensions are epitomised by the fierce disagreement between the new British Council Librarian in Ghana, Evelyn Evans, and the 'old school' Director of Education, T. Barton. Their exchange of memos between February and May 1946 reveals how the emergence of public libraries and mass education brought new challenges to the colonial Education Department. Insisting that all reading should be reading for pleasure, Evelyn Evans argued that Mr Barton's, 'graded list of books for class libraries would have depressed any children's librarian. They were mainly the retold, supplementary reader type. . . Not a single coloured attractive illustration amongst the lot of them.'[59] Holding firm to his belief that *in Africa* reading should be aimed at the practical and moral development of the child, Barton declared, 'in my opinion expensive schemes should not be embarked upon unless books are very carefully selected according to the interests and ability in reading of the class of individual for which they are provided'.[60] To this end, Barton enclosed a copy of the Department of Education's 'revised graded list of books for class libraries in primary schools' and dismissed Evans's idea for a non-curricular circulating children's library.[61]

Taken together, these various book collections provide a glimpse of the titles that were in circulation, both within and outside the tight limits set by Christian educators in the colonial period. Highly educated men such as Aggrey and Sekyi, as well as primary-school teachers and clerks, obtained books from a wide array of sources. Clearly, there was no lack of reading matter in British West Africa throughout the colonial period. While English literature was crucial to the educated community's assertion of status as a class, this brief history of book-selling and reading reveals that books in English were appropriated with remarkable rapidity by educated Africans in the colonial period. Increasing levels of literacy amongst non-elite groups in the region increased the demand for accessible reading matter on local, relevant subjects and these new readerships used English literature to their own ends.

Notes

1 I have tended to use the colonial label, 'Gold Coast', to describe the southern territory that has become part of modern Ghana. When offering historical or literary overviews of the colonial period, however, 'Ghana' is often used.

2 NAG, CSO 18/1/144: n.pag.

3 *Ibid.*

4 *Ibid.*

5 *Ibid.*

6 Rabinowitz, 1987.

7 The term 'literacy practice' is used by discourse analysts and 'new literacy' theorists to describe the ways in which meaning is made through the activity of reading in different domains. For theorists such as Brian Street (1984) and Gunter Kress (1997), literacy is a set of social practices – or 'events' – which are embedded in culture and power relations, reshaped and transformed by different cultures.

8 The material dimension of books tends to be lost in Street's work: he is so keen to emphasise the multiplicity of literacies in different cultural contexts that the significance of the book as a material object is neglected (see Stock, 1993; Collins, 1995).

9 Rabinowitz, 1987.

10 See Anderson, [1988] 1991; Hastings, 1997.

11 The writings of Ruth Finnegan (1981–82, 1988), Roger Chartier (1995) and new literacy scholars such as Brian Street (1984; 1993), have been helpful in the formulation of this position.

12 *AMP*, 3 November 1937: 2.

13 Jenkins, 1985: 27; see also Gocking, 1999.

14 Young, 1995. I am indebted to Richard Rathbone for this observation.

15 Allman and Tashjian, 2000: 222.

16 *Ibid.*, 223.

17 See Ndebele, 1990/1.

18 See de Moraes Farias and Barber, 1990; Barber, 2000.

19 Ashcroft, 2001: 72.

20 See Bartels, 1965: 4.

21 Smith, 1966: 227; Jenkins, 1985.

22 Cited in Smith, 1966. For a detailed historical account of the Presbyterian Book Depot and Printing Press, see Noel Smith's *The Presbyterian Church of Ghana, 1835–1960: A Younger Church in a Changing Society* (1966); for other extensive studies of mission schools in Ghana, see Foster, [1965] 1998, Bartels, 1965, and Kimble, 1963.

23 SOAS, MMS.257 (box), 1932: 37. In southern Nigeria, the Church Missionary Society, run by Anglicans, dominated education and the book trade in the colonial period, using innovative sales techniques such as 'book lorries' to sustain their profits. However, in the Gold Coast, the major missions and booksellers prior to independence were the Methodist Book Depot and the Presbyterian Book Depot. The presence of these missions on the Gold Coast ensured that the development of education and local creative writing in Ghana followed a different trajectory from that of Nigeria.

24 Smith, 1966: 227.

25 SOAS, MMS.257 (box), 1939: 56.

26 The Education Ordinance and Rules of 1925 prescribed subjects of instruction in Gold Coast primary schools for the first time. The curriculum for infant classes included: vernacular speaking, reading and writing; arithmetic; object lessons and varied occupations; singing; games and physical education; and simple spoken English. Children in standard classes were to be taught: language in the vernacular (Standards I–III); English; lessons on the duties and rights of an African citizen; arithmetic; writing; drawing; nature study; physical exercise; singing; handwork and domestic work (for girls) (see *GCTJ*, May 1928: 5).

27 See Gold Coast Government, 1930–31: 20, 35–9.

28 RHL, MSS.Brit.Emp.s.282, n.d: 5.

29 *GCT*, 4–11 January 1930: 14.

30 SOAS, MMS.257 (box), 1933: 8.

31 Gold Coast Government, 1930–31: 10.

32 SOAS, MMS.257 (box), 1929: 42.

33 *Ibid*.

34 Gold Coast Government, 1939–40: 33.

35 SOAS, MMS.257 (box), 1950: 4.

36 See Smith, 1966: 229.

37 See Newell, 2000.

38 See *GCT*, 25 August 1883: 4.

39 For definitions of the 'Gold Coast scholar', see chapter 1.

40 Jenkins, 1985; Gocking, 1999.

41 Miescher, 2000.

42 Wrong, 1934: 9; see also Jenkins, 1985.

43 Evans, 1956: 10. In the same period, the Carnegie Corporation of New York sponsored a survey by Margaret Wrong, which recommended the appointment of a qualified librarian to the Gold Coast. The arrival of Ethel Fegan led to the foundation of the Library Training School at Achimota College and the rapid development of the Library Service in the country (*ibid.*, 11).

44 NAG(CC), ACC.383/64, 23 September 1938.

45 RHL, MSS.Brit.Emp.s2282 (box 3/5), 5 October 1927.

46 Miescher, 2000; 2001*a*.

47 SOAS, MMS.257 (box), 1950: 4.

48 Anon., 1935: 43.

49 Miescher, 2001*a*. It would be deceptive to employ gender-neutral nouns to
   describe literacy and reading in British West Africa in the first half of the century, for education and authorship were male-dominated spheres. As late as
   1948, the census for Ghana showed that three times more boys than girls were
   enrolled in primary schools; this ratio widened to 4:1 in the secondary school
   sector (Rimmer, 1992: 35).
50 *GCT*, 5 December 1877: 2.
51 *GCT*, 16 September 1882: 2.
52 NAG, RG 3/1/15: 31.
53 RHL, MSS.Brit.Emp.s.282: n.pag.
54 *Ibid.*
55 The *Report on Achimota College* for 1927–28 records an increase in membership of the circulating library from 78 in 1926 to 248 in 1928. Similarly, the
   numbers of books sent out increased from 136 in 1925 to 368 in the first quarter of 1928 (Gold Coast Government, 1927–28: 12).
56 Gold Coast Government, 1939–40: 5. Roger Gocking notes a circulation figure
   of 10,000 daily for the *African Morning Post* during the height of the Ethiopian
   crisis in 1936 (1999: 10).
57 Cited in Wrong, 1934: 27.
58 *TWA*, 30 March 1933: 2.
59 Evans, n.d.: 3.
60 Confidential Memo Ref. 4276/34, 9 May 1946: 2.
61 *Ibid.*, 4.

1 'Paracolonial' networks: the rise of literary and debating societies in colonial Ghana

Since the Gold Coast is merely a conventional term for a portion of western Africa which belongs to the British Crown, and has no definite boundaries save arbitrary ones of European agreement, it is therefore impossible to confine oneself to works dealing exclusively with that portion of the world which we know as the Gold Coast. (Cardinall, *A Gold Coast Library*)

A major new area in post-colonial theory is the examination of 'globalisation' processes in different communities around the world. Led by Arjun Appadurai and James Clifford, cultural theory has shifted away from analyses of the impact of colonialism, towards macrocultural studies of complex global power relationships. The focus of interest is upon the ways in which local populations appropriate, succumb to, manage, regenerate or resist the cultural and economic influences which enter their communities from diverse international and 'translocal' sources.[1] These theorists have recognised the limitations of teleological and syncretic models of cultural transmission whereby the western, 'first world' centre is seen to discharge its cultural products to be received, more or less passively, by audiences in 'third world' locations. Rather, locally rooted people are seen to be on the move, entering the 'elsewhere' opened up by global electronic media, imagining themselves and their futures by refashioning goods and ideas brought in by these cultural flows, criss-crossing and interacting with one another in ways that defy the conventional definitions of culture as bounded by language, ethnicity and location.[2] As Appadurai argues, this 'elsewhere' is now a constitutive part of the social project of being local: 'If the genealogy of cultural forms is about their circulation across regions, the history of these forms is about their ongoing domestication into local practice'.[3] In consequence, he argues, 'there is still ample room for the deep study of specific geographies, histories and languages'.[4]

The categories that appear in Clifford's and Appadurai's work can be found in various combinations, with different degrees of emphasis, in a great deal of contemporary post-colonial theory: for some writers, the

emphasis is upon the complex global identifications and gender-negotia-
tions entered into by the migrant or the exile;[5] for others, the real hero of
the piece is the cosmopolitan, often an intellectual, who exhibits 'a willingness to engage with the Other' in a culturally competent manner.[6] The
marginalised Other throughout this discourse is the local who is not the
exile, nor the migrant, nor the tourist, nor the cosmopolitan. This is the
character with the fewest lines to speak in contemporary theory, who
cannot speak at all according to some scholars, who cannot begin to enter
the cultural flows. Many theorists have left these 'locals' stranded on reefs
of social and artistic solitude, picking out the odd Coke bottle from the
global culture which swells around them. Yet I hope to show that back in
the 1920s and 1930s, similar kinds of cultural flow to those specified by the
globalisation theorists were in operation, albeit without the shifting
'scapes' produced by high-speed satellite technologies. It is important,
therefore, to emphasise the diverse local uses to which even the most iconic
of international objects can be put, for in so doing we can retrieve and
begin to re-emphasise historical innovations that have been neglected or
negated in a great deal of contemporary theory.

   At each moment and in each particular location, global dynamics have
a history – globalisation has a 'prehistory'[7] – encompassing centuries of
trade relations, missionary activities, money relations, imperial ideologies
and judicial processes. In this chapter I seek to further historicise the concept of global cultural flows, to explore the 'prehistory' of globalisation
and to theorise the active role played by 'locals' in the cultural networks
that grew up alongside British colonialism in West Africa. The term 'local'
is used in this chapter to signify a rather different figure from the post-
colonial theorists' construction, for in colonial West Africa the literate
'local' was thoroughly situated in a dense network of historically condi-
tioned contexts, and was a lively participant in the business of reading.
Locals occupied culturally nuanced positions in relation to the most
canonical English texts; they developed their own aesthetic rules for the
reception of printed literature, launched themselves into printed debates
and, in the process, inserted themselves into the public sphere as a new
literati.

   While it is necessary to acknowledge the violence of the colonial
encounter, this chapter does not presume the primacy of a metropolitan
centre. In order to understand the complex local negotiations involved in
the formation of literary culture in Ghana, cultural transmission in colonial West Africa will be discussed from a *non*-colonial standpoint. In terms

of culture – literary culture in particular – the 'local' mentality has been the saving grace for many people in West Africa. Since the formal imposition of British colonial rule in the late nineteenth century, the 'local' perspective has given rise to innovative reinterpretations and reuses of what might otherwise have been hegemonic western art forms. The so-called 'colonised' generated their own specific modes of reading through which they could construct subtle, strategic commentaries about their own and others' access to money, power and patronage: through this reading culture, which often revolved around texts borrowed from the English literary canon, local people could reflect upon moral concepts such as wealth, social status and success.[8]

Focusing upon the Gold Coast in particular, this chapter retrieves a particularly intriguing group of readers from the colonial period of West African history, and traces the different ways in which they appropriated anglophone literature – especially literature from the colonial school syllabus – and redeployed it to make statements about their own social authority and modernity. The neologism 'paracolonial' will be introduced to describe these cultural processes which took place alongside and beyond the logic of British culture and colonialism. Often labelled 'mimics', this group of readers consisted of newly educated but otherwise non-status-holding youths, mostly young men, who banded together in the southern 'anglophone' belt of the region and, with increasing frequency as the twentieth century progressed, formed their own 'literary and social clubs' in order to debate moral issues and 'study the higher problems with the aid of good books'.[9] In so doing they were emulating (in the double sense of rivalling and also imitating) similar literary societies set up by the African professional elites who returned to West Africa from Britain in the 1870s and 1880s, having gained their qualifications abroad. From 1880 onwards, in Freetown, Lagos, Cape Coast, Sekondi and Accra, these literary and social clubs appeared, hosting formal debates and soirées to which educated locals would be invited.

Several theorists have presumed that there was little geographical mobility in colonial societies and that, in consequence, cultural flows within the colonies were confined to closed village networks or to bilateral exchanges controlled by the metropolis.[10] Additionally, in regions with low literacy rates, some scholars have argued that the sole channel for cultural transmission was oral, face-to-face encounters, and that the spread of particular narratives was limited by the mobility of local culture-brokers.[11] The conclusion is that colonial populations were largely cut off from world culture, with villagers in the interior glimpsing at most the occasional local newspaper or missionary pamphlet. From this two-culture standpoint, the traditional can easily be distinguished from the modern, as can the periphery from the centre, and the 'mimic' or 'Black Englishman' can be described with reference to the colonial culture.

These models of cultural transmission cannot easily be superimposed onto social formations in colonial West Africa for the simple reason that local populations had been highly mobile and commercially interactive with one another for many generations before the consolidation of British rule in the region. From the earliest days of bilateral trade and cultural contact with Europe, slave dealers, educated elites, merchant princes, middlemen, Muslim traders, pedlars and commodity traders were on the move by sea and land, particularly along the coastal belt of West Africa, but also between the coastal and inland towns in the region and between the inland towns and countries to the north. At each stop, they would have been involved in establishing and consolidating their own multi-layered relationships and networks and, as John Collins and Paul Richards (1982) have shown, they developed particular art forms which were a central part of these interpersonal exchanges. In the 1920s and 1930s, for example, musical genres such as *highlife* and *jùjú* grew up throughout the coastal zone ruled over by the British, incorporating a wide range of anglophone and vernacular references stretching from North American jazz to Ghanaian concert parties.[12] With great confidence local producers of popular culture in colonial Africa appropriated and revised foreign genres and performance styles, incorporating quotations from Hollywood movies into their discourse alongside pithy sayings from the Bible and Shakespeare.[13]

Collins and Richards provide excellent guidance for a re-examination of cross-cultural flows in colonial West Africa. The centre–periphery model which has only recently ceased to dominate post-colonial studies is ruptured by their insistence upon the incorporativeness of West Coast trading cultures. Rather than suggesting that European cultures were *grafted* onto residual and weak traditional forms, they write that 'it is the long-established characteristic of a trade-dominated social formation constantly to absorb "new" and "alien" cultural influences'.[14] The colonial state did not radically transform pre-colonial trade routes or flows of culture: colonialism represented not a complete usurpation of existing relationships, but a 'coup' staged upon established and emergent cultural and economic networks.[15] By situating British colonialism in relation to a string of regional economic power-relationships, these scholars therefore manage to historicise and localise the concept of cultural flows without resorting to blandly neutral statements about syncretism or global 'influences'.

Such a localisation of the global is particularly relevant to the literary and debating societies initiated by young male school-leavers throughout the coastal zone of Ghana in the 1920s and 1930s. Rather than bidding 'farewell to any more study, farewell for ever to any further mental culture', as African commentators complained of mimics and dandies in the 1870s,[16] the increasing numbers of male school-leavers to emerge in the 1920s and 1930s believed that 'Learning, like gold, has its intrinsic value, but if it is not polished, it certainly loses a great deal of its lustre'.[17] In the effort to establish their visibility as a social group, to polish their manners and to improve upon their educational standards, they elected executive committees from like-minded members and published schedules of lectures and debates in the African press; setting subscription rates that educated people in the white-collar sector would be able to afford, they embarked upon ambitious programmes of educational self-help.

The distinctive social groups which participated in club activities earned a variety of unflattering labels from members of the white community, ranging from Brodie Cruickshank's 'mimic' of the period 1850 to 1900 to the new, more unsettling 'scholar' class which emerged with the rapid expansion of primary education in the 1920s and 1930s. This latter group, comprising what P. Foster terms 'the lesser products of the schools',[18] aroused a great deal of ambivalence amongst European commentators. In 1928, for example, Raymond Buell wrote of the new class of West African: 'The educated African should be given clearly to understand that the future political development of the country will come through the medium of African institutions and not through misfitted European formulae.'[19] Allister Macmillan (1928) voiced similar sentiments in his account of the 'scholar', writing as the British administration intensified its long struggle to eliminate local opposition to Indirect Rule:

The 'Coast Scholar' is generally a man under 40 years of age, who has not been sufficiently educated to be able to appreciate the merit of his own natural system of education and government. He is, therefore, dissatisfied not only with those in authority over him, whom he often does not respect, but also with those who would lead him gently towards a better system of self-government under his natural leaders.[20]

Almost without exception, European commentators at the time pointed their fingers at this self-conscious group of educated, anglophone Africans who, in different ways, with great ostentation and solemnity, were asserting 'English' forms of culture throughout 'British West Africa'.[21]

The earliest literary clubs in Ghana were started by the politically active Cape Coast elite in the 1870s, and members included early nationalist politicians such as J. E. Casely Hayford and J. P. Brown, who seem to have been among the original members of the Cape Coast Reading Room, an earnest enterprise set up in 1882, involving the establishment of a library and debating club for the intellectual and moral improvement of educated youths in the town.[22] A second example is the Ladies' Mutual Club of Cape Coast, established in 1904, which had as its object 'the acquisition of accomplishments considered feminine in Europe, to which end an early rule was laid down to the effect that any members who went out in the native dress should be fined'.[23] Alongside literary discussions and public speeches, representatives of the former club insisted that 'extensive opportunities must be allowed for political debate'.[24] By contrast, the non-elite clubs started by 'scholars' in the 1920s and 1930s studiously and explicitly avoided party politics. With increasing vehemence club members insisted upon their political neutrality in the 1920s and so-called 'stormy 30s', asserting and defending their social space against the anti-colonial nationalist activity around them. Most literary clubs were outspoken in their view that 'insubordination to the Government is forbidden, and members have given a restful goodbye to all questions about the inclusion of politics'.[25] While the better-educated politicians and journalists mounted campaigns in the African press, demanding representation and constitutional change, members of the literary clubs used the same publications to describe how they took

great care in the admission of youngmen whose minds are bent on politics. Any infusion of such members will eventually cause the collapse of the club. We have many instances on record where decent societies and clubs have been ruined through unwarranted introduction and unwholesome discussion of politics.[26]

Club members seem to be preserving the unity of their associations by avoiding politics: perhaps this was the only option available to non-status-holding youths from a diversity of locations and occupations, who nevertheless felt inspired to act together publicly. They avoided challenging existing power groups, be they colonialist or African, preferring to focus their attention on academic and cultural activities. In this way, they united

in an ivory tower from which they gained cohesion as a group, and authority as intellectuals.

The African-owned newspapers in the Gold Coast contain rich details
about the activities of these clubs, to such an extent that through the press
one can map the rising aspirations of the educated West African 'scholar',
a social group which grew numerically in the 1920s and spread inland from
the coast, setting up new clubs and branches of coastal clubs in the expanding commercial centres (see Table 3).

Table 3 Literary and social clubs and other voluntary associations in the
Gold Coast, 1831–1950s

Town	Name of association	Date of formation
Accra	Youngmen's Free and Mutual Improvement Society	1873
	Social Union	c.1890
	Youngmen's Free and Mutual Improvement Society II	1896
	Social and Literary Club	1897
	Rodger Club	1905
	Gold Coast National Research Association	1910
	The Young People's Literary Club	1923
	Youngmen's Literary Club	1927
	Old Students' Union – Accra Training College	1929
	Optimist Literary Club	1932
	The Nationalist Literary Society/Study Circle	1935
	The Accra Royalist Society	1935
	The Reformers' Club (Christiansborg)	1935
	Teshie Teachers' Literary Club	1937
	Self-Improvement Literary Club	1938
	Moonlit Literary and Social Club	1938
	The Youths Literary Club	1938
	The Youths Progressive Literary and Social Club	1938
	Old Boys' Association, Mfantsipim	c.1940
	Old Boys' Association, Adisadel	c.1940
	Old Boys' Association, St. Augustine's	c.1940
	Old Achimotan Association	c.1940
Axim	Nzima Literature Society	1932
	Axim Literary and Social Club	1933
Cape Coast	William de Graft's Society for Promoting Christian Knowledge	1831
	J. P. Brown's Private Literary Club	1859

	Party of Gentlemen's Literary Club	1881
	Gold Coast Union Association	1881
	Mfantsi Amanbuhu Fekuw	
	(Fanti National Political Society)	1889
	Three Wise Men Society	1895
	Young Ladies' Christian Association	1897
	City Club	1897
	Gold Coast National Research Association	1915
	Gold Coast Youngmen's Christian Association	1919
	The Cape Coast Literary and Social Club	1919
	The Eureka Club	1921
Koforidua	Koforidua Literary and Social Club	1929
	Youngsters' Literary Circle	1938
Kumasi	Asante Kotoko Society	1916
and Asante	Optimism Club	1929
–	Literary and Social Unity Club	1930
	Bekwai Literary Society	1930
	Kumasi Eureka Club	1932
	Literary and Social Unity Club	1937
	Old Achimotan Association	1940
	Asante Youth Association	1947
	Effiduasi Youth Association	1948
	Offinso Unity Club	1948
	Nsuta Scholars' Union	1949
	Bekwai Youth Movement	1949
	Nkoranza Literary Club	1949
	Mo Scholars' Union	1949
	Bekwai Improvement Society	1950
	Bekwai Literary and Social Club	1950
Mangoase	Mangoase Literary and Social Club	1938
Peki	Peki Improvement and Protection Society	1938
Saltpond	Debating Club	1886
	Study Circle of Youth (Three Wise Men Society)	1895
	Saltpond Youngmen's Progress League	1918
	Literary and Social Club	1933
Sekondi	The Ladies' Mutual Club	1904
Takoradi	The Optimism Club	1915
	Gold Coast National Research Association	1916
	The Catholic Youngmen's Literary Club	1920
	Central Literary Club	1923
	Literary and Social Club	1924

	Cosmo Literary Club	1930
	Railway Club (Literary Section)	1930
	Ga Young People's Literary Club	1932
	The Literary Circle	1937
Tamale	Tamale African Club	1938
	Tamale Youngmen's Educational Association	1947
	Progressive Society	1948
Wineba	Debating Club	1886
	Central Literary Club	1923

Source: extracted from Hagan, (1968: 305–9)

Clubs grew up wherever there was an urban development or an industrial enterprise requiring clerical workers. One club, the Enthusiastic Literary and Social Club, was established in the large Ghanaian mining centre of Aboso; another organisation, the New Tafo Literary and Social Club, arose as a result of the setting up in 1937 of the Central Cocoa Research Station for West Africa, which led to an influx of Ghanaian employees.[27]

In August 1998 I interviewed one of the founding members of the New Tafo Club, Mr Henry Ofori, who said that the club was established 'to relieve the tedium of that rural place, where you would be coming home to nothing at the end of the day'. Members of the New Tafo club were 'mainly junior staff of the Research Station, and this was the pattern you found everywhere in Ghana'. In this interview, Ofori gives a fascinating, detailed account of the club, revealing the means through which members sought recognition as intellectuals. 'We had two clubs', he states:

First of all, there was the literary and social club and then there was the inner club, the Shakespeare Club, mainly formed by old students of Achimota School who were working in the place. The patron was a West Indian who'd come and settled in Ghana and grown rich with commerce: he had a house and family unlike us, the unmarried ones. We would choose a Shakespeare play and read through the parts in its entirety.

The other club was larger, embracing anybody who could read and write. Two or three of us were very keen Charles Dickens fans. Sometimes we would discuss a religious book. Once or twice we had a priest talk about God and Christ and everything. We asked questions, for example, Heaven: what is it like? If so many souls go to Heaven, isn't it overcrowded by now? I remember a man who believed strongly that the Second World War was the mark of the Armageddon. He was a cobbler in town – he wasn't a member of the club because he was not educated. But he was making so much noise in the church so we asked him to come and give a talk at the club.

Newspapers had columns devoted to our clubs. You were supposed to be civilised in those days if you talked literature. In other words, your horizons extended beyond the confines of your country. The people who joined literary and social clubs wanted to continue their literary education.

A distinctive assertion of status was taking place on the part of this educated class, as they acted 'civilised', 'talked literature' and sent details to the press of their eloquent debates about religion and the English classics, performed in English in the club-room.

The centrality of literary texts to their debates and lectures is revealed in this 'syllabus of work', published by the Sekondi Literary and Social Club in September 1929:

Sept 21: 'Dramatisation of the Scene of Agincourt'
Nov 18: 'Short quotations from the best English Authors with vivid explanations'
Nov 25: 'Discussion on: Who would you rather be: Martin Chuzzlewit the Master, or Mark Tapley the Servant?'[28]

In their discussions of Shakespeare, Dickens, Bacon, Ruskin, Eliot, and other authors plucked from the school literature syllabus, club members were not cowed by the difficulty or canonical status of their selected texts. In addition, it looks as if their discussions were not confined simply to the *literary* merits of authors. Rather, club members assessed the moral qualities of fictional characters such as Martin Chuzzlewit: they debated texts in terms of local ethical dilemmas, applied characters to the communities outside the club-room and even, on occasion, proposed social reforms which derived from their discussions. One active club member, Kate Riby-Williams, told me that in the 1940s, 'we discussed *Anne Hathaway* and *Wuthering Heights*, *Hiawatha*, *Treasure Island*, *The Prisoner of Zenda*, *Pilgrim's Progress*, *Animal Farm*, etc. One member would retell the story and then those who had read it would ask questions. They would add or subtract from the story and then we would all interpret its moral together.'[29] Similarly, during my interview with Henry Ofori, he mentioned that members of his literary club met once a month and chose a literary text. 'I read most of Charles Dickens', he said:

We narrated the stories to each other. We summarised the plots and
discussed the main points of the story. The idea was you wanted to talk
about the moral of the thing. Was it relevant to you? We read about
Scrooge, in *The Christmas Carol*. We discussed how some people were
mean, especially at Christmas time. We talked about Oliver Twist too,
and how he was treated and how many children suffered the same fate
in our own houses. We had a disliking for people who amassed wealth
and didn't want to spend it or share it. That was a theme of ours.

Important information about club members' attitudes towards literacy
and their perception of the uses of reading are revealed in these ethical
interpretations of English literary texts. Such a smooth transition from
English literature to West African society – from Oliver Twist to the Gold
Coast household – starkly reveals the manner in which the British 'great
masters' were appropriated through the act of reading and assimilated into
local settings. Far more than successful 'borrowers', these local readers
were demonstrating their cultural sophistication and fluent knowledge of
English literature *in combination with* and *with reference to* local values,
reusing the forms to suit their own purposes.

In one remarkable instance of Dickens-inspired creativity, a club
member – none other than Henry Ofori – produced a short comic play on
the subject of literary and debating societies. Written for the Ghana
Broadcasting Corporation in 1958, *The Literary Society* satirises the pomposity and pettiness of club members in 'a little town in the interior of the
country'.[30] Bureaucratic and hierarchical, the fictional club resembles the
worst popular stereotype of clubs in the Gold Coast.[31] The lecturers are
hilariously ignorant, assuming that the Chinese and Japanese write upside-
down script and that the Chinese 'make aeroplanes out of bamboo sticks';[32]
also, constant and hilarious bickering breaks out between club members,
culminating in a slapstick struggle between a self-important scholar and
his barely literate antagonist.

While Gold Coast clubs are clearly the target of this comedy, an unmis-
takable whiff of Charles Dickens lingers around *The Literary Society*.
Ofori's seventeen-page play reads like an act of homage to *The Pickwick
Papers*: his lively caricatures echo the opening scene of Dickens' novel,
where members of the Pickwick Club express their 'feelings of unmingled
satisfaction, and unqualified approval [for] the paper communicated by
Samuel Pickwick, Esq., G.C.M.P.C., entitled "Speculations on the Source
of the Hampstead Ponds, with some Observations on the Theory of
Tittlebats"'(see Plate IX).[33] The lecturer talks balderdash and squabbling

ruins the 'academic' atmosphere in *The Literary Society* to the same degree as in *The Pickwick Papers*, and an ironic narrator comments in both cases on the 'satisfactory and intelligible point[s]' made in the chaotic club meetings.[34] Thus, in a gesture of extraordinary circularity, Ofori employs the model provided by the New Tafo Club's favourite novelist to caricature and deride the club itself, using Dickens to highlight the faults of this most local of Ghanaian institutions.

These multi-layered connections between clubs, 'scholars' and creative writing in the Gold Coast are revealed by the fact that many of the country's earliest popular novelists were also members of literary clubs. For example, J. Benibengor Blay – described by many as the 'grandfather' of Ghanaian popular fiction[35] – joined the literary club at Aboso mines. In his autobiographical novel, *Coconut Boy* (1970), Blay describes how club 'debates centred around African intellectuals such as Dr Aggrey, Mensah Sarbah, Atto Ahumah [*sic*] and S. R. Wood'.[36] Blay's creative flame was 'kindled' by the books he read at the club, and he started to compose journalistic pieces in the late 1930s, shortly followed by political booklets and love stories which were printed at a local newspaper press.[37] Another club member, who went on to become a popular Ghanaian author, surfaces in a report on the 'Altruism Literary Club' published in the *Times of West Africa* in December 1934.[38] Speaking at a ceremony for a fellow club member who had achieved the remarkable feat of gaining an honours degree, 'Mr J. E. Edu (critic)' quotes a poem and hails the graduate's success in 'removing the stigma on the much maligned African'.[39] In the 1950s, J. E. Edu published a number of novellas and pro–Nkrumah political pamphlets for distribution to local readerships (see Plate X).

Several other new popular novelists of the 1950s were club members in the 1930s: J. Abedi-Boafo, author of one of the earliest popular novellas, *And Only Mothers Know* ([1938] 1946), is described in the *African Morning Post* as the 'Vice-President and Founder of Koforidua Study Circle';[40] and the immensely successful author and publishing entrepreneur, Gilbert A. Sam, who founded the 'Gilisam' press in the early 1950s, can be found at a Christmas dinner party in 1939 giving 'a short, but impressive opening address' as club secretary of the Cherry Ocaa Literary and Social Club.[41] After dinner, club members and their guests danced 'merrily to the music of a gramophone' until 3.35am.[42] Literary and debating clubs thus helped to produce the country's first non-elite authors, offering an intellectual space in which young men could air their ideas and put pen to paper in a closed, receptive environment.

Plate IX Seymour's
illustration 'Mr Pickwick
Addresses the Club',
from Charles Dickens,
*The Posthumous Papers of
the Pickwick Club*, 1837

Mr. Pickwick Addresses the Club.

Decades of mission schooling and contact with Europeans had generated an English-speaking element, concentrated in coastal West Africa,
whose values, social identifications and aspirations were intricately intertwined with those of other local power groups. These 'scholars' looked on
as non-status-holding Africans in the modern, salaried sector of the economy accumulated personal wealth in sufficient amounts to be able to reenter established systems of authority, making 'social investments' which
assured them of prestige and power amongst their kin.[43] As the century
progressed, increasing numbers of literary fraternities were initiated by
these educated Africans, many of whom possessed (or desired) private
property and personal wealth but had little power within the customary
state.[44] Whereas the nineteenth-century fraternities comprised members
of the coastal elite, by the 1920s and 1930s, clubs were dominated by the
relatively weak and dependent social class of clerks and teachers who, in
an effort to establish their visibility and legitimacy as a social group,
appealed for patronage among the local elites, involving African professionals, elders and chiefs in the activities of their clubs, as well as merchants, clergymen and even the occasional colonial administrator.

In order to understand how much more than plain 'replication' was involved in these cultural activities, it is necessary to situate the clubs in relation to the complex ideological conditions that prevailed at the time. Despite decades of school examination questions with titles such as, 'Give in your own words, Kingsley's description of the Armada',[45] 'Write an essay on the character of Silas Marner', 'Which writer [do] you prefer: George Eliot or Sir Walter Scott?', and 'Give in your own words the characters of Salt and Lovel as described by Lamb',[46] and despite entire library shelves of western commentary about the intellectual, moral and physical inferiority of the Negro, young scholars in British West Africa remained robust in the uses to which their English literacy was put throughout the colonial period. 'We are highly impressed by the insatiable avidity on the part of the literary clubs for intellectual enlightenment', wrote the editor of the *African Morning Post* in 1937, expressing particular pleasure to see 'the youthful element of the educated community... hand down to posterity the present-day culture and all that tends to sublimate human nature'.[47] The full text of particularly informative or eloquent lectures would be published in the newspapers, illustrating the manner in which one African readership, composed of club members, exported their debates for continuation amongst the wider newspaper-reading publics in Ghana. Summaries of lectures and debates were published in the local newspapers, and congratulations would be heaped upon particularly persuasive speakers.

It was not that club members had an essential, authentic African culture which preconditioned their responses to colonial texts; nor did they simply set out unconditionally to assimilate the imported cultural models in a show of deference to the British master-culture. Rather, throughout the colonial period, young men in West Africa – and clubs were an exclusively masculine preserve – worked hard to perfect their English literary accomplishments in order to assert their autonomy from existing power elites such as chiefs and elders. Young men set up clubs and societies at this time in which they demonstrated their collective commitment to intellectual pursuits and worked on their fluency in English, holding debates and discussions of literary classics, rehearsing their public speaking skills in the face of a colonial state which became increasingly unyielding to their demands for job promotions and political representation.

As the century progressed, club members were increasingly drawn from the geographically mobile groups of low-ranking civil servants, and also included merchants' clerks and mining clerks, catechists, cocoa-brokers, primary-school teachers, and other members of the 'white-collar'

Plate X Illustration by 'Roddy', from J. E. Edu's *How Dr Kwame Nkrumah Conquered Colonialism*, 1954

An inspired reader of that powerful booklet.

workforce, few of whom possessed the capital to trade or travel to Europe for professional training. Commenting on the Young People's Literary Club in Accra, W. E. F. Ward notes that 'none of its members (except for the one or two who were teachers) had received anything more than a primary education. They were mostly clerks in government or commercial offices; there was one bus driver and a bus conductor, and one or two men who worked in the office of one or other of the Accra chiefs.'[48]

The promotion of education was the primary objective of most organisations: 'We strive to arouse interest in education', declared one Ghanaian literary club in 1930, emphasising the membership's objective to 'help ourselves by studying good things more and more, and in so doing we shall be equipping ourselves for the future. Yes, if we study hard to know the real meaning of every matter, we will soon find that it has opened to us a new world.'[49] As the repetition of the word 'study' reveals, prospective members would have had to demonstrate that they were sufficiently *literary* to

participate in club activities. The criterion for club membership, as published in the press, was that candidates had to have obtained a full primary
education and, preferably, at least one or two years' secondary schooling.
This stipulation would have excluded large numbers of primary-schooled
men and the majority of women who left school after Standard III, but it
would have included men from diverse backgrounds and regions who
identified themselves as 'literary aspirants' and potential members of the
intelligentsia. As Ofori comments, club members 'formed the basis of the
colonial civil service and commerce – they were the educated elite of the
times, primary educated, fairly well literate and better educated than
most'.[50]

In reporting on club activities, the local newspapers provide rare
insights into the activities of this elusive, highly mobile group. None of the
white-collar occupations listed above would have carried the social status
or financial rewards possessed by members of the African professional
elite. However, what club members *did* share with the elite was literacy in
English, and what their clubs expressed was the increasing confidence of
the so-called 'scholar'. The clubs offered a positive, collective identity for
aspirant intellectuals who had not yet entered the elite, but who had
achieved the rare distinction of gaining a nominal education and entering
the salaried workforce.

Paracolonial networks

Club members belonged to precisely the class dismissed by the authorities
for being 'semi-educated', 'driven by ambition, a desire to imitate the
white man, and [possessing] an education which has fitted them only for
"literary" enterprise'.[51] The majority of teachers and missionaries failed
to recognise the autonomous 'literary enterprise' taking place outside the
formal school system, initiated by locals who were anything but simple
imitators of the white man.

It would be misleading to regard Ghanaian literary and social clubs as
if they were simply offshoots of the European presence in West Africa,
offering windows into local imitations of western cultural values. The history of clubs in British West Africa is multi-layered and complex, probably stretching back far beyond recorded memory and certainly existing
well before the colonial bureaucracy was consolidated in the region.[52]
When one examines the cultural activities of the individuals engaged in
this apparent 'replication' of European models, it becomes clear that far

more is at issue than a strategic mimicry of western culture designed to bolster trading relationships with monopolistic European firms.[53] The different types of West African club and society contain rich seams of information about the ways in which locals were interpreting and utilising 'western' education, English literacy, mission Christianity and colonial power structures for their own ends.

Whilst it is essential to avoid situating *all* local cultural phenomena in relation to a colonial source, serious consideration must be given to the personal and collective desires and aspirations that members of clubs would have expressed through their decision to wear three-piece 'Liverpool suits' in tropical West Africa, to ask colonial officials for patronage, to speak English in public and to debate the English literary classics. Embedded in choices of this kind are powerful, ongoing commentaries about changing conceptions of wealth and social status in the local community.

British colonialism occupied existing cultural and trade routes and adjusted to local pidgins and vernaculars, but the emergence of *new* West African zones in the late nineteenth century indicates the extent to which new relationships at a local level were facilitated by, if not actually generated by, the colonial presence in the region. Christian, commercial, political, musical, literary, educational, linguistic and other media networks were opened up as a result of British rule. The English language is a particularly important factor in the emergence of these new networks, being the medium of government, education (until the mid-1920s) and mercantile trade, as well as the medium of anti- and non-colonial communications between British West Africa and the United States, the West Indies and other West African countries. Without the new anglophone connections open up by the British Empire between London and territories in British West Africa, it is unlikely that newspapers such as the *Lagos Weekly Record* would have had access to journals such as *West Africa*, the *Gold Coast Leader* and *African World*, from which it culled articles on race emancipation and colonialism; nor, perhaps, would the editor of the *Gold Coast Nation* have been able to 'thank the *Nigerian Chronicle*, the plucky weekly of our friend Mr Chris Johnson of Shitta Street, Lagos, Southern Nigeria, for exchanging [articles and news] with the *Nation*'.[54] It is unlikely, too, that J. E. Casely Hayford would have been able to presume political continuity between territories and initiate the National Congress of British West Africa (NCBWA) in 1920, or to open his presidential addresses with pan-Africanist salutations such as, 'Fellow citizens of British West Africa. Greetings. The time has come for us, as a people, to take up our educational burdens.'[55] Many of these new regional affiliations were made possible by a shared language and shared political concerns. English literacy in the colonies thus opened up potentially subversive, anti-colonial networks: as African-initiated enterprises, these affiliations existed alongside and also beyond the reach of the British colonial state.[56]

The neologism 'paracolonial' aptly describes the new social relationships and cultural forms which developed in response to the British presence and the spread of the English language in West Africa. The prefix *para*-contains an ambiguity which is ideal for describing cultural flows in colonial West Africa, for it signifies *beside* and also *beyond*. The shift to paracolonial allows us to discard the centre–periphery model and instead to analyse in historical and sociological detail the local cultural productivity which undoubtedly took place over the generations, *alongside* and *beyond* the British presence in the region, as a consequence of the British presence but not as its direct product. The term is thus immensely useful if one wishes simultaneously to acknowledge the effects of colonialism and also to displace the Eurocentric and deterministic periodisation of culture and history in the colonies as being 'pre'-colonial, colonial and 'post'-colonial.

West African literary and social clubs exemplify these 'paracolonial' flows of culture, for in membership, organisation, subject matter, dress codes and language choice, they were facilitated by the British colonial presence, and yet in all of these areas they created meanings which were not anchored to meanings generated in the metropolis. Rather than adopting the master's voice, many educated West Africans were engaged in an enterprise to gain prestige in local (rather than imperial) systems from which they were often excluded as non-status-holding commoners. They actively and directly produced their own coastal cultures using as raw material English literature, the English language and fashion-styles imported from Britain.

Culturally specific notions of success, wealth and education could be conveyed through debates and lectures on topics as 'British' as 'What is a Lady and What is a Gentleman?'[57] and 'Which is the More Beneficial, Reading or Observation?'[58] English literacy was the thread upon which each club was strung, and this shared feature generated continuity between the different groups. Club activities reveal the extent to which local readers could form themselves into literate constituencies and gain public power as a direct result of their reading activities. Clubs were both literary *and* social: in appellation and activities, they demonstrated the manner in which readers could socialise and indigenise the most foreign discourse, gleaning wisdom from it which would assist in their efforts to 'civilise' the locality.

The great race activist and intellectual Edward W. Blyden exemplifies this process of appropriation when, in a lecture to the Youngmen's Literary Association of Sierra Leone in May 1893, he simultaneously refers to and recreates Francis Bacon's oft-quoted maxim, 'knowledge itself is power'. 'Mere knowledge of itself is not power', he informs club members.[59] Rather, what empowers the individual is 'the ability to know how to use that knowledge; and this ability belongs only to the mind that is disciplined, *trained, formed*'.[60] In deploying the Bacon maxim, Blyden demonstrates his command of English literary culture, but in adapting and disagreeing with the quotation, he is reorientating it to suit his Africa-centred pedagogy.[61] In the remainder of the lecture, Blyden develops his ideals for African education, continuing to emphasise the importance of applying and reusing knowledge rather than passively consuming foreign texts. The educated young African must, he tells his audience, make facts 'productive for the benefit of other minds'.[62] The manner in which Blyden reuses the 'knowledge–power' maxim perfectly illustrates the educational process he advocates.

'All the agencies at work – philanthropic, political and commercial – are tending to fashion us after the one pattern which Europe holds out', Blyden warns: 'All the books and periodicals we read, all the pictures we see beguile us. Everything says to us, "Efface yourselves". It is difficult to resist these influences.'[63] Despite these sentiments, both Blyden and the local 'youngmen' he addresses appear to be buying into a hegemonic, one-way flow of culture from the metropolitan country. Consistently in his speeches and published writings, Blyden fills his English language with quotations from an European literary heritage, and somewhat surprisingly, the syllabus of work suggested by the eminent lecturer for the Youngmen's Literary Association includes the detailed study of Shakespeare, Milton, Tennyson and Wordsworth.[64]

Such appropriations of English literature should be regarded as examples of the productive power of the 'local' mentality. Rather than abandoning 'home' as a site of subjectivity, Blyden advocates that readers adopt a distinctive, home-based position towards English literature, reading the poets for heroic images of *Africans* and seeking positive role models for themselves in biographical literature. In particular, racist representations of Africans should be ignored if readers wish to 'retain race integrity and race individuality'.[65] Operating at a local level which is many removes from Westminster, readers should select material from 'English' culture which is relevant to themselves. If they follow Blyden's suggestions, African readers will self-consciously direct their readings towards new ends, for he advises them to read with sincerity, with a purpose, and to seek personal truths in literature. This advice is hardly unique to Blyden or specific to his Sierra Leonean audience: in the Gold Coast between the 1880s and 1940s literary clubs hosted regular debates of the English classics, extracting useful local knowledge from the pages of texts by Shakespeare or Dickens.

Taken together, the activities of West African clubs reveal a fascinating and subtle interpretive process, for theirs is a 'local' appropriation of colonial culture *par excellence*, reorientating the imported materials to suit members' own assertions of authority.

The nationalist awakening and Ghanaian literary clubs

The inter-war and immediate post-war years marked a time of immense social and political change in the Gold Coast. The gradualist policies of the colonial government gave way under intense internal and international pressure for decolonisation. 'The atmosphere changed after the war. The end of the war was also the end of our literary club', revealed Henry Ofori, member of the New Tafo Literary Society in the mid-1940s.[66] In his view, 'the clubs broke down because the impression was gained by the expatriate colonial masters that such groups constituted a sense of insurrection and all the young people were not up to much good'.[67] Never far away from officials' minds, the 'Gold Coast scholar' had surfaced once again in colonial consciousness as a force for political destruction rather than for literary activity.

Ofori's interpretation of the highly charged political climate in the Gold Coast after the Second World War is echoed, with a rather different ideological bias, by colonial officials stationed in the country. 'We noted great changes', wrote Jessie Griffith, the wife of a medical officer at Achimota, upon returning to the Gold Coast in 1945: 'The peaceful happy natives we had found in 1930 were showing signs of discontent. The old tribal ways were being strained and the young men became hot-heads at times pushing for Self Rule, Self Government and their own way', causing 'disturbances and disorder' on the streets.[68] Expressing a similar, typically British resistance to decolonisation in Africa, the educationist Lionel Greaves remembers returning to the Gold Coast in 1947 after a ten-year period in East Africa: the first thing he noticed was 'racial discord, which had seemed to me alien to the Gold Coast. . . No one who left the Gold Coast before the war and returned there late in 1947 could fail to be struck

by the chilling change of atmosphere' caused by anti-colonial nationalists.[69] To these commentators, the peaceful era of literary and debating
societies was over, displaced by a new and 'chilling' American-influenced
Black radicalism among 'scholars': and much of the post-colonial West
African literature that was published for international readerships in the
1950s and 1960s reflected this radicalism.

Upholding the colonial officials' theme if not their tone, one of the
country's leading nationalists, J. B. Danquah, admitted in a wistful letter
to a follower in 1947, 'I feel rather ashamed to think of it that under the
recent administration clubism [*sic*] has been such a dismal failure both in
Accra and Sekondi'.[70] Celebrating primary-educated youths' penchant for
literary and social fraternities in the past, he continued, 'I feel strongly that
there is wanting to-day in our national life a strong living and vital cen-
trifugal force around which our national life should revolve'.[71]

As the pace of decolonisation quickened in the early 1950s, newspaper
editors in Ghana started to lament the decline of the self-help ethos that
had been so prominent in previous decades. 'It is indeed strange that one
hears practically nothing about literary clubs these days', commented the
editor of the *Spectator*: 'About three decades ago they sprang up all over
the country like mushrooms. Today they are a rarity. . . This is much to be
deplored.'[72] 'In recent years, owing, perhaps, to the political agitation that
has overwhelmed the country, literary life has received a serious setback',
complained the editor of the *African Morning Post* a year later, expressing
the commonly held assumption that literature and politics were, like
Church and State, never to overlap with one another. He wished that literary and debating clubs would be jump-started back into life: 'now that
the end of our political struggle appears to be in sight, the youth especially
are strongly advised to revert their attention to things intellectual' and to
re-establish their societies.[73]

Given these editors' laments and Danquah's nostalgia for the ethos of
'clubism', it is perhaps ironic that the clubs' abatement as a social force
seems to be related directly to the rise of international and nationwide
youth movements such as the Youth League and the Gold Coast Youth
Conference, of which Danquah himself was the General Secretary in the
1930s and 1940s.[74] The Youth Conference petitioned Ghana's diverse literary clubs for affiliation and, in the process, pulled down the fragile,
small-scale structures they had erected for themselves. Thus in December
1937, an announcement appeared for a general meeting of the Youth
Conference at the Rodger Club, to be attended by the representatives of

'all clubs and associations, city and provincial' with the aim of achieving
'unity and progress for the country'.[75] Danquah's movement aimed at
achieving unity with chiefs on the Provincial Councils and working with
the professional elite in the Aborigines' Rights Protection Society (ARPS),
as well as absorbing local literates and 'all clubs, societies, associations, city
and provincial' into a mass movement which would prepare the country
for decolonisation.[76] 'The Youth Conference like the rain came to give life
to the existing institutions', Danquah declared in his speech to the
Conference at Cape Coast in 1938: his phraseology implies that the existing clubs and associations – the intellectual soil in Ghana – were arid until
that moment.[77] Such 'rain' in this critical era was thoroughly political, for
amongst other things, Danquah used the Conference to educate Ghanaians
about the need to prevent a depletion of the country's capital on imported
foodstuffs and commodities, and about the appalling employment and
living conditions in the European-owned mines around the country.[78]

The new populist parties of the 1940s transformed people's use of
leisure time and the manner in which organisations such as the Youth
Conference assimilated the clubs took much of the initiative away from a
section of the population which had only ever established itself as an aspirant or emergent social group, lacking the power and credentials to go
national as a 'class'. As the country moved towards full-scale general elec-
tions and independence, literary and social clubs dwindled into insignifi-
cance, becoming once again the preserve of the professional elite as they
had been in the nineteenth century. Sensing this process but unable to stop
it by 1953, the editor of the *Spectator* bewailed the lack of clubs and complained, 'The intellectual light of the country is growing dim'.[79]

Released from the relatively tight controls exercised over their literacy
by Christian educationists and colonial officials, literate Africans chose to
participate in other – perhaps more exciting – cultural events in the 1940s.
Highlife dances, 'concert parties' and Hollywood blockbusters probably
held far more attraction than the reading of texts by Dickens, Scott,
Thackeray and Shakespeare. Whilst this cultural change might be viewed,
in the manner of Danquah and the newspaper editors, as an irreparable
intellectual loss to the swelling ranks of literate, economically active
Ghanaians, it might also be viewed as a comment on cultural and political
transformations in the country after the Second World War. Cultural flows
in Ghana had been steadily internationalised after the war; as a result, the
'literary gent' with his three-piece suit, love of English literature and
enthusiasm for the formal debating environment, seems to have become an

increasingly anachronistic figure to young educated people, irrelevant to their conceptions of what constituted a 'modern' lifestyle.

Additionally, in the 1950s People's Educational Associations (PEAs), adult literacy units, the Extramural Department at the University College and the Department of Education took over on a mass, national scale, the localised 'self-help' activities of the literary and social clubs.[80] In consequence, 'literary' knowledge lost some of its power after the war, for the ability to read and write no longer demarcated a small social group who cold assert their status through their textual proficiency as readers of English literature. Finally, the literary and social clubs lost their mouthpieces in the mid-1950s, when many of the local newspapers which they had used to publish their reports and programmes of activities closed down, or were taken over by high-tech and foreign enterprises that reserved press-space for national and international stories.[81]

The culture of 'clubism' continued in one quarter, however, for striking similarities can be found between the themes chosen for club debates and the content of Ghanaian novels produced in the 1940s for local readerships. This connection is hardly surprising, given that *all* of the authors discussed in this book – elite and non-elite alike – were actively involved in literary and debating societies, either as prestigious invited speakers, such as J. E. Casely Hayford and Kobina Sekyi, or as regular members of clubs. Numerous non-elite novelists graduated from Gold Coast clubs. Through their reading and writing activities in the 1920s, 1930s and 1940s, the clubs become involved in aspects of 'culture' that were civic and domestic, and likely to stimulate local interest. Thus, while other cultural forms had displaced the clubs by the early 1950s, the 'educated element' continued its literary activities: amongst the new literary forms of the 1940s and 1950s can be found the earliest locally published popular novels. In choice of subject matter and orientation, the new authors inherited the moral mantle of the literary clubs, albeit, as the decades progressed, in the form of increasingly 'thrilling' narratives, updated to attract readerships familiar with the excitement of Hollywood movies.[82]

Notes

1 See Appadurai, 1996; Clifford, 1997.
2 See Appadurai, 1996; Clifford, 1997; Shami, 2000.
3 Appadurai, 1990: 17.
4 *Ibid.*
5 See Boyce Davies, 1994.

6 Hannerz, 1990: 239; Said, 1993; Shami, 2000.
7 Shami, 2000.
8 See Collins and Richards, 1982: 114.
9 *GCT*, 29 March 1930: 4.
10 See Ashcroft, Griffiths and Tiffin, 1989.
11 See Goody, 1987; 2000; Ong, 1982.
12 Collins and Richards, 1982: 123.
13 See also Obiechina, 1973; Barber, 1987.
14 Collins and Richards, 1982: 112.
15 *Ibid.*, 115.
16 *GCT*, 17 November 1877: 2.
17 *GCT*, 13 July 1935: 6.
18 Foster, [1965] 1998: 69.
19 Buell, 1928: 745.
20 Macmillan, 1928: 169.
21 For a detailed account of Asante 'scholars', see Allman, 1993, and Donkoh, 1994, and for a discussion of Kwawu 'scholars', see Miescher 2001a and b.
22 *GCT*, 16 September 1882: 2. Studies of West African elites and of cities such as Cape Coast, Ibadan and Abeokuta in the nineteenth century reveal the extent to which they were highly differentiated from one another, separated by their own cultural and historical particularities as well as by the fact that colonial incorporation occurred at different moments in their formation as elites (see e.g. Barnes, 1986; Cohen, 1981).
23 *GCN*, 30 September 1915: n.pag. Young men's clubs also honoured this 'mystique' of Englishness (see Cohen, 1981). Well into the 1930s, literary and social clubs in Ghana continued to insist that members spoke English, wore three-piece suits and respected Christian values. Failure to do so could result in expulsion (see *AMP*, 4 December 1937: 2).
24 *GCT*, 16 September 1882: 2.
25 *AMP*, 3 September 1938: 2.
26 *GCT*, 23 October 1937: 7.
27 *GCO*, 6–13 November 1942: 400.
28 *GCT*, 21 September 1929: 4.
29 Kate Riby-Williams, Interview, 1999.
30 Ofori, [1958] 1968: 297.
31 By the time Ofori composed *The Literary Society* in the late 1950s, the decline of clubs had set in, as had this negative caricature of their 'literary' activities. Clubs were criticised in the newspapers for failing to engage with the critical political issues of the day. Labelled frivolous for debating topics such as 'which is mightier, the pen or the sword?', the clubs were exposed to increasing attacks in the 'stormy 1930s' and nationalist 1940s. See pp. 46–9 for discussion of the decline of clubs.
32 Ofori, [1958] 1968: 300.
33 Dickens, 1837: 1.
34 *Ibid.*, 4.

35 Ikiddeh, 1971; Priebe, 1988; Newell, 2000.

36 Blay, 1970: 24.

37 *Ibid.*

38 *TWA*, 29 December 1934: 6.

39 *Ibid.* Many literary clubs had an elected 'critic', whose responsibility was to correct English grammar and pronunciation, and to advise members on their prose style.

40 *AMP*, 16 September 1932: 2.

41 *Spectator*, 6 January 1939: 4.

42 *Ibid.*

43 See Arhin, 1986.

44 See Allman, 1993; Stone, 1974; Gocking, 1999.

45 Gold Coast Government, 1913: 38.

46 Gold Coast Government, 1914: 39–40.

47 21 October 1937: 2.

48 Ward, 1991: 176.

49 *GCT*, 29 March 1930: 4.

50 Ofori, Interview, 1999.

51 Buell, 1928: 738.

52 In one of the few studies of literary and social clubs in Ghana, E. Y. Twumasi (1971: 188) suggests that they originated in the early nineteenth century, when William de Graft established the Society for Promoting Christian Knowledge in 1831. De Graft set up a reading group composed of the educated elite, which met regularly at Cape Coast Castle to discuss passages of the Bible.

53 Collins and Richards (1982) develop such an argument, describing how in the 1870s and 1880s the intensification of scientific racism and exclusionary economic practices by British banks, merchants and administrators were accompanied by heightened 'European' cultural activities among African business communities. Their point seems to be that the coup visited upon West Africa by the colonial powers in the late nineteenth century involved such excessive ideological force and economic damage to local trade networks that African entrepreneurs were reduced to cultural mimicry in order to assert their status as 'civilised', 'well-mannered' individuals who had the right to continue trading as equals with European firms. Their argument is discussed in more detail in Newell (2001).

54 *GCN*, 18 April 1912: 2.

55 *SLWN*, 29 May 1926: 8.

56 We should not neglect the impact in British West Africa of non-colonial 'print-knowledge', such as the early Afrocentric writings of W. E. B. DuBois and Marcus Garvey in the United States, and the widespread reports on Gandhi's non-violent methods in India. It is essential to consider these 'subaltern' ideological currents alongside direct British influences in the colonies, for they influenced emergent anti-colonial movements as much as Colonial Office policies (see Langley, 1973; see Hill, 1986).

57 *TWA*, 8 April 1931: fp.

58 *GCO*, 22 May 1942: 41.
59 *SLWN*, 27 May 1893: 2.
60 *Ibid.*; author's emphasis.
61 See Blyden, [1887] 1967.
62 *Ibid.*
63 *SLWN*, 27 May 1893: 3.
64 *Ibid.*, 2.
65 *SLWN*, 27 May 1893: 3.
66 Ofori, Interview, 1999.
67 *Ibid.*
68 RHL, MSS.Afr.s.1985, Box 2: 11.
69 RHL, MSS.Afr.s.1755: 6.
70 Danquah, 1970: 31.
71 *Ibid.*
72 *Spectator*, 24 January 1953: 2.
73 *AMP*, 27 May 1954: 2.
74 The Youth Conference was established in 1929, but it remained more or less dormant for eight years, when it was revived.
75 *AMP*, 3 December 1937: 2.
76 *Ibid.*
77 *GCT*, 30 April 1938: 5.
78 *GCT*, 1 April 1939: 10.
79 *Spectator*, 24 January 1953: 2.
80 See Kimble, 1963; Twumasi, 1971.
81 See Jones-Quartey, 1974.
82 See Newell, 2000.

2 'Are women worse than men?': literary clubs and the expression of new masculinities

> How far were the Europeans right when they spoke of the danger from the 'semi-educated', those with enough schooling to make them dissatisfied with their tribal life but not enough to fit them for life in the towns? I felt at first that I had not enough experience of such people to answer this criticism. I wondered how to get it, and an African friend advised me to try and join one of the many African literary clubs in Accra. (Ward, *My Africa*)

The club that W. E. F. Ward joined, the Young People's Literary Club, held its fourteenth anniversary in 1934, declaring to a 'select and intelligent' audience that its work was reserved 'purely for literature, and during the whole of the year [we] have taken to the serious study of Ruskin's "Sesame and Lilies", a book which gives the idea about reading and the position of the woman in every state'.[1] When young men in West African towns joined literary clubs to discuss Ruskin's views on the duties of Christian, middle-class women, questions have to be asked about their social and political orientation, about the allegiances and aspirations they declared through such cultural choices, and about the kind of gender ideology generated by this Victorian reading matter.

A European teacher was responsible for introducing Ruskin's book to members of the Young People's Club. In his effort to gauge the 'danger' posed by semi-educated youths, Ward recollects that, 'Every Tuesday for several years I went down to Accra to attend the club's meetings'.[2] It was at one of these Tuesday meetings, long after he had established the political harmlessness of 'scholars', that Ward asked why there were no women members. Rather ironically, at the very same meeting he recommended Ruskin's anti-feminist tract, *Sesame and Lilies*, for study and debate: 'the book proved immensely popular' with members, who discussed it once a month and returned to it 'a year or two later' for another dose of masculinist polemics.[3] *Sesame and Lilies* was also cited frequently in newspaper debates linking gender with morality in the home and society.

It is not difficult to fathom why this particular book proved to be so popular amongst members of the Young People's Literary Club. In many ways, it was the perfect choice for a Gold Coast literary society, as newly educated, economically ambitious *men* monopolised the clubs. Containing moralistic advice on 'good' and 'bad' reading, *Sesame and Lilies* fulfilled the scholars' desires to increase their wisdom and to 'study the higher problems with the aid of good books';[4] and, as the Young People swiftly realised, a large part of the 'wisdom' contained in Ruskin's book related to 'the position of the woman in every state'.[5] Aimed at 'the shaping of high ideals of life', *Sesame and Lilies* advised young women to steer well clear of the public sphere and to perfect the domestic virtues peculiar to their gender.[6]

For male readers in the Gold Coast, perhaps the most useful ideological manoeuvre in *Sesame and Lilies* is the manner in which Ruskin places men and women into separate gender spheres, arguing for gender complementarity while actually insisting that male–female relations are determined by 'active–passive', 'public–private' dichotomies. 'Each has qualities not possessed by the other', Ruskin writes, and proceeds to enumerate these separate characteristics: 'The man's power is active, progressive, defensive. He is eminently the doer, the creator, the discoverer, the defender. His intellect is for speculation and invention; his energy for adventure, for war.'[7] The woman's intellect, by contrast, 'is not for invention or creation, but for sweet ordering, arrangement and decision'.[8] 'The anxieties of the outer world' do not enter into the husband's house if it is ruled by 'a true wife', for home 'is the place of Peace; the Shelter, not only from all injury, but from all terror, doubt, and division'.[9] In asserting the public–private divide, Ruskin is careful not to denigrate women: rather, he reintroduces 'the chivalric ideal of woman guiding man's actions' from home.[10] He labels women virtuous and places them on a dais from which any deviation represents a moral and national disaster, for 'she must be enduringly, incorruptibly good; instinctively, infallibly wise'.[11]

These ideas on 'the position of women' meshed neatly with the vision of 'modern' female domesticity imparted by government and mission schools in the Gold Coast. Whereas the boys' syllabus included scouting, sports and competitive games,[12] the girls' syllabus revolved around domestic activities. 'The work of a woman is in the home', declared the headmistress of Achimota at this time.[13] In 1930 an African kitchen was built for cookery lessons at the school and by 1931 antenatal and infant care had been added to the girls' timetable. Surveying these changes in his report for 1934, the Principal wrote of the transformations taking place at school:

'Instead of a science subject all the girls will henceforth study Housecraft and Needlework for the School Certificate.'[14] As British and colonial men went to war between 1939 and 1945, this 'school femininity' was enhanced still further, marking out the 'stay-at-home' sex from their soldier counterparts.[15]

As luck would have it for male readers, Ruskin's patriarchal vision could also be moulded to suit the established 'sexual division of labour' in the country, for men and women had performed gender-differentiated roles in the workplace and family for generations.[16] Ruskin thus provided a perfect model of masculine authority for newly educated young men in the Gold Coast, for he upheld the age-old concept of 'separate gender spheres' while introducing into it a nuclear, Christian domestic model which disempowered women economically and confined them to the home. The manner in which Ruskin Christianised and circumscribed women's power would have helped young men to rationalise their insecurities, particularly in the early 1930s when the Great Depression brought the Gold Coast to a standstill. Having read Ruskin, young men could get on with the business of trying to find work in the public sphere, intellectually enriched by their abundant 'good' reading matter and persuaded of their own legitimacy by the book's powerful message.

A letter discovered by Sylvia Ward on her husband's desk at Achimota School in 1927 provides an excellent example of the way Ruskin was utilised locally to assist non-elite men's attempts at self-empowerment. Possibly written by a member of the Young People's Literary Society, with whom Ward was associated, the author thanks the Secretary of the Cosmo Literary Club in Accra for inviting him to participate in a debate entitled, 'Are Women Worse than Men?'[17] 'I say yes, often and in many cases they are', the writer begins in his essay on this question, 'for the gist of it is that women are distinctly inferior to men in very many important elements of human character'.[18] What follows is a full-blown masculinist tirade against 'the weakness of "the fair sex"'.[19] The spectre of Ruskin surfaces more than once in the letter: 'I think it is John Ruskin who somewhere says in his rather sweeping fashion that he has come across very few women who seem to realise that there is anybody else in the world except themselves and their children', remarks the author, using Ruskin in support of his own 'rather sweeping' point that women are 'most wicked and vicious', for they 'recklessly undermine or damage the influence or authority which is really striving for the[ir] welfare.'[20] The 'influence' referred to, one presumes, is that of the male.

Sesame and Lilies is invoked to legitimate this furious young man's argument, but it is interesting to note that the *opposite* of Ruskin's 'true wife' features as the main feminine figure in this document. Lacking passivity, Gold Coast women are said to be 'spiteful and severe' and very 'purse proud'.[21] In addition, they refuse to remain within the privacy of their fathers' and husbands' houses.[22] In the eyes of this young man – as in the world outside the club-room – Akan women have escaped Ruskin's chivalric ideal in order to compete openly with men for the country's scarce economic resources.

Ruskin's tract was quoted widely in gender debates for several years: Mr Ward had opened a can of worms which spilled out of the confines of the Young People's club-room, affecting written assessments of female behaviour in the newspapers and influencing the terms of discussions in literary clubs throughout the country. The majority of interventions in debates about gender uphold Ruskin's ideals for a private, domestic sphere for femininity. 'Gloria', the patriarchal author of the Women's Corner in the *Gold Coast Times*, argues that woman 'cultivates a graceful humility which is more becoming to a woman than an arrogant obstinacy... she does not dabble in his work and business, but influences him, soothes him, and leads him to what is right'.[23] Throughout 1937, 'Gloria' persisted with this Ruskinesque line, repeating sentiments that had hardened into a solid position by the time the earliest non-elite authors started to produce novelettes in the early 1940s.[24] Unsurprisingly, the 'virtuous woman' produced by Ruskin proved to be an immensely popular figure in early Ghanaian literature, inspiring the creativity of male authors from elite and non-elite backgrounds alike.[25]

Sesame and Lilies thus profoundly influenced local people's perceptions of gender in the world outside the club-room. The text touched masculine minds at least as far north as Kumasi, from where a letter-writer praised the book in 1932.[26] It also provided ideological armour to young 'scholars' in their many debates upon marriage, the status of women and domestic conduct, bolstering their efforts to assert their authority as an emergent, ambitious social group and assisting in their active, collective construction of masculine power.

Given the aspirations and insecurities of the club-class described in chapter 1, it is hardly surprising that few club members seemed to be troubled by the gender exclusivity of their organisations. As an unrecognised, oft-derided social group with high hopes for the future, club members would not have wished to face competition for employment and training from educated young women. 'There was a paucity of females in the literary clubs', Henry Ofori admitted when I questioned him about the New Tafo Club: 'One time and one time only we decried the lack of women in our literary club. After that we did not discuss the matter.'[27] This failure to take action to recruit women can be regarded as a deliberate strategy: after all, the gender ideology that many club members formulated in debates was aimed at refining the masculine intellect, increasing men's social status and often – in rhetoric at least – confining women to the household sphere.

While dramatic and musical societies tended to boast equal numbers of men and women in West Africa – particularly in Freetown and Lagos – clubs requiring literacy in English and a willingness to debate in public tended to attract very few women. Ofori explained the problem thus: 'Women were not at all educated to the same standard as men. At my school from the first to the last grade – a period of ten years – there were only three girls. This was in the late 1930s in the rural area.'[28] The reason he gave for these low enrolment figures was that 'people didn't like the girls going to school. The girls would help to cook and go to the farm. Females were supposed to cook and that was that.'[29] Given the inequality in men's and women's career opportunities in the 'modern' sector, and given the tendency of parents to educate sons to a higher level of literacy than daughters, it is easy to understand why there was a lack of female members in local literary clubs.

It is necessary to note, here, the possibility that within the coastal elite, educated women did not wish to join the clubs because they preferred to regulate morality and manners in society by organising concerts and ballroom dances: in this way, as Abner Cohen argues for the Creoles of Sierra Leone, they could claim public power which did not contradict their spiritual and domestic roles as (Victorian) Christians.[30] These spiritual and domestic roles were, however, themselves European patriarchal constructions, involving the idealisation of femininity as gentle, nurturing, passive and virtuous, qualities which were amply showered upon women in the club-room as young men debated 'modern' gender roles using terms gleaned from Ruskin.

A degree of resistance to the emergent gender ideology came from one vocal quarter. In the Ladies' Corner of the *Times of West Africa*, 'Marjorie Mensah' (pseud. Mabel Dove) launched a direct attack upon Ruskin's chivalric ideal, rejecting the notion that woman should be treated as 'a being apart, a divine spirit, a wonderful inspiration'.[31] Woman 'finds it cold sitting on the clouds', she jests, adding, 'besides, she is curious to know what man is gazing at with that transformed countenance'.[32] In her column, 'Marjorie' also frequently bewails the lack of women's literary clubs. 'It is a great pity that we have no Ladies' Debating Clubs, similar to the Young People's, the La Improvement Literary Club or the Osu Debating Club', she writes in June 1932, for 'really, it is about time that we had something of the sort'.[33] However, even 'Marjorie' is a product of her times: her proposed topics for 'Ladies' Club' debates include 'listen[ing] to one of our members read a paper on domestic science; the present day housewife and her difficulties and many other things of an interesting nature'.[34] No doubt Ruskin would have approved of these feminine, 'separate sphere' subjects.

When women *did* set up their own clubs, their activities and debates were overshadowed by the attitudes described above. In the *Gold Coast Times* of 19 December 1936, for example, 'a spectator' reports on a 'Grand Concert' and variety show performed by the Young Ladies' Club of Cape Coast. After the opening glee, which includes 'Save Your Sorrows for Tomorrow', 'Just Dream of You, Dear', and 'My Cottage by the Roadside', the Club stage a 'model meeting. . . The proceedings were composed of speeches on the merits of the Club as giving to its members qualities wanting in many a lady.'[35] Clarification of the specific 'qualities' listed by the speakers comes quickly, for after a performance of 'She Stoops to Conquer', during which 'a great deal of laughter was caused by the sight of the ladies in men's clothes',[36] the Club stage their own one-act play.

This play extends and dramatises the opening 'model meeting' on the 'qualities wanting in many a lady'.[37] Entitled 'Why are there so many Divorces?', the performance contains at least two examples of *improper* feminine behaviour. The all-female cast incarnate familiar character types which surfaced as far back as 1915 in Kobina Sekyi's *The Blinkards*, and have recurred in Ghanaian concert parties in the ensuing decades.[38] First of all we encounter a 'stern father' who believes that 'women are always to blame in case of divorces'.[39] Recognising the elements of an established tradition, the reporter for the *Gold Coast Times* describes the wife as 'true to type. . . a domineering personality in the house'.[40] As with Sekyi's Mrs Borofosem, Mrs Johnson is represented as an ignorant, interfering busybody. Into this scene comes 'J. J. J. (Mr Jeremiah Joseph Johnson)', who is 'an ideal lover', and the stage is set for young Miss Johnson to progress towards a divorce with all the 'delight' of one whose maiden name and married name are one and the same, who will not therefore 'be inconvenienced in the case of divorce'.[41]

Unfortunately the full script of this play has disappeared, making it difficult to fathom the ways, if any, in which the female cast reworked these character types or subverted the familiar tale of the 'hen-pecking' wife and the fickle daughter.[42] However, from the synopsis appearing in the *Gold Coast Times*, it is possible to glean a sense of the dominant domestic model that the Young Ladies' Club upheld in their performance. A patriarchal, monogamous, nuclear family structure is reconstructed in the play: the father's domestic authority is undermined by the wife, whose 'domineering' personality is represented as illegitimate; meanwhile, the daughter chooses a partner 'who easily won the hearts of his fiancee's parents', but her own faithless nature is revealed by her pleasure at the prospect of divorce.

Clearly, the Young Ladies' Club could not extricate itself from the patriarchal domestic ideology that permeated Christian households and classrooms in coastal West Africa.[43] An area of ambivalence does emerge, however, in the debate which follows their one-act play. Echoing numerous debates in young men's literary clubs across the country, the topic for discussion is 'Are the Mental Capacities of the Sexes Equal?'[44] Curiously, the proponents of *inequality* are 'all dressed as men',[45] and they lose the debate, defeated by the opposition's 'fitting retorts' to their assertions of physical and intellectual superiority.

Why should the women decide to act out the arguments of the other side in drag? Perhaps they felt this was the only way to avoid the negative label which popularly attached to the argumentative, 'domineering' type of woman, the type who would argue for her own equality and the very personality to appear as the wife and mother in the Young Ladies' own play. Additionally, the arguments the 'men' put forward contain typically 'masculinist' views about how men alone are capable of 'the production of a Shakespeare or an Alexander':[46] in consequence, the main effect of the losers' costume is to highlight the equal, if not superior, 'mental capacities' of the winning side, for the women win the debate with 'convincing' arguments, demonstrating their brilliant reasoning abilities during the course of the discussion. Thus they prove that reasoning powers are not essentially masculine, as Ruskin suggested in *Sesame and Lilies*.

The subversive effect of this performance is to expose the socially constructed nature of men's claims to superiority, for so long as women are not allowed to take the platform alongside men, they will carry the label of intellectual inferiority. Taking the 'Grand Concert' in its entirety, then, we can sense the difficult ideological territory which members of the Young Ladies

Club had to navigate. Simultaneously supporting and subverting the masculine ideology, they managed to assert their sexual equality while *also* endorsing their gender roles as daughters of the Christian, Cape Coast elite.

Mission schools played a critical role in inculcating these gender positions. Young men and women did not simply gain literacy from mission schools: they gained *Christian literacy* and the awareness that one of the most visible, public ways in which an educated African could demonstrate his or her 'civilised' status was to be baptised and to undertake a monogamous marriage in church.[47] As far as the Anglican Church Missionary Society was concerned in Nigeria, for example, one of the most urgent tasks in the 1930s was to transform 'pagan wives' into baptised Christians. To this end, female members of the CMS would be enrolled at what Sylvia Leith-Ross hailed as the 'popular, practical and useful. . . bride-training institution', where they would be taught domestic skills: there they would also learn to read enough of the Bible to enable them to pass through the baptism ceremony.[48] Similarly, until the 1950s this bias remained pervasive in the Gold Coast. In 'vocational' classes run by schools and church organisations, girls would be taught domestic science and good wifely behaviour, trained into their roles as Christian wives and mothers. Women's study groups in Ghana concentrated upon 'sewing, knitting and childcare',[49] and Christian Ladies' Unions helped in 'educating illiterate women in housecraft, nutrition and childcare'.[50]

Boys' education, by contrast, was from the outset orientated towards the workplace, towards the training of future government clerks, civil servants, engineers and craftsmen.[51] Between the 1880s and 1920s, the government required schools to provide a pool of male recruits to the lower echelons of the civil service. Given the Victorian British culture from which administrators came, the employment of female clerks and civil servants was barely thinkable.[52] As for the missionaries – whose seminaries and schools were largely independent of the Government – while concern was expressed by some individuals about producing 'the right type of wife. . . for our [native] teachers',[53] the practical requirement to produce male catechists and schoolteachers for Christian educational work in the rural areas prevented them from paying serious attention to female education.

Female literacy levels remained low throughout the colonial period, and women formed a tiny proportion of the small percentage of literate Africans. If money was short, people preferred to give their sons a western education, fitting them for salaried, white-collar employment while girls would be withdrawn from school in Standard III. Thus the Gold

Coast Education Department reported in 1925 that out of a total of 3,824 children attending government and assisted elementary schools, there were only 453 girls, few of whom 'remained at school after passing Standard III'.[54]

Early Ghanaian literature – particularly the pamphlets produced by literary club members such as J. Abedi-Boafo and J. Benibengor Blay – reflects the ongoing, active construction of a masculine gender ideology by the country's literate classes. As with so many newspaper debates about gender-roles, moral blame often lies with the wife in this predominantly male-authored literature. Authors differ in the strength of their conviction that wives should be subordinate to husbands, but few writers challenge the image of the 'virtuous woman' described so forcefully by Ruskin. Christian chivalric discourse gives male authors a vocabulary, a logic and an ideology with which to assert control over women in the home, and many authors produce a version of domestic relations in which 'ideal wives' are paragons of sweetness and purity. Characters such as 'Emelia' in Blay's writings, for example, shine out as exemplary lovers so that 'the lessons in constancy, truthfulness and sane modesty are blazoned in the soul of readers to blossom into true relationship between two loving personalities'.[55] Of course, few 'real' West African wives would have embodied this behavioural ideal, which is thoroughly textual, divorced from the socio-economic realities of a world in which women worked and controlled their own resources outside the household.

The collective yearning amongst literate communities for 'ideal' wives in the 1930s and 1940s reveals the extent to which Christian, Victorian reading matter had ideologically impacted upon West African readers, being appropriated into debates about gender in order to vindicate the rights of local men. What is interesting in the context of this study is the way in which local readers empowered themselves through this *bizarre* female model: rather than reflecting any 'real' situation, the popular image of the 'virtuous woman' can be seen to represent local writers' attempts to rationalise their sense that gender relations had become disordered in late colonial society.[56] Victorian Christian texts are used to assist young men as they try to imagine a *new model household* in which masculine and feminine roles are clearly defined. Perhaps the very 'unreality' of this new patriarchal discourse reveals men's difficulties and anxieties in gaining and asserting power within a colonial society riven by unemployment, internal economic conflicts and the Great Depression. For the members of the Young People's Literary Club in Accra, however, it does not seem to matter that the 'virtuous woman' exists only on the printed page. Neither a wholly fictional character nor a real social being in Akan society, she is a behavioural model for a future, male-ordered world.

Notes

1 *TWA*, 4 May 1934: 4.
2 Ward, 1991: 175–6. In researching the psychology of 'scholars', Ward was responding to Governor Guggisberg's influential pamphlet, *The Keystone* (1924), which says of the club-going class, 'the very fact that they are educated tends to separate them in thought and sympathy from their less advanced relations. . . they fall a natural victim to discontent and consequently to unhappiness' (p. 25).
3 Ward, 1991: 177.
4 *GCT*, 29 March 1930: 4.
5 *TWA*, 4 May 1934: 4.
6 Ruskin, [1865] 1909: v.
7 *Ibid.*, 67.
8 *Ibid.*
9 *Ibid.*
10 *Ibid.*, 66.
11 *Ibid.*, 68.
12 See Miescher, 2001a.
13 Gold Coast Government, 1930: 17.
14 Gold Coast Government, 1934: 7.
15 See Allman and Tashjian, 2000.
16 See Amadiume, 1987; Adepoju and Oppong, 1994.
17 RHL, MSS.Brit.Emp.s.282: 28.
18 *Ibid.*
19 *Ibid.*
20 *Ibid.*, 28–9.
21 *Ibid.*, 29.
22 *Ibid.*
23 *GCT*, 26 December 1936: 10. In her recent PhD thesis, Audrey Gadzekpo has identified 'Gloria' as a woman, Mercy Ffoulkes-Crabbe (2001: 172–3).
24 See Connell, 1987.
25 See Priebe, [1978] 1997; Newell, 2000.
26 See *TWA*, 10 September 1932: 2.
27 Ofori, Interview, 1999.
28 *Ibid.*
29 *Ibid.*
30 See Cohen, 1981.
31 31 August 1932: 2. At least two other authors – one of whom was male – occasionally wrote under the name of Marjorie Mensah between 1931 and 1933, when a court case proved conclusively that Mabel Dove wrote most of the material appearing in the column since 1932 (see Newell, 2000).

32 *Ibid.*
33 *TWA*, 2 June 1932: 2.
34 *Ibid.*
35 *GCT*, 19 December 1936: 7.
36 *Ibid.*
37 *Ibid.*
38 See Bame, 1985; Cole, 1997; 2001.
39 *GCT*, 19 December 1936: 8.
40 *Ibid.*
41 *Ibid.*
42 See Sekyi, [1915] 1974.
43 See Barnes, 1986.
44 *GCT*, 19 December 1936: 8.
45 *Ibid.*
46 *Ibid.*
47 See Mann, 1985.
48 Leith-Ross, [1939] 1965: 8.
49 *AMP*, 3 May 1954: 3.
50 *AMP*, 6 May 1954: 4. For a full study of colonial femininity in the Gold Coast, see Allman and Tashjian, 2000.
51 See Mba, 1982: 61–4.
52 See Amadiume, 1987; Allman and Tashjian, 2000.
53 Fraser, 1914: 462.
54 Gold Coast Government, 1924–25: 33.
55 Blay, 1969: n.pag.
56 See Allman and Tashjian, 2000.

3 'The whole library in a pocket handkerchief': creative writing in the vernaculars

I enjoyed the two periods a week I spent 'teaching' the Twi language. I was given the top Twi set, and the position was in a way quite absurd as if an Englishman who has just managed to pass O-Level French were to be set to teach French to a class of Frenchmen. (Ward, *My Africa*)

Faced with a surfeit of school-leavers desiring white-collar work, holding Standard III certificates in one hand and poorly written job applications in the other, in the mid-1920s the Gold Coast Government decided to change tack. With little public warning, in 1925 the administration abandoned its language policy for Gold Coast elementary schools and discarded the 'literary' syllabus of previous decades. Two years later, after extensive consultation with the German missionary, Professor Diedrich Westermann, the government introduced a new phonetic-based script for Ewe, Ga, Fante and Twi; at the same time, in an attempt to invent an Akan 'national' language, officials also accepted a unified spelling system for Twi and Fante, assuming that, in time, the two Akan dialects would merge into one lingua franca which would be 'of immense political benefit, uniting, as it will, those now largely severed'.[1] Whereas in the early 1920s, 'there were schools in which notices hung forbidding the use of vernacular during school hours',[2] the government's volte-face of 1925 replaced the English language with Twi, Fante, Ewe and Ga for the first three grades of elementary school. From now on, Ghanaian children would be taught to read and write in their own mother-tongues.

These shifts towards the vernaculars represented an effort, firstly, to stamp out mimicry and reroot Africans in their own cultures, and secondly, to steer the dialects of distinctive culture-groups towards a united Akan language. The policies were designed to reconnect supposedly 'alienated' peoples with their customs and traditions, to prepare for eventual self-government through the customary rulers, and to stimulate the birth of vernacular literatures. However, the new government policy fell far short of its goals on a number of counts, galvanising neither creative writers nor future generations of African readers in the creation and reception of vernacular texts. Educationists and legislators steamrolled through unanimous local opposition, and for that and many other reasons, explored below, the local production of vernacular literature did not take off in the Gold Coast. Colonial officials failed to accept that, in the words of their favourite chief, Nana Ofori Atta, 'changes, if any, must come from within and not from without. In other words any change of words must come from the aborigines themselves.'[3] Unlike the country's British West African neighbours – particularly in western Nigeria where popular Yoruba novelists emerged in the 1920s and 1930s from a long tradition of Yoruba Christian writing – Ghana could boast no vernacular novelists of its own until the 1960s.[4]

The Education Code of 1925 stipulated that Ghanaian children should be taught to read and write in their own mother-tongues, and not be taught in English until Standard IV. The new rule was promoted by the administration as an effort to broaden the basis of literacy in the country. The central question asked by officials in the 1920s and 1930s was, 'How are we to educate the African and yet see to it that we do not take him clean away from his people?'[5] To this end, dense novels such as *Waverley* were supplanted by stories 'designed to assist the African child in learning to read and speak English in terms of his own surroundings and interests'.[6] Stories with African settings, filled with friendly and progressive chiefs, were created with 'an unusually large amount of repetition' and a limited vocabulary, chosen 'for its utility for African children'.[7]

Given the 'native' orientation of this new policy, what surprised officials most was the vehemence of local opposition to their plans. To a vigorously hostile local response, which continued unabated throughout the 1930s, educational policy under Governor Guggisberg shifted away from the production of pen-pushing clerks to the education of citizens with 'good characters', possessing respect for their vernaculars and happy to 'graft' the best of their traditions onto their new western knowledge.[8] The crux of local opposition was the withdrawal of English language teaching from the first three grades of elementary school.

The government was inspired in its educational changes by the idealistic recommendations of the Phelps-Stokes Fund commission of 1922, led by Thomas Jesse Jones: 'every people have an inherent right to their Native tongue', Jesse Jones reported, but 'the multiplicity of tongues shall not be such as to develop misunderstandings and distrust among people who should be friendly and cooperative'.[9] To this end, the vernacular rule of 1925 and the orthographic changes which followed in its wake were attempts to engineer 'national' languages for the Gold Coast. These attempts might have succeeded in kick-starting vernacular literatures but for the fact that for a period of six years after the introduction of the Westermann Script, fierce disagreements about orthography delayed the publication of vernacular texts, causing severe delays in the production of devotional and classroom material and a total hold-up in original creative writing. 'We have been severely handicapped by the lack of suitable text-books and readers and the absence of a generally accepted and agreed script', reported the Principal of Achimota in 1931.[10]

While decisions were awaited on a final orthography and on the unified spelling of Fante and Twi, the Great Depression hit the Gold Coast, causing a sudden decline of trade, large-scale retrenchments (including the publications editor of the Education Department in 1931), budgetary cutbacks and massive curtailments of publishing activities.[11] Despite the vigorous promotion of vernacular literacy at the official level, then, in the face of these obstacles and delays the Gold Coast's local authors continued to write in English. Apart from a trickle of printed vernacular plays, histories and poems, many of which were sponsored by 'nativist' organisations such as the ARPS, original creative writing continued to be composed in the colonial language until the cultural nationalist resurgence of the post-war period.

Opposition to the new Education Ordinance came from several African quarters. Whilst they appreciated the cultural value of the vernaculars, elite radicals and pan-Africanists – particularly those with Garveyite sympathies – saw the New Rules as a deliberate effort by the colonial government to suppress the internationalisation of African politics. Concluding an article on this topic for the *Gold Coast Times*, Kobina Kwaansa wrote, 'If the people in the colonies aren't taught in English they will be exploited by capitalists.'[12] The vernacular rule was viewed with suspicion by these 'been-tos', who saw it as a means to prevent the further politicisation of people who had been troubling the colonial mind for many decades. In the opinion of many anti-colonial activists, the largest section of the educated population, primary-schooled youths, would be denied the language of newspapers and government by the new Education Rules; they would be deprived of the international language which had brought them, by the 1930s, their own West African nationalist literature in English as well as the anti-colonial ideas of Mahatma Gandhi, Marcus Garvey and W. E. B. DuBois. 'We are British Subjects', wrote the author and schoolteacher, J. Abedi-Boafo, in a more patriotic vein nearly twenty years after the vernacular rule was made law: he continues, 'and as English is the official medium of the Empire, and therefore has far to go, it is vitally essential that Gold Coast school children learn to speak, read and write it correctly' in the infant and elementary classes.[13]

To some extent these commentators were correct in their suspicions about the policy: between the mid-1920s and the Sedition Ordinance of 1934, colonial officials became increasingly worried about the arrival of politically inflammatory material (and personnel) from Russia and the United States. By 1925 the government had recognised that the English language – particularly in the printed form of the newspaper and pamphlet – was a crucial factor in the development of anti-colonial and 'paracolonial' networks in West Africa, allowing the dissemination of ideas and opinions about colonial rule, and also facilitating the development of a pan-African, pan-Atlantic community of interest which had already internationalised beyond the control of Great Britain. Lines of resistance had been opened up by Africans' English-language activities, particularly in the local newspapers, which were described by one Nigerian as 'the only true medium by which the natives of West Africa can voice and give expression to their views and opinions, feelings and aspirations on questions that affect themselves and their country'.[14] Additionally, the English language was central to the paracolonial political and educational networks established between the Gold Coast and the USA, the West Indies and other West African countries. Leaders of African opinion in the Gold Coast thus had every reason to distrust the educational changes of the 1920s.

There were, however, a small number of locally sponsored initiatives to promote the Gold Coast vernaculars, initiated by the elite leadership of cultural nationalist organisations. In 1933, for example, the ARPS supported a venture to popularise 'the study, the writing and the reading of the Fanti language, with a view to the establishment of a local Press for printing and publishing newspapers and books in the Fanti language'.[15] No substantial literary canon arose from this publishing enterprise, launched as the Aborigines' Society went into decline.

The vernacular rule was unpopular with Gold Coast 'scholars' for rather different reasons from those expressed by the anti-colonial journalists. 'Many parents still regard early instruction in English as one of the essential advantages to be gained from education', ruefully admitted the Director of the Education Department in 1931, six years after the Ordinance, acknowledging that, 'English being the language of commerce and of government, parents are not unnaturally anxious that their children should acquire as great a knowledge of it as possible'.[16] For members of the non-elite, 'literacy' tended to mean *English* literacy. Thus, large numbers of parents saw in the policy another government attempt to restrict African advancement in the white-collar workforce. Why, asked one correspondent in the *Gold Coast Times*, should those interested in gaining an education 'waste time and money on vernacular education, which is intended to handicap them in their future struggle to live?'[17] According to this letter-writer, the English language 'is the key to political and economic emancipation and knowledge', without which West Africans will be isolated and incapable of achieving prosperity.[18]

Non-elite groups had a far more pragmatic attitude towards literacy than the educationists and missionaries who imagined that vernacular literacy would solidify the African's 'tribal' affiliations and touch the native's soul. Contrasting the policy-makers, 'scholars' tended to regard literacy as a tool, helping them to gain access to salaried posts in the modern sector. The aspirations of these 'never-beens' were crushed by the new rules. Given that primary schooling carried a fee, Standard III was precisely the grade at which less well-off parents would withdraw their sons from school and launch them into the salaried workforce as low-grade clerks. The new legislation was designed to hold back precisely these aspirant white-collar workers for an extra three or four years in school, enabling them to benefit from 'character training' and from the alternative career paths offered by classes in agriculture, craft-work and the trades, as well as from the English language training made available in Standards IV to VII.

Viewed in purely pedagogic terms, the legislation of 1925 ensured that the acquisition of knowledge was not hampered by the child's struggle to master an alien tongue, and educationists agreed that an African taught literacy in his or her vernacular would find it easier to learn English at a later stage of schooling.[19] The vernacular policy was, however, also motivated by complex ideological factors. It is no coincidence that Indirect Rule was formalised in the Gold Coast during the same two-year period that saw the introduction of vernacular education in elementary schools. Between 1925 and 1927, the government consolidated chiefly power by dividing the colony into three Provincial Councils of Chiefs, each one ruled over by what opponents called a 'super-chief'; two chiefs from each of the three Councils attended the Legislative Council in Accra. Meanwhile, in the educational sector during this period, the government embarked on its effort to stamp out educated Africans' apparent alienation from the custom and culture represented by these 'natural rulers'. 'Education for the present needs of the African must be based upon, and grow out of, the African's past, and his chief link with the past is his mother tongue', wrote Harold Jowitt in *Suggested Methods for the African School*.[20] However, as ex-Governor Guggisberg commented in 1927, 'it is extremely hard to give a man the highest form of education and still get [him] to retain a pride in his nationality, proud to belong to one of these African tribes'.[21] Educated 'youngmen' had to learn that they were *not* regarded as the legitimate inheritors of political power in the country.

The government was not the only institution keen to dampen the aspirations of semi-educated groups with their lilting 'Gold Coast English' accents. Throughout British Africa the vernacular policy attracted a great deal of support from missionaries and Christian educationists, to whom 'character training' and the teaching of religious values were more important in the classroom than the mere transmission of knowledge.[22] As the creator of the New Script himself pointed out in 1925, language carries 'the soul of a people' and 'direct missionary motives oblige us to cultivate and protect the vernacular'.[23] Recognising the soul-touching power of vernacular print, the problem for the missionaries was that in many African languages, 'a native teacher might easily tie up the whole library in a pocket handkerchief'.[24]

Devotional vernacular literature was a priority with the missionaries, but they also sponsored 'utilitarian' books in the vernaculars, with titles such as *40 Hygiene Lessons*, *The Vision of a Model Village* and *How Culture (Civilisation) Grows*.[25] The overarching aim of most missionaries, African and European alike, was to convey to the African 'a message that will help him on and serve and set free the fettered powers of his soul'.[26] 'We will reach a man's heart through the words he has spoken ever since his childhood' wrote Frank Laubach in 1948, echoing his predecessors in the 1920s, and for many decades the belief persisted that in order to touch the fettered African soul, literacy skills had to be fully vernacular.[27]

Despite the support generated by the educational changes of the 1920s among missionaries and administrators, the new policy was plagued with practical problems for several decades. Indeed, difficulties were acknowledged from the outset by the Director of Education in the Gold Coast, D. J. Oman, who noted the obstacles to progress caused by the 'lack of text books and infant school material, the scarcity of good teachers with satisfactory vernacular knowledge, and the variety of languages spoken by children in any one school'.[28] The most pressing problems related to the

arguments and confusion surrounding the government's adoption of the
'Westermann Script' (or 'New Script') in 1927. The new orthography ren-
dered existing publications obsolete, but no comprehensive measures were
undertaken to ensure a new supply of literature. Confusion continued for
many years: six years after the introduction of the New Script, trainee
teachers at Achimota College, an institution which led the way in African-
language teaching, were found to be confusing Twi spellings, using the
defunct 'unified spelling' system and mixing old and new orthographies
within single compositions.[29] As late as 1941, Ida C. Ward was asking questions which should have been resolved a decade earlier: 'To what "standard" is he [the African author] to conform? What dialect must he write
in? What spelling or word-division is he to use?'[30]

Perhaps the fundamental trouble with the new policy was that it was
not sufficiently radical to break free from entrenched colonial attitudes
about the superiority of English. 'The main policy' of the Education
Department remained, in the Governor's words, 'the general progress of
the people of the Gold Coast towards a higher state of civilisation'.[31] With
this 'higher state' in view, educational practice revolved around 'grafting'
English values onto the vernacular languages in Standards I to III, injecting the supposedly inferior languages with moral and intellectual standards drawn from the superior culture and communicating directly with
the African in his or her own mother-tongue. In subsequent grades,
English would be 'substituted for the vernaculars', a policy which caused
confusion and displaced the vernaculars.[32] Rather than endorsing the
vernaculars as the medium of instruction for *all* standard grades, government advisors sought to resolve the tensions that arose by re-emphasising
the superiority of English, recommending that 'the foundations of a solid
knowledge in English' should be laid early on in school.[33]

The belief persisted amongst educationists that, in the words of one
Achimota schoolmaster, 'it is almost impossible to exaggerate the importance of English', for 'the vernaculars have not, perhaps never will have,
any literature opening on to the modern world. Any Gold Coast African
who wishes to enter that world must do so by way of a European language'.[34] 'The mother-tongue' of most Africans, wrote Michael West, 'is
inadequate, both as a means of expression and in the contents of its literature, in respect of the world of modern thought and knowledge.'[35]
Original writing in the vernaculars was inconceivable, it seems, even at
Achimota where staff were hailed as the architects of an Africanised education system. Translations and adaptations of English literature were the

best innovations to be hoped for in the colony. 'English is for you in this colony the medium of your renaissance life', said A. G. Fraser, the Principal of Achimota, to an audience of Africans in 1930: 'through it flows in the energy of the new awakening. But not only that. It is the necessary tool for the production of a vernacular literature, without which the people of this land must remain backward.'[36] 'The English tongue is the gate to the world of new and powerful ideas essential to your education', he concluded, further undermining the status of the vernaculars by labelling them static and retrogressive.[37]

Despite official affirmations of faith in the vernaculars, then, English literacy continued to be regarded as the vehicle of modernity, progress, literary production and intellectual enlightenment; and foreign missionaries continued to produce inappropriate vernacular texts and set poor standards, 'presuming to write themselves' rather than 'training Africans to write their own languages'.[38] A coherent, radical language policy would have involved the wholesale replacement of the medium of English with the major vernaculars at all levels of society, from school classrooms to government chambers and churches. As it was, however, even the Provincial Councils of Chiefs – those most 'native' of British brain-children – were required to write their court reports and minute books in English.

What colonial policy-makers failed to account for in their ambitious transformation of primary education was the almost complete lack of outlets and incentives for local authors who wished to compose original literature in African languages. Whilst the Education Department and missions offered vigorous encouragement to the few African teachers and catechists who wished to produce vernacular grammars, primers, dictionaries, folktales and devotional texts for use in the classroom, they were less enthusiastic in providing avenues for local authors who wished to compose original material for circulation amongst adult readers.[39]

Until the period of decolonisation in Ghana, the government focused upon encouraging writers to produce vernacular textbooks suitable for children in schools. Provision for literate adults was left in the hands of missionaries and, unsurprisingly, efforts by Christian organisations to get African authors to produce vernacular material for adults were bound up with the problems of Christian conversion and the need to provide newly literate Africans with morally uplifting or useful reading matter. For the missionaries 'good' adult reading tended to be of a devotional or informational, self-helping nature and they were 'reluctant to print material that did not conform to their own notion of what was good for the community

for whose education they felt responsible'.[40] 'Direct exposition' was preferred to fictional narrative, and books were praised for 'explain[ing]
simply and accurately the things he wants to know about'.[41] Newly literate readers were provided with material that would assist in their development, solving their practical problems by showing them how to do things
differently.[42] Thus, novels were not easy to place with the missionary
presses, and there was no vernacular press to take locally authored secular
material until the early 1940s.[43]

Missionary efforts to promote local authorship paid off in several
quarters, however, in the form of powerful translations into the vernaculars, and it is essential not to undermine the significance of African participation in translation projects since the early nineteenth century. Some
Christian translators went on to become important authors in the twentieth century: for example, in 1941, *Books for Africa* lists a Fante translation
of *Robinson Crusoe*, written for schools by Francis A. Acquaah.[44] Within a
decade, Acquaah had become a recognised Fante author, acknowledged
alongside other Methodist Mission-trained Fantes, including J. A.
Annobil, Gaddiel Acquaah and Samuel K. Otoo.[45]

Several of these authors were members of the new literary and social
clubs which emerged in the 1940s, when country-specific nationalisms
started to supplant the transatlantic and pan-West African networks that
had previously engaged the energies of British West African activists. The
shift towards a distinctive anti-colonial discourse was manifested in the
Gold Coast by the emergence of a new type of literary society, breaking
away from the ethos of preceding decades in two respects: firstly, as with
the earliest literary clubs in the 1870s and 1880s, the new organisations
were initiated and led by the foreign-educated professional classes, including figures such as Kwame Nkrumah and S. R. Wood among their members;[46] secondly, unlike the non-elite clubs of the 1920s and 1930s with
their English-language orientation, the new groups promoted vernacular
literatures by sponsoring translations of secular material and commissioning histories and textbooks for classroom use, mounting a challenge to
decades of missionary control over the production of vernacular material.
In this reclamation of African languages, club members asserted African
spaces within the dominant culture, politicising the vernaculars and criti-
cising education policy to date.

In his autobiography, Kwame Nkrumah (1957) mentions one such
organisation: 'When I was not studying, my spare time was devoted to
forming the Nzima Literature Society', he writes, adding that 'it was

through this work that I met Mr S. R. Wood who was then secretary of the NCBWA. This rare character first introduced me to politics.'[47] Founded in 1933 by Reverend S. E. Quarm with the support of local chiefs and elders, the intention of the Society was to unite 'all educated Nzimas at home and abroad' in the retrieval of the Nzima language from the obscurity of unwrittenness.[48] The language 'seems to have been looked upon both by missionaries and officials as either too difficult or barbarous', wrote Reverend Quarm in 1934, 'and the worst part of it is that they have led the Christian natives to learn other foreign languages with the result that the natives have been discarding their own mother tongue, and the language itself has appeared to them as unbecoming in matters religious'.[49] Following in the footsteps of the earliest missionaries, but expanding the agenda to include a nationalist perspective on literacy, Reverend Quarm expressed great concern about the lack of Christian reading matter in the Nzima language and he also insisted that Nzima schoolchildren require 'better reading books in the mother tongue'.[50]

The striking feature of this African initiative is the similarity between the Society's choice of genres for vernacular writing and the missionary publications described above. 'The production of school text-books and versions of the Holy Writ' take precedence over translations and original creative writing in Reverend Quarm's list of proposed publications.[51] Grammars, dictionaries and primers dominate the agenda, closely followed by 'oral', customary and historical matters. This pattern is repeated in 1945, when another cultural organisation, the 'GSRA',[52] launched an ambitious appeal for a Ga National Library. The library was to be filled with original Ga writings alongside newly commissioned translations of 'standard works on World History, Economics, Political Science, Psychology, Philosophy, Geography, Logic, Aesthetics, etc.'.[53] Noting the 'good intentions' of the GSRA, Education Department officials rejected the scheme as 'over-ambitious', proposing instead that a Ga section should be established in Accra's new municipal library.[54]

Despite their ultimate lack of success in launching large-scale literary production in the vernaculars, these bold local ventures provide evidence of a localised, but increasingly nationalist, mindset amongst literate groups in the Gold Coast. What is revealed by these pro-vernacular organisations is the critical connection between the writing down of mother-tongues and the expression of nationalist sentiment. 'We have a firm belief', wrote Reverend Quarm, 'that God has better things in store for this Nzima nation'.[55] As Adrian Hastings (1997) argues, a shared vernacular literature

– and most particularly the Bible – is required in order for people to express a unified national identity: 'Ethnicities naturally turn into nations or integral elements within nations at the point when their specific vernacular moves from an oral to written usage', he writes, for 'it is when its vernacular possesses a literature that a society seems to feel confident enough to challenge the dominance of outsiders'.[56] In line with Hastings' argument, groups such as the Nzima Literature Society and the GSRA considered the production of written vernacular literature to be vital to their assertion of nationhood.

This neat connection between the vernaculars and nationalism is disrupted, for Hastings, by the fact that in many African states anti-colonial sentiment was expressed through pan-Africanist channels or through the vernacular literature produced by particular, highly localised ethnic groups.[57] Seen in this context, the literature sponsored by the new Ghanaian associations was of a parochial nature. Lacking a national vernacular, however, the 'national' sentiments expressed by the new Ghanaian associations remained what Hastings describes as 'proto-national' rather than truly national;[58] their literature formed one linguistic piece in a polyglot whole.

Hastings' view here seems to be predicated upon the notion, derived from Christian history, that a single vernacular is the precondition for the emergence of a stable nation-state. In a similar vein, back in 1931 a master at Achimota College commented, 'The ambitious aim of the college, I think, is the creation of a nation, and that there is a need for a common medium of speech for this nation cannot be denied.'[59] 'By encouraging the scientific study of the native languages', the teacher asserts, 'Achimota is contributing towards the evolution of a *lingua franca* out of the multiplicity of vernaculars.'[60] Hastings' conception of nationhood is similar in many ways to this teacher's Eurocentric yearning for a unified script.

Contrasting these ideals for a solitary vernacular, the Nzima Literature Society and the GSRA illustrate the extent to which the Gold Coast did not need a single national vernacular to bind the country together prior to independence. Reverend Quarm and his successors voiced a kind of 'parochial nationalism' which defied colonial fears that ethno-regional fragmentation would occur in the absence of a unified script. These new clubs held a non-hegemonic conception of their own languages, and in this they differed from the supporters of a vernacular lingua franca. Sponsoring grammars, folktales and ethno-histories in their various vernaculars, the clubs used printed literature as the basis for the formation of mini-'nations'.[61] From these diverse platforms, they expressed support for the polyphonic new nation of 'Ghana', seeming to celebrate their standing on an equal footing alongside the vernaculars from other regions. In this, they anticipated the cultural nationalism of African authors such as Ngugi wa Thiong'o by several decades.[62]

This attitude was not new to the 1940s. In 1911 the ARPS stalwart, Rev. S. R. B. Attoh-Ahuma insisted, 'WE ARE A NATION. If we were not, it was time to invent one; for any series of states in the same locality, however extensive, may at any time be merged into a nation. We have a nation, and what is more, we have a Past – "though ungraced in Story".'[63] As with many other African territories, Ghana emerged from the decolonisation process as a nation-state composed of diverse vernacular jigsaw pieces, not falling apart from the lack of a singular 'Story'. The vernacular clubs of the 1930s and 1940s illustrate the manner in which literate locals managed to steer a course through the difficult task of writing, in their numerous languages, what the GSRA proudly termed, 'the gospel of unity and constructive national effort without being chauvinistic'.[64]

Contrasting the dearth of original, locally produced printed material, a steady flow of vernacular drama was performed in the Gold Coast during the colonial period, ranging from the musical and dramatic performances put on by Methodist 'singing bands' to stage-managed Empire Day plays, translations of Shakespeare and end-of-term plays put on by schoolchildren.[65] In addition to these, Kobina Sekyi's Fante play, *The Blinkards*, was first performed in 1915 by members of the Cosmopolitan Literary Club in Cape Coast, only to be left on the shelf, unpublished for sixty years. A particular dramatic form, the 'concert party', gained in popularity with the educated public in the 1920s and 1930s, becoming increasingly vernacular as it spilled out of elite, controlled spaces and attracted less schooled audiences.[66] Meanwhile, in Gold Coast secondary schools, students composed their own original vernacular plays and performed teachers' translations of Sophocles. On at least one occasion, a polyglot version of *Antigone* was performed by schoolboys to an enthusiastic reception in Cape Coast, while in 1933 the Methodist Church Singing Band performed *The Merchant of Venice* entirely in Fante to an 'audience which was a 90 per cent illiterate one'.[67] Frequent reviews of these activities appeared in the local press, revealing a flow of unpublished dramatic material in the 1920s and 1930s in quantities which discredit the belief among western educationists of the time that 'behind all the life around me there is no vernacular literature at all except what the missionaries have created'.[68]

It is important not to neglect this 'hidden archive' of unpublished vernacular drama by local authors, for it appeared in the Gold Coast many years before the advent of vernacular prose fiction and marks the beginnings of an important dramatic tradition in the country.[69] These local dramatists did not, however, translate theatrical action into texts and produce printed scripts of their performances. This failure to get into print is difficult to comprehend, especially when in Nigeria the missionary presses clamoured for vernacular texts above all else. An explanation might lie in the different missionary approaches to literacy in the Gold Coast and in Nigeria. Unlike the Presbyterians and Methodists, who presided over the majority of schools and bookshops in the Gold Coast, in Nigeria the agents of Anglicanism were very obviously 'literary', with a vibrant diary and letter-writing tradition, particularly among the Anglicans in Yorubaland who seemed keener than most to preserve documents for posterity.

Unlike the English language plays, short stories and serialised novels which appeared in the local newspapers between the 1880s and 1930s, the first printed vernacular play probably dates from the early 1940s, with the appearance of J. B. Danquah's *Nyankonsem* ('Fables of the Celestial') (1941 in Twi) and F. Kwasi Fiawoo's *The Fifth Landing Stage* (1943 in Ewe), both of which were composed nearly thirty years after Sekyi's *The Blinkards*, only to be published more than thirty years before it.

The reasons why local authors did not publish this creative writing in the vernaculars were deep-rooted, intimately connected with the ownership and control of publishing facilities in colonial Ghana. Missionary presses dominated literary output, and the long lists of vernacular books appearing in the Christian journal, *Books for Africa*, give useful insights into the subject matter and genres preferred by these organisations. Until at least the late 1930s, translations of religious material were the priority of mission presses. In July 1937, for instance, vernacular titles are overwhelmingly biblical, including: *St. Mark*, *Messages of the Prophets*, *Christianity in Action*, *Old Testament Stories*, *St. Mark*, *St. Matthew*, *Hymn Book* and *Prophets: Their Life and Work*.[70] By 1948, topics considered suitable for new vernacular readerships included family life, heroic personalities, parenthood, Christian marriage, the Christian home, how to teach children about God, Bible stories and books on citizenship and government.[71]

This pattern was not broken by the supposedly non-official printing press set up at Achimota College in the mid-1920s. Managed by Christian educationists from the mission tradition, using government funds, its output reflected the pedagogic aspirations of its management committee:

the press produced vernacular readers, textbooks, *anansesem*, sermons, translations of Christian material and an occasional simplified narrative such as *Odysseus (Fante)*.[72] Jobs undertaken by the press at the behest of the government included political items such as, in 1937, 'Ewe, Twi, Fante and Ga leaflets to the number of several thousands on the subject of the cocoa dispute' alongside 'coronation hymns and poems in Ga, Ewe, Twi, Fante'.[73]

Devotional, educational and 'traditional' material dominated the vernacular book market in the Gold Coast for many decades. In consequence, it is probable that certain genres were associated with the vernaculars in the minds of African readers and prospective creative writers, while other genres were associated with the English language. An illustration of this language–genre connection is furnished by the African-owned newspapers, which published fiction, debates and political items in English, interspersed with occasional folktales, proverbs and 'traditional' items written in the vernacular of the region.[74] By contrast, the bulk of books about marriage, love and domestic relationships – books concerned with personal, contemporary problems – appeared in English, as did simplified versions of English literary classics. Africans could read English texts ranging from *Robinson Crusoe* and *King Solomon's Mines* to William Cobbett's *Advice to Young Men*; they could also read a wide range of English language material designed specifically for Africa, including *Christian Family Life and Bringing up of Children*, *Christian Citizenship*, *Care of Children* and *How to Build a Good House*, alongside numerous manuals in the *How To Do It* series.[75]

A compelling example of the connections between particular genres and languages can be found in the book-choices of readers during the 'book sales experiment' run by missionaries in the rural areas surrounding Owerri in Eastern Nigeria. One of the coordinators – probably Marjorie Stewart – notes the huge popularity of three English-language pamphlets, *Christian Courtship*, *How to Catch a Girl* and *Happy Homes*.[76] Folktales and vernacular pamphlets on rural issues were of no interest whatsoever to the bilingual readers who crowded around the book-lorry. Indeed, such material was purchased only by the smallest children for whom English was not yet taught at school: 'the smallest [children were]. . . often the sole supporters' of the well-stocked vernacular stall, whilst 'English reading at less than one shilling a book was sought for everywhere'.[77] The topics conveyed in the colonial language touched readers' hearts and 'traditional' material was of little consequence to people keen to seek advice on the how tos of the here-and-now.[78] As the eminent promoter of vernacular writing,

Rupert East, pointed out in 1947, 'A man who takes the important step of learning to read may have very vague ideas of what advantages he will get from it. . . but he certainly expects something more than the stories that he has known by heart ever since he was a child'.[79]

Given the subject matter of vernacular pamphlets in the Gold Coast and the lack of an autonomous, Yoruba-style literary tradition, it is hardly surprising that when local creative writers emerged in the 1930s and 1940s, they wrote almost exclusively in English, getting around the problem of finding publishers by sending their work to be printed privately in Britain and returned for distribution in the Gold Coast or submitting their work to be printed on local newspaper presses.[80] Responding to the popular demand for books on topics such as falling in love and winning a wife, they wrote novels in the language which had, over the years, come to be associated with modernity and with matters of the heart.

Comprehensive government ventures to support vernacular authorship did not start until the early 1950s, when the Vernacular Literature Bureau was established to support the extensive adult literacy drive taking place in the period of decolonisation. In contrast to Nigeria, however, where in the 1930s and 1940s literature bureaux – particularly under the direction of Rupert East in Northern Nigeria – stimulated original vernacular writing, in Ghana the Bureau tended to produce books of proverbs, African customs and folktales.[81]

In the years between the vernacular rule of 1925 and the government-led literacy campaigns of the early 1950s, the majority of Gold Coast authors continued to write original material for publication in the English language. Perhaps these authors were unable to conceive of doing otherwise, for since the first books appeared in the country, matters of tribe, tradition, soul and salvation would appear in the vernaculars, while advice on love and romances for contemporary society would appear in English. Additionally, the philosophical works and classic novels selected and debated in Gold Coast literary clubs were published in English, the common language of the very groups to spawn the first popular novelists.

By the time Ghanaian novelists emerged in large numbers, the colonial government had accepted that its quest for a vernacular lingua franca was an 'impracticable' and 'premature' step which aroused 'suspicion of an attempt to tamper with the purity of Twi and Fante' and caused long-term damage to the emergence of vernacular literatures in the country.[82] Such a realisation may have come too late, however, for when J. Benibengor Blay composed his first romantic novel, *Emelia's Promise*, in 1944, his linguistic choices may well have been determined by his decision to write a morally uplifting love story. In choosing to write what the missionaries termed 'Healthy Romances, elevating Love to its true Christian sphere and showing the Christian ideal of marriage',[83] Blay entered into an established reading context that was thoroughly embedded in the history and politics of printed literature in the country.

The Achimota history master W. E. F. Ward commented in 1937 that African art forms 'are constantly threatened by the competition of mass produced European types, and it is extremely doubtful whether they could survive if left to struggle unaided'.[84] The literary forms believed to require protection and nurturing within the confines of Achimota were, however, too old-fashioned and folklorish for the new generation of authors who entered the Ghanaian literary scene in the late 1930s. By this time, the connections between genre and language were probably too solid to break: moralistic and sensational English books on love and sex had started to appear on the streets, independent of the mission presses and English romantic novels and Hollywood movies had started to circulate around urban areas, generating great excitement among audiences and stimulating further English language creative writing in the West African press.

Notes

1 Gold Coast Government, 1930–31: 19.
2 RHL, MSS.Brit.Emp.s.282, 1937–38.
3 NAG(CC), ADM 23/1/463, 30 July 1931: 2.
4 See Gérard, 1981.
5 Fraser, 1925: 514.
6 Sibley, 1930a: n.pag.
7 Sibley, 1930b: 6–7.
8 See Gold Coast Government, 1925: 1037–116.
9 Jones, 1922: 25.
10 Gold Coast Government 1929–33: 19.
11 Gold Coast Government, 1930–31: 19.
12 13 September 1930: 11.
13 Abedi-Boafo, 1944: 31.
14 *LWR*, 28 June 1919: 6.
15 NAG(CC), ARPS Correspondence File No. 3, 1922–39: 3.
16 Gold Coast Government, 1930–31: 37–9.
17 *GCT*, 8 March 1930: 7–8.
18 *Ibid.*, 7.
19 See Jones, 1922; Westermann, 1925.

20 Jowitt, 1934: 61.
21 Guggisberg, 1927: 10.
22 See Baudert, 1931.
23 Westermann, 1925: 25–6.
24 Wilson, 1921: 378.
25 Anon., 1936: 40.
26 Meinhof, 1927: 84.
27 Laubach, 1948: 98.
28 Gold Coast Government, 1927–28: 18.
29 NAG, CSO 18/6/93, 1933: 5.
30 Ward, 1941: 51.
31 Gold Coast Government, 1922: 271.
32 NAG, CSO 18/6/96, 1930: 4.
33 *Ibid.*, 5.
34 Kingsley Williams, 1937: 6; see also Guggisberg, 1924: 20.
35 West, 1926: 2.
36 Gold Coast Government, 1930: 29.
37 *Ibid.*
38 East, 1947: 16.
39 The National Archives of Ghana hold several files of correspondence with local authors of vernacular classroom material, demonstrating the enthusiasm amongst local writers to compose books in their own languages, see e.g. NAG(CC), ADM 23/1/463.
40 Gérard, 1981: 181.
41 Ward, 1941: 49.
42 See Young, 1936: 56.
43 Gérard, 1981: 267.
44 Anon., 1941: 29.
45 See Swanzy, 1958.
46 See Nkrumah, 1957: 21.
47 *Ibid.*, 21.
48 *GCT*, 31 March 1934: 5.
49 *Ibid.*
50 *Ibid.*
51 *Ibid.* See also *GCT*, 23 October 1937: 10.
52 Documents in the National Archives do not reveal the full name of this organisation: my guess would be the 'Ga State Reading (or Research) Association'.
53 NAG, RG 3/1/315, April–May 1945: n.pag.
54 *Ibid.*
55 *GCT*, 7 April 1934: 10.
56 Hastings, 1997: 12, 31.
57 *Ibid.*, 163.
58 *Ibid.*, 12; 21.
59 Gold Coast Government, 1929–33: 50.
60 *Ibid.*, 51.

61 The word 'nation' is used constantly in newspaper reports to describe particular ethno-linguistic groups, especially the Fante.

62 The hero of Ngugi's *Devil on the Cross* (1982: 60) describes his creative role as a Kenyan composer in terms of 'harmony in polyphony': 'I ask myself a question that I have posed many times: what can I do to compose a truly national music for our Kenya, music played by an orchestra made up of the instruments of all the nationalities that make up the Kenyan nation, music that we, the children of Kenya, can sing in one voice rooted in many voices – *harmony in polyphony?*'

63 Attoh-Ahuma, [1911] 1971: 1; author's emphasis.

64 NAG, RG 3/1/315, April–May 1945: n.pag.

65 See Ward, 1991: 175.

66 See Bame, 1985; Collins, 1994; Cole, 2001.

67 *TWA*, 22 February 1932: 4.

68 RHL, MSS.Brit.Emp.s.282, 28 Feb 1927: 3.

69 See Sutherland, 1970.

70 Anon., 1937: 45.

71 Laubach, 1948: 204.

72 *Achimota Review*, 1937: 95.

73 *Ibid.*, 20.

74 These links between genre and language persisted until the 1940s, when local language newspapers such as *Amansuon* started to appear on the market (Gérard, 1981). Early attempts to produce vernacular newspapers tended to fall into the genre-trap described above, producing vernacular 'traditional' material and stories of the tribal past which were not particularly interesting to newly literate, expectant readerships (see Jones-Quartey, 1974).

The lack of original vernacular literature in Ghana is a regionally specific phenomenon. In South Africa by the 1920s, mission presses were publishing a steady stream of original Xhosa and Sesotho novels by local authors, including Thomas Mofolo's *Chaka* (1925); in East Africa, increasing numbers of Swahili novelists found secular publishers for their work; and in Nigeria, Hausa creative writing was stimulated by Rupert East in the 1930s, while in the south-east of the country, original Yoruba compositions appeared as far back as 1857, continuing to be sustained in the 1920s by the 'lively vernacular press' in the south (see Gérard, 1981: 247–9).

75 Anon., 1940: 36.

76 Anon., 1951: 21–6.

77 *Ibid.*, 22–3.

78 A similar instance can be found amongst the prize-winning authors in the annual competition for vernacular writing, organised by the International Institute of African Languages and Cultures. In the 1930s, runners-up were allowed to select titles from a list of approved books. Several exam-orientated winners would choose books such as *The Complete Key to Baker's and Bourne's Elementary Algebra* or *The Tutorial Press Matriculation Course*. 'A very frequent request', however, was 'for books giving sex instruction' (Brackett,

1934: 23). Lacking titles on this topic, the Institute could not fulfil these needs, causing observers to conclude that 'there is evidently a great need for books on the physiology of sex written specially for the African' (*ibid.*).

79 East, 1947: 14–15.
80 As in the Gold Coast, in Nigeria in the mid-1920s a complex debate took place around the Phelps-Stokes Commission's recommendation that the vernacular be taught in schools. Cultural nationalists allied themselves with the vernacular-promoting missions, over against many African businessmen and modernisers, who promoted the English language as the vehicle for gaining entry to international cultural and economic forms. The Yoruba community was as divided as the European community over this issue (Barber, personal communication).
81 Gérard, 1981: 267.
82 NAG(CC), ADM 23/1/463, 1933: 1.
83 SOAS, MMS.257 (box) 1924–50, December 1929a: 35.
84 Ward, 1937: 19.

4 The 'problem' of literacy: 'good' and 'bad' literature for African readers

Life being very short, and the quiet hours of it few, we ought to waste none of them in reading valueless books. (Ruskin, *Sesame and Lilies*)

Christian teachers in West Africa, particularly within Protestant circles, considered the ability to read to be so fundamental that by the 1920s sprawling networks of mission schools and bookshops had been established throughout the continent.[1] Except for old-aged converts, literacy was the prerequisite for full membership of many Protestant churches.[2] Bible-reading was believed to effect a communion between God and the individual soul like no other form of worship. Such an unequivocal belief in the power of the written word explains the seminal role played by print in the Christian project in West Africa, for in the act of imparting literacy skills to Africans, missionaries hoped to recruit converts to the church and to rescue locals 'from the swamp of darkness, of heathendom and establish them in the sunshine of God's kingdom'.[3]

Booklists were sent to the journal *Books for Africa* from African and European teachers stationed in mission schools all over the continent, containing recommendations of uplifting and useful books alongside advice on adapting the syllabus to the African's moral and spiritual needs; and a 'self-help reading list' was available on request to teachers in Africa, listing booklets which were described by the International Committee on Christian Literature for Africa (ICCLA) as 'a means of evangelism in any reading class'.[4] Home committees were asked to endorse ever-increasing budgets for the production of this 'good' literature, providing the churches and the reading public with titles designed to meet the needs and tastes of newly christianised readerships.[5]

By the late 1930s missions were the main distributors of vernacular literature in Africa, and mission schoolteachers were responsible for over 90 per cent of educational work on the continent.[6] Until Colonial Office policy shifted towards mass education after the Second World War, mission schools dominated education in British West Africa. Side by side, education and Christianity progressed through the region, inseparable to such an extent that in many communities 'the Christian was marked out from his fellows by his literacy'.[7] Indeed, by 1926, 'in some parts of Africa to discover if a man is Christian the appropriate question is: "Are you a reader?" The Christians of Africa are the "People of the Book".'[8] The following pages explore precisely what the 'marked out', mission-schooled African was able to read and write between the 1920s and 1940s, and the ways in which Christian beliefs and teaching techniques influenced local interpretations of literary texts.

Many European educators in the colonial period were convinced that literacy magically or miraculously generated a new mental state in the native. Particularly in the post-war period, as the discourse of 'development' replaced that of conversion, literacy was regarded as 'the magic key to unlock the door of escape from custom and stagnation';[9] it was 'the equivalent on the intellectual side to the sudden healing of a cripple'.[10] Illiterate individuals, on the other hand, whatever their status in local communities, were described by the same educationists as 'virtual slaves' who were 'doomed to poverty, oppression, and fear until they are rescued from illiteracy'.[11]

Literacy was not a neutral acquisition, however, which in itself changed the minds and outlooks of its recipients: it came prepacked with literature to work upon relating to monogamous marriage, the Christian household, gender roles, morality and personal salvation. For example, subjects covered by the Sheldon Press's immensely popular 'African Home Library' included *The Christian Home*, *An English Family at Home*, *Man's Work in the Home*, *Prayers for the Daily Task* and *A Clean House*.[12] Similarly, the 'How To Do It Series', published by the United Society for Christian Literature (USCL) in London, included topics such as letter-writing in English and making a success of marriage.

During a century of Christian educational work in Africa, newly literate people were furnished 'with reading material containing the Christian ideals', particularly in relation to marriage and the maintenance of a Christian home.[13] 'Only good and useful books for Christians' were provided for African readerships.[14] Concerned for the moral welfare of their flock, religious leaders advised African readers to select only 'good and devout spiritual books',[15] or 'the utilitarian type of book', conveying useful information on agriculture or fishing methods.[16] Following pedagogical practice in Britain, educationists in Africa also promoted the uplifting moral value of the English classics – albeit communicated via 'simplified' versions of great novels. In Africa, as in Britain, 'to use books rightly was *to go to them for help*: to appeal to them when our own knowledge and power of thought failed. . . and receive from them the united sentence of the judges and councils of all time'.[17]

Not all mission-sponsored literature promoted the Christian lifestyle. By the 1940s it was generally agreed in missionary circles that low-cost manuals on 'health, proper nutrition, or the evils of soil erosion and bad farming meet as great a Christian need as do pamphlets on the evils of drink or gambling, child marriages or sexual errors'.[18] The vital connection between these different topics relates to their genre. Whether or not authors promoted explicitly Christian opinions, *readers* were receiving a constant stream of 'how to' books from the mission presses. Through such literature readers were learning to treat books as instructional manuals providing answers and advice on personal, domestic issues. Apart from these utilitarian books, until the mid-1930s few other titles were available to local readers in British West Africa. This was a cause for celebration amongst some missionaries, who noted with relief that 'it is doubtless a great advantage to the progress of civilization in Africa that such books as exist are all of Christian origin'.[19] Didactic publications thus formed the reader's intellectual fodder, and one probable consequence was that early generations of West African readers *learned to expect* to acquire moral and spiritual knowledge from printed texts. The impact of these expectations upon 'the literate element' in West Africa was profound.

In 1926 an article in the *Sierra Leone Weekly News* amply demonstrated the extent to which the Christian reading practices encouraged by mission schoolteachers had been accommodated and endorsed by West African readerships. 'Reading the right sort of books etc., is a decided improvement of the mind', writes Cujoe, suggesting that schools throughout the region should purchase library books which will stimulate students' 'moral nature'.[20] Bewailing the fact that, in society at large, 'Young men are rogues. Young women are unchaste', Cujoe sets out a literary aesthetic aimed at countering all social ills, defining 'good books' as those 'which teach moral courage, thrift, bravery, honesty, truthfulness, perseverance, and so on'.[21] This list of moral qualities is accompanied by a list of Christian-sponsored titles, including *What a Young Man Ought to Know* and *What a Young Woman Ought to Know*.[22]

The affinities between the reading matter produced by missionaries and the literary tastes of mission-schooled Africans persisted well into the period of nationalist awakening in British West Africa. In the late-1940s

Igbo readers crowded around a book-lorry belonging to the Eastern Nigeria Literature Bureau, demanding pamphlets with titles such as *A New Child is Born, Christian Courtship, Local Government, How to Catch a Girl* and *Happy Home*.[23] Just as Cujoe listed self-helping texts for Sierra Leoneans, so literate Igbos in Eastern Nigeria selected titles that were relevant to their own personal predicaments, helping them to resolve emotional dilemmas and succeed in the most intimate areas of their lives. The personal, self-helping dimension of this literature is revealed by the demand for particular titles by particular groups of reader. Hence, '*Marriage*, 4d, did not have such popular demand' amongst young unmarried men as *How to Catch a Girl*: '"I am not yet ready, I will get it when the time comes" grinned a young teacher.'[24] As these readers reveal, by the 1940s literate Africans were spontaneously demanding the material Christians had produced for them since the turn of the century. These texts were regarded by readers as the 'magic key' described by educationists,[25] unlocking a door leading to moral enlightenment and personal growth.

Abiola Irele has argued that the material produced by missionary publishing houses has had a decisive impact upon the production and development of West African literatures: 'the missionary presses', he writes, 'for a long time provided a model of publishing for the new, educated class which the missions were helping to create.'[26] In 1958 South African novelist Peter Abrahams powerfully summed up this connection between Christianity and literacy in Africa: in a speech at the ICCLA's silver jubilee conference, he stated, 'in the process of "educating" me, the missionaries taught me a new set of values'.[27] Abrahams bears witness to the fact that mission schools helped to generate fundamental literary and social values amongst readers, values which are evident from the reading matter produced for African readers.

Alongside the especially published 'how to' books, low-cost novels were also commissioned for readers in Africa: these were 'brief, simple stories in which the Christian ideal could be introduced', and 'healthy' stories exploring 'actual problems based on "real life" incidents'.[28] 'Penny helpfuls' of this nature were designed to counter the influx of 'penny dreadfuls' into newly Christianised, newly literate communities. When faced with a novel, local readers were advised by their teachers to dwell upon striking plots, '*applying them to ourselves and our own case*. In this way reading becomes a kind of meditation.'[29] The far-reaching effects of Baeta's prescription are revealed below, for evidence in the archives points to the existence of a Christian reading mode in West Africa, applied by readers to secular material and novels as much as to religious material and 'how to' books.

Christianity filled West African classrooms with a literary culture and a set of expectations about the meanings and morals that a book would yield. These expectations harmonised with existing interpretative conventions for genres such as the folktale and dilemma tale. The central difference between established local genres and the missions' comprehensive publishing and educational activities relates to the *content* of texts: the latter ensured that 'as a person learned to read *he learnt also* something about the saving Grace of Jesus Christ'.[30] At the very moment of learning to read, then, students were also learning a set of *Christian* literary expectations and *Christian* interpretative conventions, adapted by their African and European teachers to suit local classrooms.

Christianity in West Africa was internationalised well before the First World War, but it was only after 1914 that increasing numbers of pamphlets started to appear in West Africa. Educated local worshippers could make use of their literacy in English to read the Pentecostal and evangelical pamphlets which started to be imported in bulk from Britain and the USA after 1914, and by the 1920s they could access relevant ideas from the increasing range of foreign publications available in urban bookshops.[31] As a result, local variants of foreign Pentecostal organisations, including the Faith Tabernacle (now the Christ Apostolic Church) and the Assemblies of God and Apostolic Church were established in urban centres throughout the region at this time.[32]

Some African members of the mainline missionary churches responded with hostility to the imported literature that was influencing these new religious movements. Bewailing the 'misuse' of literacy, editorials and articles in the national newspapers labelled the books 'harmful literature' and called for bans on further imports. Complaining about publications arriving from North American outlets such as the Grace and Truth Press, the Faithful Words Publishing Company and the Moody Press, one journalist in the *Nigerian Pioneer* commented in 1918 that:

The evil which the reading of pernicious literature does in a community is becoming increasingly felt in Lagos. Earnest and devoted Christians behold young men, some in their teens, identifying themselves with doubtful movements and so-called literary societies whose real aims are opposition to and vilification of Christian teachings.[33]

These complaints reveal that literacy was fundamental to the dissemination and success of new religious movements in the early twentieth century. The period after the First World War was a time when mission-educated West Africans started to make revisionist readings of the Bible, injecting it with local relevance and organising independent groups in which the Word could be reapplied to the debates taking place within their own communities on subjects such as polygyny, witchcraft, the sources of misfortune and the pouring of libation.[34] As the newspaper report reveals, newly literate young men were joining 'literary societies' and gaining inspiration from the promises of personal salvation contained in imported publications.

The expansion of these 'doubtful movements', achieved in large part through their publications, became unstoppable in the 1930s and the mainline churches were forced to accommodate their presence. The growing popularity of evangelical and Pentecostal Christianities in West Africa permeated the whole spectrum of Christian churches, affecting new prophet-led movements and missionary institutions alike, generating theological, cultural and moral shifts in their orientation.[35] By the 1930s in Ghana, the Presbyterian Church had accepted prayer-healing into its liturgy and the Roman Catholic Church followed in its wake by recognising the Pentecostal prayer groups that hitherto had been operating independently of the Church hierarchy.[36] With the exception of the Anglican Church in Ghana, by the 1950s most established churches in the region had accommodated these movements, seeking to prevent schisms by allowing groups to organise and function alongside the formal church hierarchy.

Faced with declining book sales for Christian literature, many missionaries in the mainline churches started to wonder whether the literacy they had initiated and nurtured over the decades had been such a good idea. 'Great perils threaten those who have only just learnt to read and yet are lacking the right books', wrote Charles Wilson in 1926: 'Non-Christian forces may find a simpler conquest among people whose first desires have been awakened for the knowledge which the printed page can bring.'[37] Also, with the onset of the Great Depression, budgets for Christian book production were failing to meet the perceived need for well-illustrated, interesting and 'good' reading material. 'If they cannot get good literature they will read bad', warned Margaret Wrong in 1934, having observed a hospital patient in Dakar reading a 'lurid French novel' with great relish.[38]

Perhaps in response to the collective refusal of many African readers to be passive consumers of 'good' or 'sweet' literature, missionary journals and governmental reports in the 1930s were filled with an almost obsessive concern about the uses (and misuses) to which African literacy was put. In response to growing concerns about 'pernicious' literature, a 'definitely Christian' magazine, *Listen*, was launched in 1932 by the ICCLA, aimed at village needs, containing religious articles, items on hygiene and the village school, biographies and renditions of folklore.[39] Despite the popularity of *Listen*, however, a sense of crisis increasingly pervaded Christian writings about literacy in Africa. 'Can we, strangers in an Africa still so largely unknown, attempt to locate or define African need?' asked the Reverend Cullen Young in an article for the missionary journal, *Books for Africa*: 'Would such people be *likely* to feel the need of the kind of literature which we are preparing for them? If so, is it the *form* in which we present the material that is wrong?'[40] 'What reason have we for supposing that the [reading] material which we think it right to supply is the material which the African needs?' Young continued, 'Has the African anything at all to say?'[41]

Responding to such crises of legitimacy, to the low sales of vernacular books (except for the Bible) and to the influx of 'pernicious', un-Christian literature from foreign publishers in the 1930s, the Methodist Book Depot in the Gold Coast launched an essay competition for elementary schoolchildren in December 1935. Students in Standards IV to VII were asked to write about 'My Favourite Book – and Why'. The prize-winning entries were selected according to relatively neutral criteria: judges looked for the demonstration of original ideas, comprehension of the plot and ability to discuss literature in correctly spelt, clearly written English.[42] The purpose of the competition was to enable the Book Depot's management to address the question of Gold Coast students' literary preferences and the resulting report, held in the National Archives of Ghana, contains a detailed record of two hundred students' aesthetic tastes and opinions.[43]

The most popular types of book fall under the headings, 'Stories of Great Men', 'Books of Information' and 'Stories with a Moral', and titles listed on a regular basis by entrants include *Self-Help* by Samuel Smiles alongside numerous simplified English classics and titles from the *African Home Library*. Uncorrected extracts of several essays are included in the report, and what is conspicuous about them all is the students' efforts to draw personal moral lessons from their favourite publications. In one winning essay, for example, a Standard V student comments that *Morte d'Arthur* 'teaches me to obident [*sic*] and loyal to my seniors, my teachers and to do what I am told'.[44] The biography of Booker T. Washington is praised by another student for portraying 'the kind of life which encourages young children who find many hindrances in their school career'.[45] A book entitled *Shakespeare's Plays* – probably a simplified, reduced version of the Lambs' *Tales from Shakespeare* – is labelled 'good literature' for the manner in which good characters are separated from evil ones, and the reader is moved 'to mend his mistakes, in habit or character. It makes a man aim higher in his daily life. The book teaches that before man becomes successful in life he has to struggle hard. . . Above all, it is the second book to the Holy Bible.'[46] Whether fiction, drama or 'informational' literature is chosen, these young literary critics bring a similar interpretative mode to the text, detailing the moral lessons they have learnt from their favourite European texts. No African-authored text was selected, nor any book in the vernacular.

The essay competition reveals the way in which, by 1935, students from mission schools had been trained to interpret all fiction as 'helpful' and edifying, to seek didactic plots and moral advice in secular as well as religious novels. In the students' view *Morte d'Arthur* is as much a 'penny helpful' as *What a Young Woman Ought to Know* and *How to Catch a Girl.* Clearly, these readers have been trained to regard all 'good' literature as self-helping, moral and useful, and to select favourites on that basis. This ethical reading mode overlaps in many ways with the responses encouraged by 'traditional' folktales and dilemma tales, where audiences are invited to participate in the tale, making moral interventions and drawing personal lessons from the actions of characters.[47] Christian doctrine might have supplanted the morals and beliefs contained in local folktales, but in both cases readers were required to adopt similar interpretive positions, to participate in a similarly active way in the narrative.

To some colonial educationists, West Africans were obsessed with self-help, taking 'penny helpful' literature far too seriously and over-investing in the concept of reading for self-advancement. Amongst Ghanaians, however, there was one influential and oft-cited British writer who vindicated these aspirations. Samuel Smiles' lengthy motivational text, *Self-Help* ([1859] 1997), was listed by schoolchildren as a 'favourite book' in the 1930s and quoted extensively by local authors in order to justify their writing activities. For literate West Africans, Smiles' assurance that poverty may be 'converted even into a blessing' through reading and self-help allowed for a positive interpretation of their difficult situations.[48] Also, his promotion of achievement through hard work and through the emulation of great men and women meshed perfectly with Akan conceptions of the self-made individual.[49]

Smiles stressed that many national heroes started life in 'the lowliest calling' but, through hard work and self-education, achieved 'the loftiest results'.[50] As we have seen, numerous literary and social clubs sprang up in the Gold Coast in the 1920s and 1930s, organised by young men who enshrined this ideal of mutual improvement. In their 'aims and objectives', which were published in the local press, these 'youngmen' defined themselves in Smiles' terms as gentlemen without riches or rank, who were hard-working and 'truthful, upright, polite, temperate, courageous, self-respecting, and self-helping'.[51]

One crucial difference separates Smiles' literary agenda from the reading modes generated in colonial Ghana. In the process of promoting literacy, Smiles warns against excessive novel-reading, for in his view fiction is 'positively pernicious' when forming the bulk of a reader's literary diet.[52] Novel-reading is a type of 'intellectual dram-taking, imparting a grateful excitement for the moment, without the slightest effect in improving and enriching the mind or building up the character'.[53] As the two hundred entrants to the Methodist Book Depot's essay-writing competition reveal, however, Ghanaian novel-readers largely escape the accusation of frivolity. Fiction, for these readers, is firmly regarded as a 'self-helping' genre, containing exemplary and errant character types who are interpreted in an ethical and utilitarian manner. Thus, for these colonial readers, novels assist in character-building to the same extent as non-fictional 'how to' books.

As in Britain in the 1870s, when the 'masses' first gained access to elementary education, literacy started to be perceived as a disturbing 'problem' by educational authorities in the colonies, providing 'a ready channel for the agitator', with African-owned newspapers and other printed texts placing 'ideas within the reach of millions who otherwise might have to wait years before they would hear these opinions spoken'.[54] By the mid-1920s, the press had become 'intensely political' and 'sometimes highly scurrilous'.[55] Texts judged to be 'against Christ. . . pandering to depravity or hate' were believed to be in circulation by the early 1930s;[56] by the end of the decade, 'frank, outspoken, practical' mail-order books with titles such as *Love and Marriage*, containing '*sex secrets*. . . hitherto known only by doctors, now laid bare to all!' were advertised on the front pages of Gold Coast newspapers.[57] Some advertisements invited readers to purchase esoteric, occult pamphlets from America and India, whilst others asked provocatively, 'Have You Read "The Red Light"? It's sex in a nutshell.'[58]

In response to this uncontrolled growth in available literature, Christian writers continually emphasised the dangerously addictive potential of 'seemingly harmless' books, and warned the new reading public against misdirecting their literacy. The reading of frivolous novels 'engenders a distaste in us gradually for all Spiritual Reading' wrote one journalist in the 'Sunday Corner' of the *Gold Coast Times*: 'The most valuable works, full of religion, good sense and talent, do not compare in our minds with those with which we have become fascinated', and the reader of non-spiritual material will decline into 'miserable perversion'.[59] Similarly, in 1935 in the Women's Corner of *The Times of West Africa* 'Marjorie Mensah' complained that 'many of our girls are reading books that can do them no earthly good', including 'the Penny Dreadful type of novel' with titles such as *From Shop Girl to Duchess*, *Married to a Millionaire*, and *From Dancer to Princess*.[60] Momentarily supporting the introduction of a censorship bill, 'Marjorie' adds that 'Steps should be taken' to halt the influx of this 'harmful' fiction to West Africa.[61]

The influential post-war literacy campaigner, Frank Laubach, agreed with the sentiments of these African commentators: 'Literacy needs the Bible', he wrote, 'Every time I pass a railroad newsstand and see the books sold there, I shudder to think of the possibilities for evil in literacy.'[62] Concerns about misdirected literacy continued to be expressed well into the 1950s. 'Cheap, secular, often pornographic literature is probably a greater danger than communistic literature' in Africa, stated Claude de Mestral.[63] Faced with a 'fantastic drop' in sales of Christian literature by 1959, he added that it is 'essential that the producers of Christian literature make certain that their publications get a solid hold on this growing market – which the printers of communist literature and sexy tabloids cultivate already'.[64] In these circumstances, for many Christian commentators censorship seemed justified.[65]

African literacy also became a 'problem' in government circles. By the early 1930s Garveyism, and to a lessser extent, communism, were gaining ground amongst Africans as an oppositional discourse relevant to colonised populations.[66] Colonial officials watched in consternation as members of the Ghanaian intelligentsia disseminated 'inflammatory' publications from North America through African newspapers and oral networks, influencing literates and illiterates alike. This 'agitation' caused particular sensitivity in the Central Region around Cape Coast where Kobina Sekyi, the politically uncompromising leader of the ARPS, waged continual propaganda wars against the government and the provincial councils of chiefs. During one fact-finding campaign against the ARPS the Acting District Commissioner of Saltpond sent an infiltrator to the settlement of Baa, who reported back that:

It is learnt that one H. J. Martin of Cape Coast a writer of stories in the vernacular tours the Twafu Division. . . to sell his publications which find a ready market and it is on the occasion of these visits that Martin alias Kweku Martin circulates the Aborigines' pamphlets which he interprets to the illiterate masses.[67]

These tours are blamed for the story circulating amongst 'illiterates' that the Stool Treasury would claim a fee each time a woman lay with her husband.[68]

In the view of many officials, not only could semi-educated Africans obtain 'bad' literature from the intelligentsia, but they and their illiterate kin would also listen credulously to the false news conveyed orally by literates. Thus the danger was two-pronged and pointed to the need for mass secondary education for Africans or else, in the words of Governor Guggisberg, 'we shall be continuing our present system of providing the easy prey of the demagogue'.[69] 'If we are to protect the masses from the hasty and ill-conceived schemes of possible local demagogues,' continued Guggisberg, 'we must hasten as rapidly as our means will allow to fill up the gap between the two classes.'[70] Well-educated Africans on the coast were seen to be leagues ahead of their compatriots, both intellectually and politically; their ideas were described as 'dangerous' by government officials and missionaries alike, and the only methods of defending the masses would be through a careful combination of censorship and mass education.

By 1934 the Gold Coast administration had become convinced that illiterates and primary-educated 'scholars' would be vulnerable to the types of anti-colonial reading matter that had caused trouble for the British on the Indian sub-continent. As a result, Governor Sir Shenton Thomas forced through the Criminal Law (Amendment) Act – known locally as the Sedition Bill – which forbade the importation or local production of any printed material judged by the authorities to be inflammatory or politically subversive. The legislation was prompted by the Inspector General of Police's report to Shenton Thomas that 'in 1931 the number of copies of various publications found and destroyed was approximately 76; in 1932 it was approximately 940; and in 1933 it was 1,750, of which 1,100 copies were of the "Negro Worker"', a communist North American journal which preached revolution against colonialism and white domination.[71]

In response to the sustained press outcry against the Bill, the Governor released an Extraordinary Minute in which he claimed that the Ordinance was intended to 'protect the public' from the ever-increasing quantities of 'seditious literature' arriving in the Gold Coast, inciting violence and rebellion.[72] 'I say that the people of this country are being threatened to-day by a danger of which they know little or nothing', Governor Thomas told the population, 'and it is my bounden duty to protect them against it.'[73] Clearly, the long, monogamous marriage between Christianity and literacy was over. Literacy had attracted other bedfellows, and reading and writing had been politicised by educated Africans who looked to North America for their English-language material. In the words of one prominent European educationist, 'Marcus Garvie [*sic*] muck' was entering the country alongside 'literature from subversive Negro societies in America and revolutionary stuff from communist blokes [*sic*]', causing political excitement reminiscent of 'jolly old India'.[74]

Surprisingly, however, the English-language creative writing which appeared alongside this troublesome literature in the 1930s and 1940s upholds the domestic, personal orientation of Christian 'how to' books. Local authors produced ethical tales about marriage and love, albeit from a culturally nationalist perspective: 'big fish' such as Kobina Sekyi and J. B. Danquah joined 'small fry' such as J. Benibengor Blay and R. E. Obeng, offering moral interventions in people's daily lives and stimulating public debate about social issues. Authors focused upon men and women in the search for ideal life-partners, the ill-effects of jealousy and a wide range of other personal dilemmas. Rather than openly challenging the colonial regime in this period of nationalist activism, then, they deployed creative writing to suggest ideal domestic arrangements and to create the new nation in miniature: if a nation is being invented and fought for in this literature, it is situated within the intimate space of the home.

The Sedition Bill arose directly from the perception that small numbers of trouble-making literates – especially Kobina Sekyi and the detested I. T. A. Wallace-Johnson – were influencing large numbers of volatile semi-literates, who would be vulnerable to revolutionary material from North America and Russia.[75] Government and missionary authorities had been happy to promote the Ghanaian's preference for 'how to' books and 'Stories of Great Men', for these genres were regarded as ideal for character-training and the teaching of 'citizenship'. Facing the failure of 'educated natives' to be good readers of good literature, however, legislation was introduced across the region to limit supplies of literature from abroad and to constrain what it was possible to publish locally. Literacy was the problem. Whilst the educationists' ideal remained the promotion of 'sweet emotions' recorded for posterity in literature by 'great men and women',[76] as the century progressed, outside the classroom West Africans redeployed their literacy for political, anti-colonial ends, producing newspaper articles and political commentaries which increasingly challenged the regime.

Notes

1 Christian missionaries in Africa were responsible for most of the earliest translation work and publishing activity on the continent, printing grammars, vocabularies, religious texts and didactic material for dissemination through hundreds of different language zones. Much of this local-language material was printed on the first presses to be shipped into Africa from Europe. There is an extensive secondary literature in this area (see e.g. Sanneh, 1983; Gérard, 1981). By 1851, for example, the Basel Mission was using the Methodist Mission printing press at Cape Coast for its educational material (Sanneh, 1995). As with the Christian presses that followed in its wake, the Methodist Mission produced not only conventional religious publications but also instructional pamphlets on good behaviour and agricultural methods. Literate converts were thus initiated into the earliest of Africa's 'how to' genres.

2 Sanneh, 1983.

3 Richter, 1929: 74; see also Thomas, 1931.

4 Christian Council of the Gold Coast, 1952: 8. Several of the Christian publishing houses and bookshops that grew up around these printing presses are still in existence today in Ghana, releasing inexpensive pamphlets about love, sex, marriage and etiquette (see Sanneh, 1995; Gérard, 1981).

5 SOAS, MMS.257 (box), 1950c: 4.

6 Wrong, 1938: 509. In Accra alone the Methodist Book Depot was the dominant supplier of books by 1950, with a turnover of £50,000, supplying 500,000 school text books, i.e. 60 per cent of the country's total requirement (SOAS, MMS.257 (box), 1950: 4).

7 Smith, 1966: 231.

8 Wilson, 1926: 508.

9 Laubach, 1948: 20.

10 USCL, 1944: 11.

11 *Ibid.*, 19; Laubach, 1948: 13.

12 Anon., 1951: 9; Anon., 1940: 36.

13 Laubach, 1948: 127.

14 Anon., 1929a: 14.

15 *GCT*, 7 August 1937: 3.

16 Baeta, 1946: 14.

17 Ruskin, [1865] 1909: 57–8; emphasis added.

18 USCL, 1944: 16.

19 Wilson, 1926: 509.
20 *SLWN*, 22 May 1926: 13.
21 *Ibid.*
22 *Ibid.*
23 Anon., 1951: 21–4.
24 *Ibid.*, 21. Onitsha market literature was influenced by this missionary material, especially pamphlets such as *How to Get a Girl in Love* and *How to Speak to a Girl about Marriage*. Africans who read this self-helping literature are satirised by Kobina Sekyi in his play, *The Blinkards* ([1915] 1974).
25 Laubach, 1948: 20.
26 Irele, 1972: 7.
27 Cited in Mestral, 1959: 2.
28 SOAS, MMS.257 (box), 1929: 34.
29 Baeta, 1946: 14; emphasis added. The African schoolteacher was expected to exemplify the lifestyle ideals proposed in this reading-matter. In the view of one hard-line commentator on the uses of literacy, the Gold Coast teacher, 'has accepted this employment because he has accepted a way of life, a tradition and civilisation that is based on the English language, on Christianity and on the whole of Western European thought' (Walker, 1956: 33).
30 USCL, 1944: 11; emphasis added.
31 See Hackett, 1989: 197–203; Ojo, 1988b.
32 Atiemo, 1993: 20; Assimeng, 1986: 140–56.
33 Cited in Assimeng, 1986: 138.
34 See Peel, 1968; Sanneh, 1995; Ojo, 1988*a*.
35 Hackett, 1997.
36 Atiemo, 1993: 31.
37 Wilson, 1926: 509.
38 Wrong, 1934: 9.
39 Wrong, 1931: 18.
40 Young, 1933: 5–6; author's emphasis.
41 *Ibid.*, 5.
42 NAG, CSO 18/1/144: n.pag.
43 Prizes were given in two classes: (i) Standards IV and V: entries were received from 53 boys and 3 girls; (ii) Standards VI and VII: 133 boys and 11 girls entered in this category.
44 *Ibid.*
45 *Ibid.*
46 *Ibid.*
47 Oduyoye, 1995.
48 Smiles, [1859] 1997: 16.
49 McCaskie, 1986; Ackah, 1988.
50 Smiles, [1859] 1997: 12.
51 *Ibid.*, 328.
52 *Ibid.*, 269–70.
53 *Ibid.*, 257.

54 Walton, 1929: 111.
55 Ward, 1991: 177.
56 Walton, 1929: 111.
57 *AMP*, 3 December 1937, fp.
58 *GCO*, 3 July 1942: 141.
59 *GCT*, 31 July 1937: 3. Sentiments such as this almost precisely echo the views of Samuel Smiles, John Ruskin and other nineteenth-century educationists. Smiles wrote: 'The habitual novel-reader indulges in fictitious feelings so much, that there is a great risk of sound and healthy feeling becoming perverted or destroyed. . . the heart that is touched too often by the fiction may at length become insensible to the reality' ([1859] 1997: 270).
60 *TWA*, 26 January 1935: 2.
61 *Ibid.*
62 Laubach, 1948: 122; see also Anon., 1938: 7–9.
63 De Mestral, 1954: 436.
64 De Mestral, 1959: 8.
65 See RHL, MSS.Brit. Emp.s.282.
66 See Cunard, [1934] 1970.
67 NAG(CC), ADM 23/1/726.
68 *Ibid.*
69 Guggisberg, 1924: 10; see also Jones, 1922: 35.
70 *Ibid.*, 30. Here were political reasons for mass education which echoed the reasons for legislation in Britain in the 1870s (see Watt, 1956; Webb, 1955).
71 RHL, MSS. Afr.s.1527, 27 June 1934.
72 *GCT*, 3–10 March 1934: 3.
73 *Ibid.*
74 RHL, MSS.Brit.Emp.s.282, 17 March 1934.
75 A large dossier of 'seditious' articles by Wallace-Johnson was compiled by the Gold Coast government and submitted to the Colonial Office in justification of its repressive legislation in the 1930s (RHL, MSS.Afr.s.1527). These articles include the infamous piece, 'Has the African a God?', which was published by Nnamdie Azikiwe in the *African Morning Post* and caused new legislation to be created to enable the Gold Coast Government to deport 'undesirables' such as Wallace-Johnson and Azikiwe.
76 *AMP*, 3 November 1937: 2.

5 Why read *The Sorrows of Satan?*: Marie Corelli's West African readerships

> I went. . . to teach in one of the so-called private schools in my district and
> discovered that the school 'library' consisted of a dusty cupboard contain-
> ing one copy of the Holy Bible, five pamphlets entitled *The Adventures of
> Tarzan*, and one copy of a novel called *The Sorrows of Satan*. (Achebe,
> *Morning Yet on Creation Day*)

Throughout the first three decades of the twentieth century a regular
advertisement appeared in the commercial supplement of *The Sierra
Leone Weekly News*. Each week, the representative of 'T. J. Sawyerr –
Bookseller, Stationer and General Dealer (estd. 1856)' of Water Street,
Freetown, filled a column with book reviews, book bargains and details
of new titles dispatched from Britain, suitable for all classes of West
African reader. Weighty tomes and simplified English classics were advertised alongside calendars and diaries containing quotations from the
European literary greats. Customers in search of epigrams and witticisms
could choose from the variety of Dickens, Tennyson and Shakespeare
diaries, while those seeking calendars containing 'a quotation per day'
could select from Bacon, Dickens, Longfellow, Ruskin, Shakespeare,
Napoleon and – perhaps most popular of all in Britain's colonies during
this period – Marie Corelli. In the evenings, readers could leaf through
non-fictional works obtained from Sawyerr's, such as *The Memoirs of
Paul Kruger*, or they might prefer to buy Marie Corelli's most recent
novel, newly arrived from Liverpool. Should they develop eye-strain or
poor health in the process, 'T. J. Sawyerr' could also furnish them with
spectacles, slippers and cod-liver oil.

For those who could read, or who mingled with literate individuals in
British West Africa, *The Sierra Leone Weekly News* would have been a
familiar title: indeed, by 1933 it claimed to be 'The Paper in every Home,
well-known, the most extensively circulated throughout the principal West
African Colonies'.[1] Similarly, Sawyerr's client-list extended across British
West Africa: through the column he sent regular greetings to customers in

'the Colony and its Protectorate, Sherbro, Gold Coast Colony, Northern and Southern Nigeria and Gambia', and items were sent out by mail to customers all over the region who were unable to visit the shop in person.[2] Upon picking up the newspaper, readers could not have missed Sawyerr's column, for the commercial pages of the *Weekly News* were wrapped around the inner news-sheets like a dust-jacket. As a result of this format, which echoed that of the London *Times*, the bookseller's commentaries made front page reading each week, and the colony's political pages and society columns were enfolded by eye-catching headlines and illustrations about locally available books and services.

Occasionally, the name of T. J. Sawyerr slipped out of the commercial section and into the news pages, revealing the effect of his bookstore upon the literary tastes of locals. In a letter to the *Weekly News* in 1908, one joyful reader stated:

I think all lovers of good, not trashy and degrading books, in Sierra Leone – especially our young men and women to whom we look for 'light and leading' in the near future – are greatly indebted to Mr T. J. Sawyerr for placing within the reach of the poorest literary aspirant such masterpieces of English literature as comprise *The People's Library* at the nominal cost of a shilling each volume.[3]

Responses such as this reveal the central role played by the local bookseller in influencing the leisure-reading choices of the literate community. Sawyerr's combination of low prices, good advertising and well-known writers would have gone a long way towards helping the 'poorest literary aspirant' to realise his or her ideal of assembling a personal book collection.

Sawyerr's advertisements are striking, both for their longevity and for their morally authoritative tone. Week after week between 1901 and 1930 the bookseller 'pressed on in his efforts to create a state for reading' in anglophone West Africa.[4] His mission was to throw light into his compatriots' intellectual corners, to fill their minds with improving literature and knowledge. Demonstrating his own encyclopaedic knowledge while advertising his wares, 'Mr Sawyerr remind[ed] the young men of Sierra Leone and its Protectorate in the words of Channing:– "It is chiefly through books that we enjoy intercourse with superior minds".'[5] In this manner, commercial considerations were presented as if they were secondary to the bookseller's intellectual and aesthetic projects. In Sawyerr's view, not only did the ability to read make it possible for literate West Africans to connect with 'superior minds' but, in conformity with current educational bias, a certain mental superiority was accorded to the literate individual, for in and of itself reading meant that, '(1) the children's curiosity can be gratified (2) the youth's thirst for knowledge can be satisfied and (3) the man's craving for further light can be met at nominal cost'.[6]

In spite of his efforts, the bookseller's mission finally faltered during the world recession of the 1930s, and the store folded after eighty years of business. Taken together over a thirty year period, however, the articles released by 'T. J. Sawyerr' form a unique collection of responses to the increasing flow of English literature into colonial bookshops from British and American publishing houses.[7] 'Novels! Novels!!' the column proclaims, 'Mr T. J. Sawyerr has the largest stock of Novels in the colony both new and old ranging from sevenpence upwards'.[8] What these advertisements reveal very clearly is the way in which West African booksellers made themselves responsible both for producing literary values and also for responding to popular local taste for specific titles.

Sawyerr's sensitivity to local literary preferences is revealed in relation to one particular novelist, whose name shines out repeatedly above even the most classical author listed in the column. What is astonishing, given the elite status and professional qualifications of a large proportion of the literate community in Sierra Leone and in anglophone West Africa generally, is the name of the author: Marie Corelli.

From the moment that her first novel, *A Romance of Two Worlds*, was published in 1886, to the moment she died nearly forty years later, this best-selling authoress was baited and derided in the British press. Observing her meteoric rise, many literary critics believed that Corelli personified the 'bad reader' brought forth by the Education Acts of 1870 and 1876, for she was judged incapable of writing real literature: her mind was described as 'ridiculously inadequate to the issues raised',[9] and her novels as 'the pretentious treatment of lofty themes by the illiterate for the illiterate'.[10] Adding insult to injury, her face was likened to that of 'a bulldog in ectoplasm'.[11] The public was deemed to have shown its true colours in choosing to read books by 'this pretentious and imperious little nonentity' above other, more literary, authors.[12] Corelli's name was invoked to criticise the reading choices of the masses who, as with the low-status 'scholars' of West Africa, preferred florid prose and moral wordiness to the precise, unadorned English of highly educated writers. In the ensuing forty-year battle between novelist and critic, Corelli played to the gallery by praising the reading public's preference for her type of fiction. In *The*

Sorrows of Satan (1895), for example, a publisher explains to the protagonist, whose novel has crashed despite his efforts to 'boom' it, 'people have
got Compulsory Education now. . . preferring to form their own independent opinions'.[13]

Queen Victoria, Prince Albert, Gladstone and the Prince of Wales
praised Corelli's work, but in British journals and newspapers the all-male
literati ridiculed her 'full-blooded Turkey-carpet style of writing with its
half dozen words where one would do'.[14] She split her infinitives, made
grammatical and theological blunders, saturated her prose with adjectives,
used an over-abundance of adverbs, and had an ethical agenda that would
put a saint to shame. In short, she subjected the English language and the
English novel to her own moral agenda, making them both work in the interests of her idealistic vision of society.[15] The British public loved her inflated
moral tone and applauded her prescriptions for the purification of society.
Whilst her romances made the reviewers wince, the reading public bought
her books by the tens of thousand, making her eighth novel, *The Sorrows of
Satan* (1895), the first best-seller in British publishing history.[16]

Marie Corelli's writing career spanned forty years, from 1886 to 1924,
overlapping with the most successful years of the 'T. J. Sawyerr' bookshop
in Freetown. Such a coincidence renders the column in the *Weekly News*
all the more interesting for the way in which the bookseller's comments on
Corelli shadow (or outshine) the output of the metropolitan reviewers.
Contrasting the dismissal of Corelli in the British press, 'T. J. Sawyerr' –
who might be seen as the voice of the Creole establishment carried over
from the mid-nineteenth century – proclaims his praise for this 'wonderful' author of 'deeply valued' literature.[17] Specimen copies of her novels
were held in the shop for inspection and her publisher's advance notices
were rewritten as tantalising cliffhangers: 'All that Mr Sawyerr is at liberty
at present to say about this book is that it will prove to be another *Uncle
Tom's Cabin*', Sawyerr concludes in his promotion of *Holy Orders* (1908),
having commented on its 'powerful style and plot', without giving either
away.[18] Clearly, Sawyerr is presenting Corelli as a prominent *literary* writer
worthy of close attention. 'This brilliant novelist', he writes, will 'delight
and enthral' all who read her in West Africa.[19]

This was not a case of poor quality literature being foisted upon naive
or unwilling colonial readerships, as Brian Masters (1978) suggests in his
biography of Corelli. 'Some remaindered Corelli titles were dumped in the
West Indies after Marie's death', Masters writes, 'with the result that a
whole generation has been brought up on Corelli, has even learnt English

with her, and has been introduced to literature through her'.[20] Ever since the 1920s, Masters implies, passive (post-)colonial readerships have been inundated with and influenced by this Victorian pulp literature.

Other commentators recognise that people's leisure-reading preferences involve choice and discernment, but they view Corelli's tenacious hold over readers in the colonies with puzzlement. 'It is clear that the English style and taste of many educated Gold Coast adults is firmly rooted in the nineteenth century', Helen Kimble (1956) comments, noting that the name of Marie Corelli appears first, above Shakespeare, Rider Haggard and Dickens (the three runners-up), in a reading survey of 159 people conducted in Accra in the early 1950s as part of the post-war commitment to mass education.[21] 'This limitation of taste is disappointing and yet challenging', Kimble continues, unable to offer any explanation for the conundrum of Corelli's popularity. She simply suggests that, given the popularity of self-help pamphlets and books aimed at solving modern problems, the Gold Coast reading public *should* choose contemporary novelists above the Victorians.[22] Perhaps the puzzlement of Kimble and other commentators derives from their failure to take historical and material conditions into account. Such critics ignore the possibility that West African readers preferred Corelli precisely because she assisted them to comprehend the moral obligations and ethical foundations of 'modern', colonial and Christian social formations.

Uncomfortable as the fact might be to Western literary critics, Corelli's metropolitan publishers were not disposing of unwanted stock through the commercial channels opened up by the British Empire. Sawyerr's weekly column reveals that, well in advance of the publication date, orders for Corelli's new novels would arrive from diverse West African locations, and customers waited expectantly for the arrival of their copies. A sophisticated commercial apparatus was in place at Sawyerr's, whereby first editions and special colonial editions of Corelli titles could be obtained within weeks of the originals' release in Britain. As Kimble's survey reveals, these titles, hot from the press in the early years of the century, remained favourites with West African readers well into the 1950s.

It was not simply the anglicised Creole community, dotted around West Africa, who ordered Marie Corelli en masse from their local bookshop. Her spiritual and didactic romances were immensely popular with men and women throughout Britain's colonies and foreign territories. Special 3/6d editions were produced for Corelli fans in Australia, New Zealand and the colonies, and by 1894 pirated editions of her novels were being imported into South Africa from America and sold at an uncontrollable speed.[23] In 1899 sixty New Zealand troopers in the South African trenches passed *The Soul of Lilith* (1892) between them, one page at a time; during the same war, a Colour Sergeant under siege in Natal described the 'invaluable' comfort obtained by the First Battalion Gloucestershire Regiment from *The Sorrows of Satan*; so widely read was Corelli that pages from *The Murder of Delicia* (1900) were discovered in the evacuated trenches of the Boer army, demonstrating the rapidity with which her novels dispersed around different communities of readers.[24] Besides the distribution channels opened up by the Boer War, Corelli was read as far afield as India and South East Asia. The Maharajah of Kartarpur sent gifts of 'hand-woven silk heavily embroidered with gold' to her,[25] and another Indian prince addressed her as 'one who is inspired with the truths of the Divine'.[26] Several titles were translated into Hindustani, Gujarati and also Thai, and translations were available in the major European languages.

The extent of Corelli's impact on literary values in the colonies is revealed by the way her name infuses the writing of diverse early novelists. Between 1901 and 1903, for example, a Thai translation of *Vendetta* (1886) was serialised in the magazine *Lak Witthayā* (trans. 'Plagiarism'), inspiring other translations from Western prose fiction and influencing the first generation of Thai novelists.[27] Similarly, early Ghanaian fiction is peppered with direct and oblique quotations from Corelli novels, particularly *The Sorrows of Satan*, which proved to be the most popular of her titles in the Gold Coast. A range of best-selling Corelli novels was still available at Sawyerr's bookshop in 1930, providing food for the 'intellectual appetite', sold alongside more practical 'how to' books such as *Mrs Beeton's Cookery Book* and *What a Young Wife Ought to Know*.[28] As for Nigeria, according to Chinua Achebe, 'so high was the admiration for Marie Corelli that in a little book just published in Nigeria she is numbered among the world's superwomen, in the company of Joan of Arc and Mary Magdalene'.[29] 'I tell you, that woman was a genius', declared another Nigerian author, Akachi Ezeigbo.[30]

Unlike her contemporary, H. Rider Haggard, on no occasion was Marie Corelli listed on the English literature syllabus of West African secondary schools.[31] In government and mission schools, it seems that Haggard's masculine adventure stories were regarded as better written and less damaging to young African minds than Corelli's steamy sagas of feminine purity struggling against the moral and sexual degradation of the age. In Britain and the colonies during the 1920s and 1930s, educationists and cultural commentators became increasingly concerned about the influence of popular literature on the reading public, and the general tone of their response to Corelli was that, 'Nothing can better illustrate the immense drop from the highly critical and intelligent society led by Charles Fox to later Victorian taste than the nature of Marie Corelli's success'.[32] Christian missionaries and colonial officials knew very well about the effects of 'bad' literature on African attitudes. Indeed, certain types of text were believed to play potentially dangerous games with the volatile emotions of any 'lowbrow', semi-educated reader, whether in Britain or the colonies. Not only did authors such as Marie Corelli combine 'Bad writing, false sentiment, sheer silliness, and a preposterous narrative', but they were also seen to be insufficiently intelligent to realise that their moral prescriptions encouraged 'social, national, and herd prejudices' amongst readers.[33]

In British West Africa, mission schoolteachers and educationists struggled to keep the reading of Corelli to a minimum amongst pupils. 'Students, left to themselves read with apparent enjoyment and profit most unexpected books', reported the Reverend L. B. Greaves of Wesley College, Kumasi: 'if we bought books in accordance with students' desires, we should have bought Marie Corelli and Hall Caine in bulk'.[34] As it is, the Reverend reined in student's literary desires and redirected them towards Rider Haggard's novels, *King Solomon's Mines* and *She*.[35] As late as 1955, the Gold Coast Library Board noted the idiosyncratic reading preferences of Gold Coast library users, registering the popularity of 'Novels by a few authors who, for varied reasons, have a special appeal to Africans such as Rider Haggard, Somerset Maugham and Marie Corelli';[36] and as we have seen, in 1956 Helen Kimble noted with astonishment the esteemed position of Corelli, a writer 'who can hardly have been recommended in any school syllabus'.[37]

As a result of the institutional bias against Corelli, for the first half of the twentieth century West African readers were required to make a proactive literary *choice* each time they wished to obtain one of her novels. 'The reading of Marie Corelli's novels was discouraged by our teachers', the Nigerian novelist Akachi Ezeigbo told me, describing how in the early 1960s, Corelli's novels would circulate in secret amongst girls at the Archdeacon Crowder Memorial Girls' School in Port Harcourt.[38] Left to their own devices, West African readers forged interpretations of these novels that were isolated from the contemptuous reviews appearing in the British press. The meanings they generated would, of course, have been preconditioned to a large extent by aesthetic values learnt at school, by the Christian framework surrounding literacy in general, by the value placed upon literacy by the colonial state, and by each reader's personal and inherited definitions of eloquence, beauty and narrative skill. However, their readings would not have been coloured by European literary prejudice but by the ways in which literary values were being negotiated and established in the region at this time: the comments of metropolitan reviewers would have had less impact on West African readers than the intense social debates occurring locally about morality and marriage.

Given her exclusion from the syllabus and her 'number one' status amongst readers, it is necessary to ask why Marie Corelli remained popular for so long in the region.[39] Her reign spanned the colonial state-building period. What aspects of her work were attractive to 'British West Africans', impelling each new generation of African readers from diverse language groups in diverse communities to seek out her books over a fifty-year period? When Achebe's Nigerian pamphleteer – probably an 'Onitsha' writer – lavished praise upon Corelli in his 'little book',[40] surely he must have been using interpretive skills that were different from the criteria employed by the Freetown Creoles in 1911? Likewise, T. J. Sawyerr's turn-of-the-century readers could not have been more different in lifestyle, occupation and outlook from the newly literate Ghanaian readers surveyed by Kimble in the early 1950s. Yet the former group read Corelli with as much relish as the latter group, finding themes of value in her vast, moralistic tomes. How was it possible for Corelli's writing to retain its appeal during five decades of seismic social and political shifts in British West African territories?

It is difficult to address these fascinating questions, not least because the effort to 'retrieve' historical readerships is beset with obstacles. Interview material is absent from the archives and we have few ways of discovering exactly how West African readers responded to foreign popular fiction between 1900 and 1950. One of the available strategies is to reread a novel by Marie Corelli, using it to speculate about changing West African literary values during the colonial period. To this end, the remainder of this chapter will examine the most frequently mentioned Corelli title in West Africa, *The Sorrows of Satan*. A series of 'openings' will be located in the novel, into which can be slotted many of the aesthetic debates and social questions to have emerged during the colonial period.

As with most Corelli novels, *The Sorrows of Satan* is heavily didactic and the plot is driven by the conflict between the forces of good and evil, defined in Christian terms to the extent that an angel complete with halo makes regular appearances in the form of Mavis Clare, a novelist who lives in the country and produces uplifting Christian romances; at the opposite end of the moral spectrum, 'Lucifer, Prince of Darkness' is realised as a full-blown fictional character named Prince Lucio Rimânez, a handsome foreigner who arrives in London complete with a retinue of demonic servants and snorting black horses. By the end of the novel, as his identity is revealed to the narrator, a spirit-chorus chants 'Ave Sathanas' and terrible cries, groans and flapping wings rent the air.[41] On the worldly level is the story's narrator, Geoffrey Tempest, who narrowly misses selling his soul to Satan after a friendship with Rimânez that involves a great deal of drinking and gambling in the elite clubs of London. Crucially for West African readers, the sign of Tempest's decline into evil is his choice of wife, for Lady Sibyl Elton is a 'fallen' society beauty who is so self-aware about her debauched sexual desires that she is capable of detailing the causes of her moral corruption for pages on end.

All of the characters carry their own particular pieces of moral baggage for the duration of the novel: Sibyl's sections of text detail the effects of pernicious novels on young ladies. Over against Sibyl, the 'ideal woman' is personified by the genius from the lower social ranks, Mavis Clare, the 'quiet and graceful creature, so slight and dainty' with a 'golden halo',[42] who struggles in her writing to overcome the powers of evil personified by the upper classes. Mavis Clare is 'poor – but unspeakably happy',[43] directly contrasting with Geoffrey Tempest, whose portions of narrative demonstrate the evil inherent in unearned wealth and the corruption of class society. Finally, Lucio's cynical speeches emphasise the lesson that friends may be fiends, that personal appearances and protestations of love often are masks worn by individuals intending harm.[44]

All of these characters occupy set places in a Christian grid, divided by thick lines. In a similar vein, when we turn to the plot and themes we find that the novel contains multiple moral pieces, any number of which might be grouped together by readers for purposes of contemplation and personal development. The vital constraint on this 'free flow' of meaning is that, as Q. D. Leavis points out, the reader of Corelli must follow the writer in being 'passionately in favour of the Christian ethic, the accepted social and moral code, family affection, altruism, and self-sacrifice'.[45]

In *The Sorrows of Satan*, 'evil' characters such as Sibyl and Prince Rimânez condemn themselves by their own words and behaviour. In moments of self-loathing they employ the same absolute moral framework by which they are conceived in order to point out their failings. For instance, Sibyl knows full well that she is morally corrupt, the product of degenerate upper-class parentage, environment and education. 'I cannot feel. I am one of your modern women', she warns Tempest upon his pro-posal of marriage: 'I am a contaminated creature, trained to perfection in the lax morals and prurient literature of my day.'[46] She follows her name-sake as a prophetess and fortune-teller, carrying this message through the text, writing it into her suicide letter which contains a lengthy condemna-tion of Realist and Naturalist narratives – particularly novels by Emile Zola – for their sensational depictions of 'base humanity', corrupting read-ers such as herself.[47]

It is important to note that Sibyl's downfall has been induced by the *fictional texts* she reads, and not primarily by the influence of people in soci-ety. Her evil nature is shown to have been created by her bad reading habits, a point she acknowledges again and again in her self-knowing monologues. 'Do you think a girl can read the books that are now freely published. . . and yet remain unspoilt and innocent?' she asks Tempest on one occasion, describing how modern novels promote 'polygamy' and 'free love', ideas which lead directly to her suicide the moment she attempts to practise them with Rimânez.[48] Into Sibyl's mouth goes a set of aesthetic values which are proved worthy by her own counterexample, for she dies in the knowledge that she has sold her soul to Satan and is heading directly for hell.

From the depths of depravity Sibyl comments on 'the serious and even terrible responsibility writers incur when they send out to the world books full of pernicious and poisonous suggestions'.[49] Whether romantic or real-istic, the written word is shown to have a discernible impact upon the behaviour of readers – particularly women readers – influencing them for better or for worse in their daily lives. Thus, Sibyl's reading makes of her a cold-hearted, unfaithful wife. 'All the finer and deeper emotions which make a holy thing of human wedlock, were lacking, – the mutual respect, the trusting sympathy, – the lovely confidence of mind with mind', Tempest comments, defining the ideal before encountering his wife sitting by the lake reading 'one of the loathliest of prurient novels that have been lately written by women to degrade and shame their sex'.[50] In fury, he snatches the novel and throws it into the water, but he has intervened too late to save Sibyl from the sticky end brought about by her literary tastes.

Given the extent to which the theme of 'misused', misdirected literacy is dramatised in *The Sorrows of Satan*, it is ironic and surprising that

Corelli's novels were excluded from the school syllabus in the colonies. *The Sorrows of Satan* plays out many of the debates about the links between Christian morals and 'good' reading matter taking place across British West Africa in the inter-war years. In legislative assemblies, missionary journals, schools, newspapers, social clubs and school common rooms, similar concerns to Corelli's were raised. Well into the 1930s, the social consequences of 'pernicious' – and, in the colonies, 'seditious' – literature were being discussed at an official level, and were taken up locally by new readerships to be debated and renegotiated in the social clubs and newspapers.

If the educationists chose to ignore *The Sorrows of Satan*, Corelli's mission-schooled West African readers must have seized upon it for its descriptions of good and bad reading modes, useful and damaging reading matter. The 'defective reader' modelled by Sibyl would have caused a strong reaction in Sierra Leone, Nigeria and the Gold Coast, where the majority of new literates would have learnt to read christianised texts in christianised classrooms, and where a tradition of independent, self-helping literary clubs was firmly established amongst school-leavers by the 1920s. 'I preferred *The Sorrows of Satan* for its religious angle. It is very morally inclined and it tends to structure your thinking about life', Ezeigbo stated, remembering her youth in Port Harcourt during the 1960s: 'At the mission school they taught us the moral angle in certain books. Reading *The Sorrows of Satan* brought into your mind the enormity of the power of the devil.'[51] Clearly, the idea of reading what Tempest labels 'the loathliest of prurient novels'[52] would have repelled readers such as Ezeigbo whose aim was to refine their intellects by reading 'improving' novels. *The Sorrows of Satan* thus validates readers' pre-existing conceptions about the reasons for reading particular types of text.

In other ways, too, *The Sorrows of Satan* is an exemplary narrative for colonial West African readerships. Within the first paragraph themes emerge that would appeal to certain groups of reader in the region. The novel opens with a vivid, first-person description of abject poverty, narrated by Geoffrey Tempest. Tempest is an aspiring novelist and hopes to become a member of the intelligentsia; he possesses one threadbare suit, one rejected book manuscript and one set of Christian ideals which are worn down and finally abandoned as a result of the influence of his decadent society. Being a 'commoner' with no funds for social and political investments, Tempest is similar to large numbers of educated West African men in the inter-war period who were struggling to gain status in a relatively closed colonial society. He is ambitious to succeed, desperately poor, intelligent, well-versed in Christian ethics and a follower of Christian marriage ideals.[53] Given what we know about newly educated West African men in the 1920s and 1930s, then, it is clear that interest in Geoffrey Tempest's situation would have been immense, particularly amongst readers in the Gold Coast.[54]

The story is recounted with hindsight by Tempest, whose sudden inheritance of five million pounds renders him so open to the forces of evil that he becomes the passive plaything of Lucifer, indulging in gambling, drinking and sex in the upper-class dens of London. From the outset he voices his one hope for those in possession of similar quantities of unearned or ill-gotten wealth, that 'other men currently in sin, [will] learn from this lesson narrated here'.[55] As for the colonies, 'other men' will learn this and many other lessons from the narrative, and one of the most pervasive messages retained and reiterated from *The Sorrows of Satan* concerns women's roles in marriage. Early Ghanaian literature is saturated with similar marital ideals to those laid forth in this novel, and until the 1970s much Nigerian popular literature contained traces of Corelli. Direct quotations from *The Sorrows of Satan* abound in stories by J. Abedi-Boafo (1938) and J. Benibengor Blay (1944), and 'softer' quotations can be found in many other authors' work in the form of women who resemble Corelli's saintly and sinful female characters.[56]

Ironically perhaps, it is the devil himself who is most often quoted by West African authors, for in *The Sorrows of Satan* Lucio is in charge of describing the ideal Christian household ruled over by morally pure and faithful wives. Any reader wishing to extrapolate the *marital* moral from the novel will end up quoting Lucio, who has the most to say about women's wifely duties. 'Women have always done me harm', he tells Tempest, 'And why I especially abominate them is that they have been gifted with an enormous power for doing good, and that they let this power run to waste and will not use it.'[57] For Lucio the saintly wife exists *in absentia*, and Corelli endorses the devil's cynical sermons by creating in the character of Sibyl an extreme example of wifely infidelity. Lucio offers regular sermons of this type and his misogynistic comments are proved accurate by the female 'society' portrayed in the novel, for the physical beauty of characters such as Sibyl and her mother, Lady Elton, mask their avarice and sexual promiscuity. 'Ah, what fools men are!' Lucio exclaims, 'How little we dream of the canker at the hearts of these women "lilies" that look so pure and full of grace!';[58] 'The idleness, wickedness, extravagance, and selfishness of women, make men the boors and egotists they are', he comments after Sibyl's attempted seduction of him, adding, 'Let us put the whole mischief down to the "new" fiction!'[59]

Many of the saintly and sinful women who surface as characters in early West African narratives demonstrate the process whereby Corelli's West African readers were impressed by her writing to the extent that they reimagined her stories, filling out her characters and quotations with local colours and opinions. Lucio is the driving force behind early novels such as *And Only Mothers Know*,[60] appearing in the narrative in the form of a named, quoted character and informing the narrator's running commentary against unfaithful African wives; women resembling Sibyl appear in many Nigerian pamphlets and Ghanaian popular novels, flashing their 'violet eyes' seductively at young men in order to deprive them of their money. 'You don't see these characters as white people', Ezeigbo explained, for 'the moral threads in their characters are far more real to you than their personalities as foreigners.'[61]

In quoting Lucio and in recreating 'Sibyline' characters, these writers had not necessarily read through the entire five hundred pages of Corelli's *The Sorrows of Satan*, following the downfall of the bad wife and skim-reading the sections dealing with other, less relevant themes. Instead, authors might have had *The Marie Corelli Birthday Book* to hand, or a copy of *The Marie Corelli Calendar: A Quotation from the Works of Marie Corelli for Every Day in the Year*. There they would have found Lucio amply quoted, alongside epithets on the qualities of the ideal wife extracted from the numerous Corelli novels containing this theme. Such texts would have taken on the status of encyclopaedias, containing moral facts and fragments of knowledge to be pulled from the page and reconstituted elsewhere. Similarly, quotations from *The Sorrows of Satan* in the local newspapers might have inspired local authors to pick up on particular themes. Corelli had not therefore necessarily *initiated* the ideas expressed through the quotation of her work. It would be ludicrous to claim that this author alone launched the theme of unearned, malign wealth into West African literature, or that Corelli inspired every description of the ruination of young women by the sexually lax mores of the city. These themes cannot be 'sourced' in such a simplistic manner, and they antedated *The Sorrows of Satan* by many decades.[62]

Corelli's cultural significance in West Africa relates to the remarkable way in which her novels meshed with local aesthetic and moral values. Whether seeking to express old themes or new, readers could turn to her novels and 'pick' epigrammatic, quotable material suitable for a wide range of moral debates. Her work permeated literary output to the extent that quotations from her novels would form the starting point for newspaper articles and novels alike, used to convey sentiments imbued with local concerns. In an editorial in the *Gold Coast Times*, for example, the death of a local 'man of affairs', Josiah Afari Mills, is announced and bewailed through the quotation of Lucio in *The Sorrows of Satan*. The editor writes, 'This dark world of ours is replete with Joys and Sorrows. Rightly has the late Marie Correli [*sic*] termed it the "Sorrowful Star". Across which threshold the skeleton form of death has now thrown his fearsome shadow.'[63] In another issue of the same newspaper, 'Gloria', the author of the Women's Corner announces, 'Mother moulds the life, character and destiny of man. . . The beautiful words of Marie Corelli are worth quoting here, "Who shall deny you the right of angelhood, ye patient self-denying, noble women. . . A true mother is Heaven's own creation".'[64]

Taken together, the didactic characters, quotable chunks and 'improving' themes help to explain the resilience of *The Sorrows of Satan* in West Africa during the colonial period. The novel is constructed as a series of moral tableaux – or *tableaux vivants* – each one containing quotable sentiments and themes which can be extracted and reused by readers in their own moral assessments of local and personal situations. The abstract Christian moral, that by not choosing to follow the path of good a person embarks on the path of evil, is grounded at every stage of *The Sorrows of Satan* in the concept of British class society. Corelli's London setting is portrayed as a rigidly hierarchised society, filled with aristocrats in possession of country houses and seats in parliament. Excessive amounts of money are frittered away by the ruling classes on sex and bribes, fashion items, entertainments and vanity projects. In Tempest's degenerate society, genius is less valued than gold, and immoral novels are more publishable than upright Christian literature. Each successive aristocratic character to appear in the novel develops this theme, particularly the arch-aristocrat Prince Lucio Rimânez. As Lucio tells Geoffrey, 'If. . . you happen to be truly great, brave, patient, and enduring, with a spark in you of that genius which strengthens life and makes it better worth living', yet have no gold to distribute, then 'you shall be spurned' in English society.[65] These sentiments undoubtedly would have appealed to British West African readerships in the 1920s and 1930s, many of whom developed nationalist sympathies as a result of witnessing or experiencing inequalities in their own racially hierarchised societies.

The class dimension of the story also opens up the possibility of a 'seditious' reading of *The Sorrows of Satan*. When Corelli's domestic novels are transported to colonial West Africa and when her meritocratic social ideals are transplanted into segregated or hierarchised colonial soil, a whole new dimension attaches to Lucio's remark that 'I foresee a new aristocracy. . . when the Low educates itself and aspires, it becomes the High'.[66] Self-education and aspiration to be 'high' played a major part in fuelling the nationalist movements in British West Africa.

Politically frustrated readers of *The Sorrows of Satan* certainly would have found ideological ammunition in the novel, for Corelli's portrayal of the ruling class reveals that every institution in the metropolis – publishing houses, private schools, the police force and government itself – is saturated with evil. This theme is developed to such an extent that the final scene shows Satan entering the Houses of Parliament, absorbed in conversation with a minister with whom he walks arm in arm: they 'ascend the steps and finally disappear within the House of England's Imperial Government, – Devil and man, – together!'[67] Evil permeates and pollutes the very heart of the British Empire, and London is revealed to be a lost city. Thus, Corelli's novel might have assisted West African readerships to comprehend, from a Christian perspective, the unethical foundations of the British colonial state. One of the messages to be gleaned from *The Sorrows of Satan* is that, until the social hierarchies give way to a meritocratic work ethic, the forces of evil will continue to thrive in the metropolis.

No printed evidence exists of such a 'seditious' reading of *The Sorrows of Satan* in colonial West Africa, and it is unlikely that Corelli's exclusion from the school syllabus had any more sinister motive than the educationists' attempt to prevent students from emulating her overblown literary style. 'Marie Corelli. . . was a Victorian fashion, and remains so in the Victorianised Gold Coast', Helen Kimble comments in her survey of readers in Accra: 'anybody who has marked Gold Coast students' essays knows how deeply ingrained is the Victorian style and how difficult it is to convince people that "plain words", in Gower's [sic] sense, are better'.[68] Reports by education committees and school inspectors over the forty-year period between 1910 and 1950 reveal the efforts that educationists put into eliminating Corelli's type of verbosity. However, the point remains that an important anti-colonial reading can readily be made of *The Sorrows of Satan*. London is not portrayed as the democratic centre of a great empire. From his life mingling with the English ruling class in London, Tempest learns that the polity is characterised by political corruption, cruelty to others and unfair access to gold. Albeit in antithetical form, the key concepts of democracy and equality are embedded in these lessons, concepts which also characterised anti-colonial discourse in the colonies.

In an age of colonial adventure stories – which *were* included on the literature syllabus in West African schools – Marie Corelli wrote uplifting, ethical romances aimed at readers who 'want their thoughts raised or purified in the novels they read for amusement'.[69] In tone and choice of subject matter, Corelli, the 'Queen of Victorian best-sellers', differed greatly from H. Rider Haggard, who emerged in the 1880s as the 'King of Romance'.[70] In Haggard's stories, brave white men set out from the metropolis for adventures amongst natives, albeit noble ones, on the darkest fringes of the Empire. Corelli's novels reverse the moral direction of these journeys: in her stories it is the *rural* folk who attempt to bring spiritual healing and civilisation to those in the metropolis. Forced to live on the margins of British society, these pure characters make forays into the capital city, revealing the extent of its corruption before fleeing back to their countryside dwellings. Perhaps this helps to explain Corelli's resilience in colonial West Africa. She influenced the early West African novelists in a manner that Haggard did not because her domestic dramas appealed directly to the literary tastes, ethics and ideals of West African readers. Morally and politically, her writing helped to *centre* readers who were constantly under threat of marginalisation or erasure from political processes which were managed by Europeans.

Corelli detested any system in which an underclass was excluded from power, and she used writing as a tool to fashion her critique.[71] In *The Sorrows of Satan* alone, she condemns unearned wealth, rejects atheism and, in the manner of Bunyan, signposts a route to personal redemption through hard work and Christianity. She was dismissed in Great Britain as 'a rigid moralist denouncing the shams and follies of Society',[72] and it was for these very reasons that her writing was applauded in West Africa. Her novels offered 'light and leading', qualities sought by Sierra Leoneans in their letters to the newspapers in the early years of the twentieth century; and in colonial Ghana, lists of 'good books that grip one straight from the beginning' frequently include Corelli, who is recommended in the 1930s as a novelist who 'adds to culture and often makes one a welcome member of refined society'.[73]

After the achievement of independence in most British colonies, a sign appeared of Corelli's final acceptance into the West African school system.

In 1962 a 'special reading edition' of *Thelma* (1887) was published by Longmans in simplified form, 'intended as a help in building vocabulary' and adapted for 'bilingual' readers by Margaret Maison and Michael West.[74] Michael West in particular had many decades' experience in 'reducing' English classics and adventure stories for West African elementary schools: in the 1920s he wrote books on the teaching of English to students in the Empire, and his 'creative' repertoire included a simplified *Silas Marner*, an adaptation of *Return to Treasure Island* and many other 'New Method Readers' for Longmans in the 1930s, 1940s and 1950s. English educationists such as West thus appear to have accepted Corelli into the canon of 'reduced' novels for foreign readerships by 1962, the only condition being that they simplify her elaborate diction, limiting it to a basic vocabulary.

The Africa into which this simplified edition of *Thelma* was released had undergone dramatic political, social and economic transformations since Corelli's decades-long peak in popularity. Indeed, by the 1960s literary tastes had changed sufficiently for references to Corelli to have become less flattering and more ambivalent than in previous decades. For instance, in his cynical post-colonial novel, *A Man of the People* (1966), Chinua Achebe refers to Corelli in order to expose the uneducated, low-grade literary tastes of 'Chief the Honourable M. A. Nanga', the corrupt and uneducated Minister of Culture who is unable to name the country's leading writers and believes that Michael West is a 'great writer' on a par with Shakespeare and Jane Austen.[75] At one point in this novel the protagonist, Odili, wanders into the Minister's library and finds there 'a decorative set of an American encyclopaedia. . . *She* by Rider Haggard, and also *Ayesha, or the Return of She*; then there were a few books by Marie Corelli and Bertha Clay – I remember in particular *The Sorrows of Satan*'.[76] Achebe's description reflects an ongoing preference for Corelli amongst lesser-educated Nigerians, but the presence of *The Sorrows of Satan* in Chief Nanga's library signifies a more sinister theme, for the Chief's literary preferences reveal that he has preserved a neo-colonial cultural liaison with the British at the expense of locally produced literature. Corelli, Haggard and Clay – Victorians all, writing in the Age of Empire – have displaced the new African fiction from the library shelves of the political leader, and to this extent they symbolise the novel's concern with Nigeria's failed, or partial, achievement of independence.

Except for a few members of the intelligentsia who remained ambivalent about her work, Corelli gained recognition in West Africa as a 'literary' author. Judging by the information presented in this chapter, the reception of her work in Sierra Leone, Nigeria and Ghana indicates that for the duration of the colonial period her writing was valued in West Africa for precisely the stylistic and thematic features that caused her to be derided by the intelligentsia in Britain. The Christian themes and manichean characters in novels such as *The Sorrows of Satan* provided colonial readers with a moral framework within which they could work on producing their own sets of meanings, particularly in relation to gender ideals. For this reason, in West Africa at least, Corelli's novels were regarded as the antithesis of 'trash'.

The African responses presented in this chapter reveal that Corelli's work was regarded as well written and morally educative, and that she was greatly in demand by local readers. Her novels provided infinitely requotable morsels of wisdom on general topics such as poverty, marriage, evil, literature and inequality. Readers could chew over their Corelli quotations as they progressed through each day. In addition to providing epigrams for daily use, it is probable that her novels had a deeper impact on West African literary production. Even if my 'seditious' reading of her work is put to one side, it is clear that her writing contributed to the repertoire of themes and characters which emerged in the earliest novels produced for local readerships by new writers in the 1930s and 1940s. When Corelli has a character say, 'It is because we make for ourselves "ideal" men, "ideal" women, and endow these fair creatures with the sentiment of "imaginary" love, that we are still able to communicate with the gods',[77] it is almost as if *she* is quoting from a corpus of West African narratives stretching back to J. E. Casely Hayford's *Ethiopia Unbound* (1911) and forward to R. E. Obeng's *Eighteenpence* (1943). Whether or not Casely Hayford and Obeng read Corelli – the literary establishment might shudder at such a proposition – her work was 'in the air', intermingling with other, equally powerful ideological forces which combined in these writers to bring forth the first locally authored narratives in the Gold Coast.

Notes

1 *SLWN*, 8 July 1933: 15.
2 *SLWN*, 5 January 1907: fp.
3 *SLWN*, 8 February 1908: 6.
4 *SLWN*, 9 January 1909: fp.
5 *SLWN*, 12 October 1907: fp.

6 *SLWN*, 20 April 1907: fp.
7 What complicates the intimacy and directness of 'T. J. Sawyerr's' weekly address is the fact that Thomas John Sawyerr died in 1894, several years before January 1901, when the first advert for his bookshop appeared. Despite the very real 'death of the author', his successors, the barristers A. J. and J. C. Sawyerr, continued to generate texts in the name of their father. The patriarch remained the protagonist – albeit in the third person – of the 'T. J. Sawyerr' column, very much alive and well, sending 'hearty Christmas greetings to his numerous customers' in 1907 (*SLWN*, 5 January: fp) and offering an 'Easter Letter to his Customers' in 1930 (*SLWN*, 30 March: fp). The sons' strategy is a clever exploitation of the 'invisibility' conferred on authors by the medium of print, enabling them to rouse the spectre of their father for a once-weekly airing, during which he called on customers' loyalty to the firm, invited them to visit and peruse the shelves, and advised young readers on the benefits of study. The 'Sawyerr' I am referring to in this chapter is thus a spectral figure who stands for (and stands in for) the 'House of Sawyerr'.
8 *SLWN*, 7 January 1911: fp.
9 Leavis, [1932] 1965: 64.
10 Sampson, cited in Masters, 1978: 292.
11 Connolly, cited in Masters, 1978: 8.
12 Masters, 1978: 31.
13 Corelli, 1895: 212.
14 *Morning Post*, 22 April 1924, cited in Ransom, 1999: 6.
15 See Federico, 2000.
16 See Ransom, 1999; Federico, 2000; Masters, 1978.
17 *SLWN*, 22 August 1908: fp.
18 *Ibid.*, 22 August 1908: fp.
19 *Ibid.*, 29 July 1911: fp.
20 Masters, 1978: 305.
21 Kimble, 1956: 80
22 *Ibid.*
23 See Ransom, 1999: 76–8.
24 Carr, 1901: 61–3.
25 Masters, 1978: 8.
26 Carr, 1901: 55.
27 Senanan, 1975: 39, 64. I am indebted to Bill Watson, University of Kent at Canterbury, for this reference.
28 *SLWN*, 30 March 1930: fp.
29 Achebe, [1972] 1975: 39. The 'little book' referred to by Achebe was probably the Onitsha pamphlet, *Spiritual Renaissance in Nigeria* by Joseph Okwuobari Ekezie. I am indebted to Anita Kern for this information.
30 Ezeigbo, Interview, 2000.
31 She does get a mention in the *Achimota Library Catalogue* (1935), which lists four Corelli titles and several Sabatinis amongst hundreds of popular editions and 'reduced' versions of English literary classics. Also, as the epigraph

reveals, *The Sorrows of Satan* could be found in at least one Nigerian school 'library' in the 1950s.

32 Leavis, [1932] 1965: 137.

33 Leavis, [1932] 1965: 61–70. With nearly a century's hindsight, it is easy to criticise Q. D. Leavis's elitism and her construction of 'lowbrow' readers as passive fantasists, their emotions easily influenced by the sensational writing of under-educated authors. What must be remembered is that Leavis was expressing commonly held concerns about first- and second-generation readers in Britain, the early products of compulsory mass education after 1876. Similar concerns were echoed in the colonies in the 1920s and 1930s, with the additional worry that 'bad' reading would inspire seditious 'native' publications, resulting in civil disobedience and anti-colonial protest (see Newell, 2000). Leavis's comments on Corelli are thus relevant to the colonies, articulating the concerns of an epoch about the dangers of mass literacy.

34 Greaves, 1932: 36.

35 *Ibid.*

36 Gold Coast Library Board, 1955: 72.

37 Kimble, 1956: 80.

38 Ezeigbo, Interview, 2000.

39 The reasons for Corelli's popularity also exercised British critics of her fiction. As one contributor to the *Westminster Review* – a man who went on to establish firm links with West Africa as a 'coaster' and inhabitant of Onitsha – wrote in 1906, 'The questions which I have asked myself with marked insistence have been, "Who are chiefly Marie Corelli's admirers?" "Why is she so popular?" and "What relation does the popularity of an author bear to the quality of the writer's books?"' (Stuart Young, cited in Federico, 2000: 61).

40 Achebe, [1972] 1975: 39.

41 Corelli, 1895: 458–70.

42 *Ibid.*, 226.

43 *Ibid.*, 259.

44 This 'deceptive appearance' theme dominates Nigerian market literature, which was produced in bulk by young school-leavers in and around Onitsha in the 1950s and 1960s (see Newell, 1996).

45 Leavis, [1932] 1965: 160.

46 Corelli, 1895: 200, 202.

47 *Ibid.*, 405.

48 *Ibid.*, 201–2.

49 *Ibid.*, 201.

50 *Ibid.*, 304–5.

51 Ezeigbo, Interview, 2000.

52 Corelli, 1895: 304–5.

53 The character of the self-made woman, Mavis Clare, also reinforces this theme, for as one character comments, she 'hasn't a penny in the world that she does not earn' (Corelli, 1895: 142).

54 See Agovi, 1990; Holmes, 1972.

55 Corelli, 1895: 1.
56 See Newell, 2000.
57 Corelli, 1895: 83.
58 *Ibid.*, 130.
59 *Ibid.*, 386; 388.
60 Abedi-Boafo, [1938] 1946.
61 Ezeigbo, Interview, 2000.
62 Many Yoruba-language narratives published or performed since the mid-nineteenth century gave a positive spin to both themes, celebrating the larger-than-life figure of the urban prostitute and applauding the sudden influx of unearned wealth as the sign of an individual's spiritual health (see Barber, [1981] 1997).
63 *GCT*, 13 March 1937: 6.
64 *Ibid.*, 28 January 1939: 12.
65 Corelli, 1895: 130.
66 *Ibid.*, 88.
67 *Ibid.*, 487.
68 Kimble, 1956: 80.
69 Corelli, 1895: 35.
70 See Dixon, 1995; Showalter, 1991.
71 Ransom, 1999.
72 Cited in Ransom, 1999: 6.
73 *TWA*, 22 January 1932: 3.
74 Masters, 1978: 305.
75 Achebe, 1966: 61–5.
76 *Ibid.*, 40. I should like to thank Lyn Innes of the University of Kent at Canterbury for this reference. Bertha Clay remains widely available, and widely read, in Ghanaian bookshops: she was listed as a favourite novelist by readers filling in questionnaires between 1996 and 1999, one hundred years after her departure from British literary memory.
77 *Marie Corelli Calendar*, 1913: 24.

6 White cargoes/black cargoes on the West Coast of Africa: Mabel Dove's *A Woman in Jade*

(The exquisite lines of her sensuous young figure are displayed by the manner in which she has draped her body in a soft, many-colored cloth ... Her features are small and regular after the fashion of the Hindoo girl, with the exception of the lips, which are over full) ... 'I am Tondeleyo.' (Gordon, *White Cargo: A Play of the Primitive*)

Then he remembered where he was; that the woman was black; and disgust flooded over him. (Simonton, *Hell's Playground*)

Anxieties about the negative moral influence of foreign novels and movies upon young people were raised on a regular basis in Ghana in the 1930s and 1940s, running alongside the debates about good and bad literature discussed in chapter 4. On occasion, concerned parents would halt young people's displays of western culture: the young socialite of the 1930s and 1940s, Kate Riby-Williams, revealed in an interview that during one dance at school, 'a boy from town sang a love-song, "I Love You for Sentimental Reasons", and the mums stopped it. They closed the function at once.'[1] Unlike these mums, 'Marjorie Mensah' (pseud. Mabel Dove) adored the new romantic musicals; but she was no exception to the prevailing mood, especially when it came to literature. In one review of Marie Corelli's *The Sorrows of Satan*, for example, she praises 'the grim pathos of the whole piece: the cunning, ingenuity and mysterious dignity of Prince Romanz [*sic*] – and then, what a wonderful climax that takes me almost out of breath'.[2] However, Corelli, 'cannot rank or be claimed to be a classic. She was a great romancer and viewed life entirely from this standpoint. . . I would like to see our girls reading more of the works of really classical authors.'[3]

The ambivalence surrounding the western romance is perfectly captured in Dove's punning typo, where the devil incarnate of Corelli's novel, Prince Rimânez, is renamed as 'Prince *Romanz*', a kitsch incarnation of 'Prince Romance', the hero of the Western love genre. The expression of 'love' – complete with pulsing crimson hearts and dense purple prose – is shown by writers such as Dove to be a discourse which masks the cunning of lovers, who are invariably revealed to be rogues operating in a world outside the value systems and vocabulary of the 'happy ever after' narrative. With 'honey mouth' and forked tongue the prospective lover becomes a 'sly friend' to his victim, invading her rose-tinted world and offering her so much 'counterfeit' love that she falls to her moral ruin.[4]

Dove's ambivalence towards romantic love symptomises her broader ambivalence as an educated African towards the mass-produced films and popular novels flowing into West Africa from America and Britain in the mid-1930s.[5] Increasing numbers of cinemas opened in the expanding Ghanaian cities during this period, screening movies 'full of super sensation' such as *Gold Diggers* – which remained 'the sensation of Accra' for a number of years[6] – as well as the *Tarzan* movies, *The King of the Kongo*, *Gentlemen Prefer Blondes* and many 'powerful stories of great love and sacrifice'.[7]

The problem for Ghana's moralists was that, while Hollywood helped to uphold images of women as chaste and loyal lovers, it also generated celebratory images of single women, depicting them as dark seductresses or as liberated, fun-loving 'gold diggers' who, if they married at all, would marry a man for money not love. 'Those of us who were a trifle shocked at the gold-diggers crowd will find Sally after our own heart', Dove writes with apparent relief, responding to one of the new romantic *Sally* movies showing at Ocansey's Palladium in January 1933.[8] Unlike *Gold Diggers*, where the only sincerely held emotion is the love of money, the new film 'is a picture which should inspire and give courage to those who have suffered in "love"'.[9]

The glamorous western life- and love-styles represented on the silver screen were made all the more dangerous, for Dove, by the presence in the Gold Coast of a certain type of European male, 'who appears to be absolutely desperate as far as African girls are concerned', who spends his time 'orgling [*sic*], winking and taking his chance' with local young women, turning them into good-time girls and ruining their prospects of attaining positions of respect as married women in African society.[10] The play to be examined in this chapter represents Dove's moral response to local women's liaisons with this type of man in colonial Ghana. Given that local women 'always prefer doing wrong than right', following the glamorous gold-digger rather than Sally for behavioural models, Dove reveals her ambition as a writer to 'attempt some adjustment in these channels'.[11] The play, *A Woman in Jade*, can also be regarded as Dove's 'reader response' to the images of Africa – particularly of African women – generated by the popular texts and movies circulating around British and colonial cultures in the 1920s and 1930s. The former response is played out through the latter, for Dove judges European men in West Africa by borrowing from a western repertoire of black and white character types: however, the difference in Dove's case is that she inverts the racial bias of her borrowed texts, transforming the image of the pith-helmeted, idealistic colonial officer into an 'orgling, winking', immoral character who craves sexual experiences with local women and is incapable of committing to long-term relationships.

In expressing her reactions to inter-racial relationships in the form of a play, Dove draws upon one particularly influential representation of West Africa, epitomised by the character of 'Tondeleyo' in Leon Gordon's *White Cargo: A Play of the Primitive* (1923). *White Cargo* proved massively successful in Britain and America in the 1920s and 1930s, and the motion picture, starring Hedy Lamarr as Tondeleyo, was an instant success in 1942. Portraying the seduction and degradation of Allen Langford, a morally impeccable but emotionally weak Englishman, by Tondeleyo, a 'sensual and sinister half-breed', *White Cargo* capitalised on long-standing fears at home about the sexual (and thus moral) temptations facing 'our' men in the colonies. These concerns dated back at least to the turn of the twentieth century, for *White Cargo* itself was based upon a novel by Ida Vera Simonton, *Hell's Playground*, first published in 1912 and reprinted at least four times in the 1920s.[12]

In the context of metropolitan culture, the ideological staying-power of this theme arises from the way in which the downfall of European civilisation is symbolised at the most intimate level by the sexual liaison of coloniser and colonised. 'You bring out everything that's rotten in me', says Langford, the hero of *White Cargo*, as he gives Tondeleyo the first in the series of lingering kisses that leads to their disastrous marriage.[13] Stated plainly, the moral of the play is that 'if you marry. . . [a] nigger you're going to a hell that no man can stand up against'.[14] Even if the African woman is 'more than half-white', like Tondeleyo, the European man will quickly discover the extent of her unbridled sexual instincts and 'just how shallow her poor little soul' is.[15] The 'native' portion of the 'half-caste' woman will reject Christian monogamy, plotting murder to escape the marriage contract.

The idea that the 'savage' could be civilised through marriage rather than through the intellectual and moral leadership of the white man is completely debunked in *White Cargo*. As we discover, Tondeleyo 'is more than half white, but her blood and her instincts are all nigger' like the 'natives' around her.[16] The play thus makes the point that when the civiliser mingles his blood with that of the savage the moral justification for imperialism is undermined.

Stern warnings followed the white man into Africa, advising him against liaising with 'the savage' – including the 'half-caste' – whose 'native superstitions, beliefs, abominable practices and nudity are as much a part of him as are his peculiar odour, his black skin and his kinky hair'.[17] Where this cardinal rule is broken, a new race of sexually voracious Africans is born, represented in *White Cargo* by Tondeleyo, 'a notorious harlot' who is shown taking domestic and economic power from her master in a cunning and murderous manner.[18] The very presence of Tondeleyo symbolises the failure of the white man to civilise and christianise the natives, for her father has made a mistress of her mother when he should have been setting a moral example to the polygynous natives. As Reverend Roberts says in the movie, 'half-castes' such as 'Tondeleyo can only mean another example of our failure'. When they use sex to rise up and take power, they place the final nail in the coffin of a morally weak imperial masculinity. To demonstrate this point, at the end of *White Cargo*, having barely survived his wife's attempt to poison him, Langford is carried from the scene and transported downriver, a piece of 'white cargo' to be loaded on board a steamer, an emasculated echo of Conrad's Mr Kurtz.

Heart of Darkness inspired countless derivative texts depicting the retrogression of white men in West and Central Africa and the need to uphold rigorous moral standards in order to survive the corrupting climate. For example, Ida Vera Simonton's best-selling *Hell's Playground* (1912), upon which *White Cargo* is based, depicts 'the debauching life of the African tropics', particularly how, when 'freed from all restraint, deprived of the society of white women', white traders and officials 'early shed the veneer of civilization. They revel in tyranny, licentiousness and brutality. . . they outsavage the very savage.'[19] A specific difference separates Conrad's tale from these successors, however: Kurtz's African mistress symbolises the moral retrogression of Kurtz, but she does not bring about his corruption. Autonomous and noble, draped in the trinkets and bangles presented by her lover, she appears as the white man's sexual other, the untamed savage onto whom Kurtz has, incomprehensibly, poured his affections. By contrast, Tondeleyo is not the symbol of Langford's downfall but the agent of it. Goading and tempting the lonely man with her sexual displays, she fits the western mold of 'seductress' far more readily than Kurtz's 'other' mistress, whose sexuality is alien to the narrator of the tale.

From the first appearance of the 'half-caste adventuress'[20] in *Hell's Playground* to her appearance as the semi-clad seductress in the war-time movie, the 'Tondeleyo' figure resonated with symbolic potential, signifying all that was desirable and yet terrifying and untamed in colonial Africa. With each passing decade the weak-willed hero becomes increasingly limp, while the black woman is punished more severely for her sexual power. In Simonton's novel of 1912, for example, the fallen man makes a reasonable comeback as a West Coast trader after sending his treacherous lover packing down the coast; a decade later, in Gordon's stage-play, Tondeleyo's power is neutralised by the canny Witzel, who forces her to make 'tiffin' for him after Langford's departure; in the screenplay of 1942, however, the audience's final vision of Tondeleyo is of an unconscious figure, sprawled dead or dying on the forest floor while Langford is transported downriver. Tondeleyo is the opposite of the fantasy image of the woman *civilising* the man, a tradition of representation stretching from Richardson's *Pamela* to Brontë's *Jane Eyre*. In psychoanalytic terms, the repression of the desired element, which proves repulsive to the colonial ego, has been achieved, but the effort has been so monumental as to symptomise the ongoing power of the denied element.

British popular novels focused on the theme of 'the debauching life of the African tropics'[21] with increasing fervour during the inter-war years. At this time, opportunities were increasing for middle- and working-class men to find employment in West Africa. With the expansion of the colonial civil service, positions became available throughout the Empire;[22] additionally men could find employment in the European trading companies positioned along the Coast; or they could set up their own stores and trading stations to do business with African customers.[23] In this climate of masculine enterprise, the 'half-caste' woman was deployed in popular narratives as an attractive, exotic vessel into which authors and ideologues could pour their concerns about the moral dangers facing youthful traders and administrators. *White Cargo* dramatises 'the trouble with mixed blood. The color always predominates.'[24] Tondeleyo's mother is 'Accra woman. Much black. (*She spits contemptuously.*) Tondeleyo most white.'[25] This African matrilineage is shown to pollute and overpower the western blood of her father. Being of mixed parentage, 'she knows how to purr her way into your mind and scratch her way out'[26] and, being of African woman born, she symbolises the moral 'damp rot' that would, it was feared, set into young men after several months in the interior.[27]

In the eighteenth and nineteenth centuries, European traders and travellers had remarked upon (and helped to sustain) the numbers of 'mulattoes' on the West Coast of Africa, to the extent that one early mission school in Cape Coast, set up at the Castle in 1751, was dedicated to the education of these by-products of European expansion.[28] In the best-selling novels of the early twentieth century, however, we witness the full 'horror, the horror' of the white man's loss of moral and political control in black Africa. Writers produced and reproduced the image of the falling man, who became a resonant figure expressing anxieties 'at home' about the activities of white workers stationed in the heart of the Dark Continent. By the time that *White Cargo* was staged, sexual contact with the African had come to be represented as the ultimate in the white man's moral degradation: 'You'll stagnate and you'll deteriorate and *in the end* you'll mammy-palaver', the experienced 'old coaster', Witzel, tells Langford when he arrives.[29]

White Cargo was an immediate box-office success in Britain and the United States, opening for a long run on Broadway in November 1923 and, having toured Chicago and Boston, moving to London's West End in 1924. A production was still running in London in March 1927. After a decade lying fallow, the play surfaced again as the Metro-Goldwyn-Mayer movie, released in 1942. The little-known author of the stage and screen play, Leon Gordon, made his fortune from his depiction of what the theatre programme described as 'the primitive unvarnished life in the Tropics'.[30]

It is important to remember that *White Cargo* was performed to audiences familiar with racist caricatures, including the natives in *Tarzan* movies and narratives in which, when a hunter sets 'two grinning skulls ... side by side; a negro's and a gorilla's. It was difficult to tell them apart.'[31] With few exceptions, travellers' tales, colonial exhibitions, adventure stories and popular anthropology in the period fed the reading public's fascination for the 'savage', exotic side of Africa.[32]

London reviewers seemed to be rather tired of the theme even before the play had commenced its long run in the West End. 'The white man on the West Coast had become almost a classic figure in literature through the genius of Mr Conrad', wrote one theatre critic in the London *Times*: 'He has now found his way to the stage, where he speaks with less sense of style, but drinks even more whisky.'[33] 'Too often have we had the white man's views on the subject of the dusky enchantress', wrote Kathleen Hewitt in 1933. 'The tale is always the same; the hero – blue-blooded, public schooled, varsity-veneered – finds himself among the mangoes and coconuts. He is a white man, but a waster!'[34] Clearly referring to the mythical Tondeleyo of *White Cargo* and the plethora of popular narratives that appeared in its wake, Hewitt continues, in an ironic tone, 'A coloured lady swings a rope of hybiscus flowers or waggles a beaded hip, and he is ensnared. After which, having failed to Play the Game, he sheds a basin full of tears over his Old School Tie. Alas, alas!'.[35] 'This hero, in West Africa, would never last', comments the 'old coaster', Warren Henry, in his autobiography.[36] 'Something awful was bound to happen to such a person [as Langford] – anywhere. And West Africa will do as well as Westcliff-on-Sea.'[37]

Despite their sense of boredom with this theme, the critics had to admit that 'the applause last night was overwhelming', especially for 'the coarse. . . she-animal', Tondeleyo,[38] who 'slip[s] in and out of the action to purr, to claw, or to shriek as in convulsion'.[39] 'Immense audiences watched with breathless interest' as Tondeleyo played her part.[40] 'With much skill and little clothing', white actresses took on the part of Tondeleyo,[41] culminating in Hedy Lamarr's memorable performance in the movie.

West African audiences appear to have had no opportunity to watch *White Cargo* on the stage or the big screen.[42] African movie-goers were not sheltered from western representations of 'natives' in the interior of their continent, however, for cinema schedules in the cities included films such as *Tarzan* and *The King of the Kongo*, in which tribal savages wearing little except war-paint were liable to put white men into cooking pots. It is important to note that the enjoyment of African audiences would not necessarily have been lessened by the fact that an African skin signifies savagery and otherness in the imperial imaginary. Expressing a hearty 'not-I' towards the barely clad film-natives, many Africans on the West Coast would have shared the colonial sense of shame about un-Christian, unclothed people in the interior, and would have applauded the urge to 'develop', 'enlighten' and 'civilise' these others.

Whether or not West African audiences had seen *White Cargo*, the fact that Tondeleyo is portrayed as both a 'savage' *and* a coastal 'half-caste' caused public discomfort and reaction in at least one African quarter. Some time in the late 1920s, Mabel Dove returned to Accra having completed her studies in England. Dove was in a unique position to 'write back' to colonial representations of Africans, for she had been a regular theatre- and movie-goer in London, and an avid reader of British popular novels and newspapers alongside the literary greats.[43] The vital difference separating Dove from the defensive, critical 'empire writes back' model developed by Ashcroft, Griffiths and Tiffin (1989) is that she writes for readers of the *Times of West Africa* rather than for audiences abroad. While colonial officials might have formed part of her readership in Ghana, the colonial capital is at several removes from her primary constituency, for Dove borrows from diverse international source-texts – incorporating some elements, explicitly rejecting others – in order to intervene in and 'attempt some adjustment' in local readers' lives.[44]

Published in the *Times of West Africa* between 7 November and 31 December 1934, *A Woman in Jade* responds to white fictions about Africa. Whilst in her articles Dove agrees wholeheartedly that, 'There is no doubt that the morals of our young ladies of fashion are deplorable and the *brown skin girl seems to be a class by herself*',[45] she suggests that it is not the African mother but the European father of such racially mixed offspring who carries the burden of moral responsibility for the 'deplorable' state of affairs in Ghana. Following in Tondeleyo's genetic footsteps, at least one of the heroines of *A Woman in Jade* is of mixed parentage. As Beryl explains to her lover, 'my father was a white man' who disappeared when he discovered that her mother was pregnant.[46] In Beryl's case, then, the tables are turned against the white father and the problem is presented as social rather than biological. In Dove's version of the 'white man on the West Coast' narrative, the blame for immorality is laid squarely at the feet of the colonial man who dallies with local women and refuses to take responsibility for the outcome.

Cross-racial liaisons did not appear to offend Dove, whose own family was of mixed race and who mingled with an elite, many of whom had European ancestors. Indeed, the type of narrow racial prejudice which characterises *White Cargo* is satirised in the play through the figures of Mr and Mrs Tollemache, two 'missionary looking people' who believe that the officers' antics with the local women are destroying the racial balance of power in West Africa and causing the natives to criticise and laugh at their overlords.[47] The moral of Dove's play is not that local women tempt white innocents, but that 'it is terrible to see these young girls waste the sweets of their life in dissipation with profligate and senseless white men who have neither religion nor morals'.[48]

Dove's 'reader response' to the character of Langford in *White Cargo* is inscribed in the play in the form of three 'orgling, winking' British officers, Captain Hawke, Lieutenant Bradley and Angus Fitzgerald. Unlike Langford, these Europeans are portrayed as the seducers and corrupters, displaying a type of colonial masculinity which is dangerous to the local girls. 'If anything happened to me, do you think that you would marry me?'

Beryl asks the silent Captain Hawke as he pulls her into bed.[49] The popular representation of 'Africa, the woman, the savage' who tests European man 'to the uttermost'[50] is rewritten by Dove to include attention to the 'menacing' type of European man, who 'begins to play the role of a modern Don Juan. . . as soon as he dons the Colonial garb and steps ashore'.[51] This is precisely the type of European man written out of *White Cargo*, where Tondeleyo pesters any lonely young man, offering him 'tiffin' until he is no longer in control of his emotional and physical responses. By contrast, 'Marjorie Mensah' uses her play to warn the 'chronic bachelor' that his relationships with local women will destroy the very class of enlightened, progressive Christians that colonialists and missionaries had helped to create. Indeed, as a consequence of the white men's sexual interference, 'Our girls have now crossed the last ditch. They are beyond recall.'[52]

In *White Cargo*, Langford's loss of moral control is played out through his increasing sexual desire for an African woman. Dove's version of this theme is more socially and politically situated than Gordon's, for she lays the blame on Europeans in colonial Africa. 'You finally go home and blame the country', she has a character tell the three 'Don Juans' of the piece, reinterpreting the message of *White Cargo* in the process:

You drink far too much and live a life of comparative wasters. You come on in all the beautiful prime and flash of life, and limp back pale, whisky-sodden, physical wrecks, and the tale you tell is the same. . . purely a matter of malaria and the terrors of unhealthy swamps in the so-called white man's grave. Wine and women, yes. But the wage is death. You sneer and jeer at marriage. . . It is a pity.[53]

These white men are criticised in the play by the very women they have seduced and plied with champagne, money and cigarettes. 'Do you know why most black girls interest themselves in whitemen [*sic*]?' Baake asks the Europeans, 'Not because they love them or that they feel some strong sex appeal. The poor classes do it for money; the better classes because they know that it is wrong – from curiosity and novelty.'[54] In this way, Dove reorders the moral bias of narratives such as *White Cargo* by switching the cast of characters around; and, in true 'Women's Corner' style, the plot unrolls from the African woman's point of view.

The meaning of 'white cargo' in Leon Gordon's play – passive white flesh, ruined by a woman and transported downriver – is reversed by Dove, for the women in this play are openly referred to as 'the black cargo'. The sixteen-year-old Beryl describes herself and her friends as 'just a bit of black cargo in a posh limousine'.[55] Here lies evidence of Dove's familiarity with Gordon's play. 'The women. That's the cargo', confirms a white soldier at the end, 'A bit of *it*. A mere car load full of Black Cargo.'[56]

In order to depict life in the vibrant modern city of Accra, Dove borrows glamorous images of *America* from western popular movies and she rejects all images of a 'tribal', 'primitive' Africa.[57] No space is given to the racist representations of Africans that were prevalent in western narratives of the inter-war period: 'the violence of dark secret things, of ugly half-hidden atavism, and uglier half-grown civilisation',[58] and the pidgin-speaking, child-like Africans of the movies are replaced with sophisticated city women, well-educated, eloquent and carefully individualised by their author. In the view of their white lovers, these heroines are 'too brilliant for mere coast girls', but through them Dove reveals how witty and intelligent – how unlike Tondeleyo – local African women can be.[59]

Out of 'the black, sweating violence of the crowd'[60] emerge three 'young women about town', Baake Quaynor, Aba Mensen and Beryl Nurse, and the curtain rises on 'a fashionable cafe' in the heart of Accra which closely resembles the hotel in which the movie *Gold Diggers* is set.[61] Baake, Aba and Beryl frequent this exclusive setting, drinking pints of champagne, wearing 'resplendent tea gowns in the latest fashion' and enjoying the sound of the orchestra as it plays 'a beautiful pianissimo passage from an entrancing romantic song' in the background.[62] 'Life would be so dull without a little sin to give it some colour', Baake says, echoing the 'hostess' character in *Gold Diggers* as the heroines await the arrival of their British lovers, champagne glasses in one hand and cigarettes in the other.[63]

Dove borrows from *Gold Diggers* in order to lend glitter and modernity to the African characters, but she does not endorse the movie uncritically. Criticisms of the moral impact of Hollywood films are aired regularly within the very play that depends on such movies for its sense of urban sophistication. 'A very distressing impression was created in the mind of some of the youth of the country', says Clement, the young African lawyer and voice of moral probity in the play, when cinemas in Accra showed 'a Hollywood film depicting women or chorus-girls trying to entwine men in their dissipate coils'.[64] 'Would you believe it', he continues in alarm, 'all our girls started to style themselves with the pet names of the Hollywood women with similar designs and pretensions.'[65] In order to illustrate this point, Dove borrows the racy, decadent chorus-girls from *Gold Diggers*, placing them in the city of Accra and watching the moral outcome of their antics. Incarnating the gold-diggers of the big screen, the three heroines of *A Woman in Jade* are also locally situated, typifying the kind of 'young girls' who come out of the cinemas and loiter in the streets and, in 'Marjorie Mensah's' view, 'must be made to practice morality'.[66]

In the process of rejecting racist images and narratives, then, Dove draws inspiration from 'non-colonial' movies, poaching characters and plot-lines, and modelling her heroines on the decadent white stars of the big screen. In this way she dilutes and reinterprets the symbolic seductress of *White Cargo* by reincarnating her in the form of the three fun-loving girls. By Africanising the glamour-girls, Dove contests the prevalent western representations of West Africa as 'savage', but she also critiques the western celebration of women as 'gold diggers', revealing how this type of heroine is morally lost, dangerous to the future of Gold Coast society.

Another young African lawyer, Harry, voices the moral of the play: 'It is for us the coming generation to make it [society] perfect and beautiful.'[67] Similarly, for Dove, the 'object of all writing is to make our society beautiful, pure and perfect'.[68] To this end, *A Woman in Jade* picks up themes and threads from 'Marjorie' articles dating back to 1932 and 1933. Offered as a fully fictionalised exploration of the romantic liaisons between African women and European men, the play can be read as a moral commentary on the effects of novel-reading and movie-going upon African women in the city and the dangers of romantic discourse when no marriage is intended. The three heroines are African 'Sibyls', destroyed by morally corrupting reading matter and movies imported from the West. In the manner of Corelli's fallen heroine, they are fully conscious that they have learnt their debauched lifestyle 'from reading English novels and. . . by going to the cinema';[69] 'Your English civilisation has made me what I am' Baake says, describing herself as a marvel 'in corruption'.[70]

A Woman in Jade develops Dove's critique of the ideology of romantic love which presents young women with false ideals and desires. 'To me, it [romance] has become like the food upon which the body must feed', Baake admits to her lover,[71] having told her friends that 'marrying. . . is like becoming a bride to eternal solitude.'[72] She confesses that, like Sibyl, her cultural and sexual influences have made her addicted to romance, the very 'honey' that African men are incapable of offering to local women.[73]

This is not a monological Christian play preaching a simple message against female promiscuity, and criticism is not reserved solely for the atheist heroines and their seductive European partners. An underlying message seems to be that the effect of Hollywood movies and romantic novels, combined with the presence of 'romantic' European men in Accra, has left local men looking solid, over-virtuous and dull. Gold Coast men are shown to be stranded outside the international cultural flows and untouched by the western influences affecting the women, while European men are shown to be free to seduce African women, achieving in their victims 'a delicious, rapturous romantic surrender' through a few choice words from a romantic vocabulary.[74] Upright and unromantic by contrast, Harry Quashie and Clement Asiedu are two young lawyers drawn from the Gold Coast's 'own wonderful stock of solid manhood'.[75] The former character is engaged to Baake, seeking his marriage partner within the morally flawed class of women represented by the heroines. 'The fellow can't even kiss a girl properly', she continues behind her fiancé's back.[76] Local men's 'kisses have no thrill and the touch of their most passionate embrace carries a peculiar chill with it. They talk about love as schoolboys would talk about books', Baake says, whereas from the Europeans, 'I have since learnt to view life, romance and love from a different sexual angle'.[77]

A Woman in Jade dramatises many of the issues raised in Dove's semi-fictional commentaries, published in the *Times of West Africa* in previous months. A large number of 'Marjorie Mensah's' articles take the form of didactic tales which are written in 'purple' prose and filled with melodramatic characters designed to warn young women of the dangers of falling in love. On each occasion, men are shown putting on the language of love like a mask in order to seduce young women. 'Girls, we must indeed be very careful', Marjorie concludes each time, predating the 'beware women' message of Nigerian market fiction by twenty-five years and inverting its gender bias: 'Young men today are no more young men; they are so much counterfeit';[78] 'the methods of these slim dreadfuls are so clandestine in the extreme', she writes, for 'the menacing male' is taking 'undue liberty of the generous and unsuspicious disposition of any woman'.[79] The implication seems to be that the language of romantic love, when deployed in the non-fictional world, assists young men in their deceptions and prevents young women from seeing the truth. Clearly, when a woman falls in love with a man, she runs the risk of falling in a different way, of succumbing to illicit desires and sexual temptations, of being abandoned by her lover to a life of promiscuity and sin.

'It takes a woman with a woman's sympathies and fine feelings to speak to women on a subject specially designed for women', Dove wrote in 1935.[80] Her contributions to the women's page form a vital part of Ghana's

literary heritage, not least because she was one of the few women in a sea
of male authors until the mid-1960s, when Efua Sutherland, Ama Ata
Aidoo, Kate Abbam and other women emerged onto the literary scene.[81]
Dove predated and anticipated these authors by several decades, writing
woman-centred stories which explored sexual inequalities and the down-
side of romantic love. *A Woman in Jade* raises female promiscuity to centre
stage and rewrites the immensely popular 'white man in Africa' formula
which circulated around Britain and the colonies almost without break
between 1900 and 1942. When women are regarded as 'black cargo' to be
enjoyed by white men, she seems to be saying, the ethical debates and marital models promoted in the Women's Corner will be placed in jeopardy.
Simultaneously borrowing and 'writing back' to western popular texts,
Dove engages in a complex critical response to the popular art forms entering British West Africa in the colonial period. As I hope to have shown, her
responses are incarnated in the form of characters plucked from *White
Cargo* and *Gold Diggers*, but contained within these characters is a critique
of the local effects of the international cultural models.

Notes

1 Riby-Williams, Interview, August 1999.
2 *TWA*, 22 January 1932: 2.
3 *Ibid*.
4 *TWA*, 1 May 1931: 2.
5 It was not until the 1940s that Hindi popular movies and pamphlets started
   to arrive in the region (see Larkin, 1997; Obiechina, 1973).
6 *AMP*, 27 October 1937: fp.
7 *AMP*, 20 November 1937: 4.
8 *TWA*, 28 January 1933: 2.
9 *TWA*, 7 February 1933: 2.
10 Mensah, 1933: 29.
11 *TWA*, 16 March 1933: 2.
12 In Simonton's novel readers saw the prototype of Tondeleyo – a character
   with firm antecedents in the eighteenth century – and witnessed the African
   woman as she 'advanced toward him [the European newcomer] with the slow,
   languorous abandon of the savage woman of the torrid zone' ([1912] 1928:
   240). Similar rhetoric can be found in novels such as *Gone Native* by
   'Asterisk', published by Constable in 1924. This novel is described in one
   review as revealing 'the lure and the ultimate undoing which awaits those who
   forget their pride of race in the languorous life of the South Sea and "go
   native". It is, of course, the old problem of the white man and the black
   woman. We get a glimpse of the sordid business it may become in the old

trader who alludes to the black mother of his eleven children as "that cow of mine"' (*Daily Mail*, 1 May 1924: 13). For a vision of black *male* sexuality to parallel Tondeleyo's, see Lady Dorothy Mills' novel, *The Arms of the Sun* (1924) in which an Afro-Arabic prince abducts a beautiful English rose (her name is Rose) intending to rape her and make her his queen.

13 Gordon, [1923] 1925: 78.

14 *Ibid.*, 82.

15 *Ibid.*

16 *Ibid.*, 30.

17 Simonton, [1912] 1928: 8.

18 Gordon, [1923] 1925: 71.

19 Simonton, [1912] 1928: 8.

20 *Ibid.*

21 *Ibid.*

22 See Lewis, 2000.

23 Ironically, even when local populations were the patrons and providers of profit in white-owned stores, they would be represented as savages in metropolitan newspapers. In an article published in the *Daily Mail* in 1924, storekeeper Clifford Collinson remarks, 'To see a loin-clouted savage sniffing the scented rival merits of "Shem-el-nessim" and "Phul-nana" and topping off his purchases with a tin of talcum powder is no uncommon sight in the shop which I run in the tropics' (*Daily Mail*, 9 April 1924: 8). It seems that, until the racial caricature has been driven home, the white man's sense of racial superiority is undermined by his role as server of the black man, dependent for a livelihood upon the other's cash.

24 Gordon, [1923] 1925: 99.

25 *Ibid.*, 78.

26 *The Doctor*, Movie, 1942.

27 *Witzel*, Movie, 1942.

28 See Foster, 1965.

29 Gordon, [1923] 1925: 41; emphasis added.

30 *The Times*, 16 May 1924: 12.

31 Simonton, [1912] 1928: 181.

32 See Lindfors, 1999; Dixon, 1995. Ward Price's sensational adventure tales were published in the *Daily Mail*. Opposing the entire genre, Warren Henry writes that *White Cargo* is a 'travesty' of the relationships struck up between white traders and local women, especially in its portrayal of African women as 'vamps'. Women in the region are, he insists, 'ordinary, simple and often virtuous', living in carefully worked-out 'pseudo-connubial' relationships with coasters (1927: 159–60).

33 *The Times*, 16 May 1924: 12.

34 Hewitt, 1933: 6.

35 *Ibid.*

36 Henry, 1927: 150.

37 *Ibid.*, 166.

38 *The Times*, 16 May 1924: 12.
39 Parker, 1925: 10.
40 *The Times*, 14 September 1925: 10.
41 *Ibid.*
42 I have found no record of *White Cargo* in cinema listings or reviews columns in Ghanaian newspapers from that period.
43 See Denzer, 1992. Although Dove does not mention attending a performance of *White Cargo* in London, the contents of her *A Woman in Jade* reveal that she knew enough about the play to quote directly from it and to incorporate it into her own work.
44 *TWA*, 16 March 1933: 2.
45 *TWA*, 11 June 1934: 2; emphasis added.
46 *TWA*, 24 November 1934: 4.
47 *TWA*, 12–13 November 1934: 2.
48 *TWA*, 29 November 1934: 2.
49 *TWA*, 24 November 1934: 4.
50 Simonton, [1912] 1928: 318.
51 Mensah, 1933: 31–2.
52 *TWA*, 28 December 1934: 2.
53 *TWA*, 24 December 1934: 2.
54 *TWA*, 19 December 1934: 2.
55 *TWA*, 15 November 1934: 2.
56 *TWA*, 27 December 1934: 3.
57 See also Dove's novella, *Adventures of the Black Girl in Her Search for Mr Shaw*, where a tennis racquet symbolises the heroine's modernity. The story was serialised in the *Times of West Africa* between September and October 1934, and is discussed in detail in *Ghanaian Popular Fiction* (Newell, 2000).
58 Mills, 1924: 100.
59 *TWA*, 12 December 1934: 3.
60 Mills, 1924: 100.
61 *TWA*, 7 November 1934: 2.
62 *TWA*, 11 December 1934: 2.
63 *TWA*, 3 November 1934: 2.
64 *TWA*, 3 December 1934: 2.
65 *Ibid.*
66 See e.g. *TWA*, 10 January 1935: 2.
67 *TWA.*, 31 December 1934: 2.
68 *TWA.*, 16 March 1933: 2.
69 *TWA.*, 12 December 1934: 2.
70 *TWA.*, 14 December 1934: 2.
71 *TWA*, 20 December 1934: 2.
72 *TWA*, 19 November 1934: 2.
73 *TWA*, 21 November 1934: 2.
74 *Ibid.*
75 *TWA*, 20 December 1934: 2.

76 *TWA*, 17 November 1934: 4.
77 *TWA*, 20 December 1934: 2.
78 *TWA*, 1 May 1931: 2.
79 Mensah, 1933: 67.
80 *TWA*, 7 January 1935: 2.
81 Dove also wrote numerous short stories, several of which – especially 'Anticipation' – have been anthologised (see Opoku-Agyemang, 1997). The literary contributions of Gladys Casely Hayford to the *Gold Coast Leader* in the 1920s must not be ignored (see Gadzekpo, 2001).

7 Ethical fiction:
J. E. Casely Hayford's *Ethiopia Unbound*

Thus developed a tradition in which the westernised Africans wielded
intellectual weapons against British colonial domination. It was a tradition based on the production of books and newspaper articles which
argued the irregularity of British power and jurisdiction, informed the
Gold Coast African of his past and exhorted him to greater achievements
and combatted European racist ideas about him. (Baku, 'An Intellectual
in National Politics')

J. E. Casely Hayford's remarkable novel, *Ethiopia Unbound: Studies in Race
Emancipation* (1911), is often denied its status as a front-runner for the
position of 'first West African novel in English' and 'first true novel to be
published by a Gold Coaster', appellations which are reserved for R. E.
Obeng's *Eighteenpence*, published more than thirty years later in 1943.[1]
From the moment of its first appearance in 1911 until the present day, the
majority of literary critics have reacted to the novel with caution. 'Mr
Hayford has now cast his ideas on the subject of racial problems more or
less in the form of fiction', wrote one contemporary reviewer in London,
continuing, 'We say "more or less", because some of the chapters. . . break
quite away from the slender thread of story on which most of the episodes
are strung'.[2] More than eighty years later, the Ghanaian scholar Margaret
Nkrumah concurred with this critic, commenting, 'by the end of the book,
all pretensions to a story-line have been abandoned; similarly the characters are merely vehicles for speeches' delivered in 'Bertie-Wooster mode'.[3]

Rather than concluding with the critics that *Ethiopia Unbound* is 'more
an elucidation of Casely Hayford's cultural and political philosophy than
a novel'[4] and that the author 'is using the fictional element as a mere
crutch',[5] this chapter will function as a kind of palate-clearing exercise and
ask *why* Casely Hayford opted to write fiction above non-fiction. Three or
four decades before nationalism is said to have taken hold of West African
literature, Casely Hayford wrote this vehement, race-conscious critique of
colonial policy, suggesting reforms to the legislature, imagining an ideal

African leader, an egalitarian education system for all West Africans and a post-independence utopia in which equality of opportunity would take precedence over colonial hierarchies.

What did the novel offer to this brilliant political thinker and activist which other genres such as the political treatise, historical study or legal petition – all of which Casely Hayford wrote at one time or another – could not provide? In posing these questions, this chapter will assess the fictionality of *Ethiopia Unbound* in terms of non-realist aesthetic and narrative conventions. Such a reconceptualisation of fiction is hardly new, for it is assisted by the declarations of pre-realist novelists such as Samuel Richardson, in whose eighteenth-century view, '*story* or *amusement* should be considered as little more than the *vehicle* to the more necessary *instruction*'.[6]

Casely Hayford was one of the handful of high-born, highly educated West Africans to enter national politics after obtaining his professional qualifications abroad.[7] Trained as a barrister in the British legal system, he understood the legislative structures with which 'British West Africa' was burdened and worked for twenty years as a nominated member of the Legislative Council to change the colonial system from within.[8] Politically reformist rather than revolutionary, he believed that the educational opportunities which had transformed the British masses into a 'reading public' should be made available to Africans in the colonies, allowing them to realise their full potential as a cultured, literate race capable of matching European achievements.[9] In conjunction with his political activities, and as proof of his own hyper-literate status, Casely Hayford was, at various times, editor of the *Gold Coast Chronicle*, the *Gold Coast Echo* and the *Wesleyan Methodist Times*;[10] he founded the *Gold Coast Leader* in 1902 and, alongside *Ethiopia Unbound*, wrote several books on Akan-Fante institutions, inheritance laws, land tenure, local leadership and traditions. As this brief curriculum vitae reveals, Casely Hayford was a prolific writer, translating his ideology and speeches into texts at every opportunity, generating material that demands inclusion in Ghana's literary history.

In Casely Hayford's hands, the novel becomes an infinitely expandable rag-bag into which multifarious political and spiritual concerns can be placed. *Ethiopia Unbound* seems to operate according to principles of digression and flexibility rather than conformity to rules.[11] The novel expertly incorporates non-fictional genres, including lectures by the author's mentor, Edward W. Blyden, and educational articles published by Casely Hayford in the West African press. What holds the 'rag-bag' together – the black ribbon at the top – is the author's ideological consistency as an early pan-African thinker and cultural nationalist whose primary aim was the eradication of racial inequalities. With no apparent sense of unease at the unruly nature of his manuscript, Casely Hayford adapts the genre to suit his own purposes, using it to explore the spiritual integrity of 'pagan' belief systems outside mainstream Christian doctrine, the sophistication of African languages and customs compared with their European equivalents, the intersections between colonial exploitation and racism in the colonies, and the design of an educational syllabus that will help Africans to attain the peak of their abilities.

Whilst *Ethiopia Unbound* has been criticised for being 'too much of a history lesson to make it successful fiction',[12] a key difference separates Casely Hayford's fictional and non-fictional writing. His histories and ethnographies show a keen sense of customs and institutions that have been displaced as a consequence of colonialism,[13] but his novel plays around with time-scales, manipulating the reader's sense of a 'narrative present' and demonstrating the currency of bygone customs and art forms. For example, the opening scene represents a utopian moment, taking place during a hiatus in European systems of knowledge. In a wry swipe at the scientific discourse of racial types, the narrator reveals how, by the turn of the twentieth century, 'it had been discovered that the black man was not necessarily the missing link between man and the ape' and 'Negroes' were, in fact, the intellectual equals of 'Aryans'.[14] 'The art of the caricaturist had by now been played out', states the optimistic narrator, removing to the recent past one of the ideological struts of the British Empire.[15] Into this gap in western knowledge Casely Hayford inserts the new African, described with racial pride as 'anatomically perfect' and 'the scion of a spiritual sphere peculiar unto himself'.[16]

This scene is rhetorically flawless: Casely Hayford binds the British Empire into a web of its own making and places the African in a discrete space, untouched by western prejudices. If one of the core justifications for direct colonial rule – the racial inferiority of Africans – is disproved by the Empire's *own* scientists, then fundamental transformations are required in the systems of governance by which Africans are ruled. Clearly, Africans' need for European protection and tutelage is undermined when their intellectual equality is recognised by their rulers. The tables are thus turned on the promoters of 'progress' and 'enlightenment', for whom a leap into modernity involves the abandonment of 'uncivilised' ideas about the African.

Ethiopia Unbound is rich with ironic inversions of this type, particularly relating to the constant challenge posed by educated Africans to direct British rule in the colonies. From the outset, the protagonist's articulate, 'civilised' voice and complete mastery of world literature reveal the 'backwardness' of European beliefs about a 'backward' Africa. Comically, Kwamankra describes the British as 'those who occupy those tiny islands somewhere in the English Channel';[17] and from the start he 'found himself thanking the gods that he was a poor benighted pagan according to the formula of the church'.[18] By ironising the imperial centre and ideology in this way, Casely Hayford sends a 'cultural nationalist' message to his European readership, alerting them to the fact that this English-language novel does not derive from a fawning desire to imitate the colonial civilisation.

Whereas in his non-fictional writing Casely Hayford explores historical events and examines the minutiae of customary laws as they have evolved over time, fiction allows him to operate on the futuristic level of ideals. A prophetic and utopian vision of Africa is described as if it were current or about to become real, attainable in the lifetime of the protagonist. For example, an idealised version of Mfantsipim School, called Mfantsipim National University, is described as 'doing good work. . . about the time that these studies open'.[19] Built from local funds and labour, led by the national redeemer, Kwamankra, the institution represents a nationalist success for 'Fantiland' Africans: in particular, the University is shown to have taken over teacher-training and translation work from the missions and the government, distancing the acquisition of literacy from both God and Empire.[20] Interweaving idealised leaders such as Kwamankra with real historical achievements such as the construction of Mfantsipim School from local resources, the novel describes a political fantasy in the 'near future' tense, showing readers the ease with which their ideals can be translated into the real world: all this, of course, occurs in the real-time of turn-of-the-century West Africa, a period when nationalism was the vehicle for the expression of both sub-national and trans-national ideals. Thus, not-yet-achieved goals such as the wearing of 'national dress' in school, the mass training of African teachers, increased salaries for teachers, mass enrolments of children into schools, teaching in Fante, Yoruba and Hausa, and textbook translations into Fante, all are shown to be *succeeding already* in the University.[21] Launched in the dream, the narrator describes how, after the opening of the National University, 'the thirst for knowledge spread so rapidly that men and women took to attending night schools where they quickly picked up reading and writing in their own languages'.[22]

Casely Hayford's admixture of history and fiction led one British reviewer to comment in 1911, 'it is impossible to follow the author to the heights of idealism to which he would lead us when he preaches the doctrine of an African nationality'.[23] Believable or not, what the technique reveals is the way in which creative writing allows Casely Hayford to imagine idealised outcomes whilst, in African readers' own worlds, the political configuration might be more oppressive and gruelling, less easy to transform.

The fictional and the real exist in a complex, ethical relationship in the novel. As we have seen, at times *Ethiopia Unbound* represents the political struggle in West Africa as if its goals had been achieved already. At other times, prophecies for the near future are narrated in the past tense. The final chapter opens, 'By the year 1925 a mighty change had come over the thought of the nations', due in large part to the pan-Africanist newspaper launched by Kwamankra and circulating throughout Africa, uniting 'the entire race';[24] likewise, by 1925 race warfare has been replaced with 'a mighty truce', brought about by the realisation that 'the white needed the black and the black needed the white'.[25] By shifting ideals into achievements in this way, the novel shows great optimism about the speed with which the British Empire would accommodate the demands of intelligent, self-determining Africans.

In its vivid descriptions of the ideal future society, the novel functions as a manifesto for political change. Indeed, eight years after the publication of *Ethiopia Unbound*, when Casely Hayford cofounded the NCBWA in 1919, he created a platform to argue for many of the political and philosophical ideals put forward in the novel. Borrowing themes from his novel, Casely Hayford argued for the racial integrity of 'Ethiopians' and the necessity for elected African representatives to enter the colonial political institutions. We can thus regard the novel as a kind of *ur*-text containing details of the stories, heroes, prophesies and ideals which motivated the African elite for many years to come.

In a similar vein, Casely Hayford employs fiction to effect spatial manipulations. The novel allows him to demonstrate – rather than simply to describe – the easy fusion of the 'real' world into the non-Christian realm of the ancestors. In one of the most inspirational, poetic chapters of the book, the world of the ancestors (*Nanamu-Krome*) is fused with the domestic world, narrated in a manner which shows both to be 'real'. In the process, the Christian concept of heaven is replaced with *Nanamu-Krome* and the Fante afterlife is shown to be more relevant to Africans than its European counterpart.

Under an anaesthetic, Kwamankra is translated into the form of pure spirit and crosses a great lake into Fante 'heaven' to meet the spirits of his dead wife and child. The hero *is* 'Ethiopia unbound' in this scene as he moves out of his physical body into a visionary realm which is, despite its Fante protagonist, intertextually loaded with references to classical and Christian parables. Entry to the Afrocentric heaven is mediated by quest narratives such as the *Odyssey*, the *Divine Comedy* and *Pilgrim's Progress*.[26] These prestigious pre-realist texts function as stepping-stones away from the earthly world of the previous chapter, in which Kwamankra attended the theatre, proposed to Mansa and lived in domestic bliss after the wedding. Now a being appears beside Kwamankra, half-man, half-beast with a 'woe begone' expression distorting his features.[27] 'I hoped to scale high heaven by knowledge and by the work of man's imagination', says the being, but he so angered the gods with his arrogance that they made him stay in this purgatory for a thousand years, pointing others to 'yonder city' beyond the great lake.[28] Casely Hayford freely borrows from Homer, Dante, Bunyan and the Bible in this scene in order to effect the hero's movement into Fante heaven, and the eminent pre-texts enhance the moral and emotional veracity of what comes next.

With lilies around his head and a prayer to the God of Love, Kwamankra walks on the water to the other side, where children wave palm fronds and direct him to Mansa, his wife-turned-goddess, who dwells in the eastern-facing part of the city. At this point the narrative moves beyond its Christian prototypes, Africanising the spiritual quest motif by describing how, instead of a one-way path leading from earth to heaven, there is traffic and continuity between the two realms: 'a thin veil divides Nanamu-Krome from the nether world' Mansa says, and 'the veil is drawn, whenever it pleaseth heaven, for converse between immortals and men';[29] in keeping with this two-way traffic between worlds, Kwamankra feels that he has been sent from *Nanamu-Krome* as 'a witness unto the truth. . . a thinker among the thoughtless', into the world of mortals in the nether sphere.[30]

By building these non-Christian cultural references into a Christian model of messianic salvation, Casely Hayford transforms Kwamankra's domestic tragedy into a moment of cultural rediscovery and rebirth. When he comes round from the anaesthetic, the hero has become a fully reborn African, sent back to earth as an African saviour 'to testify against corruption and wrong in high places, in the name of truth'.[31] Whilst the domestic ideal has been shattered by Mansa's death, the tragedy has brought about Kwamankra's inner journey and understanding of the spiritual life cycle of Africans.[32] In this chapter, then, the use of fiction gives Casely Hayford a unique opportunity to layer times and realms upon one another, to demonstrate the complex intercourse between the nether world and the ancestral realm.

Alongside the temporal and spatial manipulations made possible by fiction, the novel provides space for Casely Hayford to construct black leadership models. In this he continued a long-established – and long-to-continue – West African practice of honouring 'men of genius', 'big men' and 'men of affairs'. By the beginning of the twentieth century this eulogistic discourse had acquired Christian overtones, for European evangelists brought their own biographical traditions to Africa, inspired by nineteenth-century educationists such as Samuel Smiles who considered 'biographies of great, but especially of good men, [to be] most instructive and useful, as helps, guides, and incentives to others'.[33] Unlike fiction with its dangerous capacity to fuel escapist fantasies, Smiles declared that biographies of 'good men' were capable of 'teaching high living, high thinking and energetic action' to newly literate readers.[34] 'The chief use of biography consists in the noble models of character in which it abounds', Smiles states towards the end of *Self-Help*, for 'it is a record of greatness which we cannot help admiring and unconsciously imitating while we admire'.[35]

Inspired by these educators of the British working classes, missionaries provided new African readers with plentiful 'lives of the saints' and biographies of admirable Europeans and Africans. For example, *Lives of Eminent Africans* was recommended in the July 1932 issue of the missionary journal, *Books for Africa*, as were *Honourable Men*, *Victors of Peace*, *A Shorter Boswell* and *Story of a Great Schoolmaster*.[36] Within this Christian tradition, E. W. Smith's *Aggrey of Africa* (1929) proved immensely popular, listed by West African schoolchildren in the 1930s as 'my favourite novel' and purchased by the thousand per month when simplified versions of it appeared in the Methodist Book Depot.[37]

The West African response to this Christian-sponsored literature is significant for the manner in which local writers reject the Eurocentric booklist whilst retaining the genre of biography for precisely the qualities applauded by Smiles. Thus, Magnus J. Sampson's *Gold Coast Men of Affairs (Past and Present)* (1937) is modelled explicitly upon Smiles' *Self-Help*, but the author confers upon himself the mantle of *nationalist* biographer, asserting that his object in writing the book is that 'of awakening a passionate patriotism' in Gold Coast youths and lighting 'the flame of emulation' in readers by presenting a line-up of exemplary, talented

Africans from local history.[38] 'Outstandingly interesting and instructive' life-stories have been chosen 'to serve as an example' to African readers, Sampson writes, 'for as Dr Smiles has wisely said, "Their great example becomes the common heritage of their race, and their great deeds and their great thoughts are the most glorious legacies to mankind"'.[39]

Decades before Sampson's nationalist biographies, in April 1903, Edward W. Blyden delivered an 'Address at the Opening of the New Library by Old Boys of the Wesleyan High School' in Freetown, in which he emphasised many of Sampson's themes. 'I often see a man going about selling books in town and calling out, "The Life of Napoleon Bonaparte, The Life of Admiral Nelson", etc., etc. Such books can be of no earthly use to you.'[40] 'History furnishes examples for your inspiration and guidance from your own race', Blyden continued and recommended, in place of Napoleon and Nelson, the purchase of locally authored pamphlets and biographies of prominent black heroes such as Touissaint L'Ouverture, designed to meet African readers' needs rather than to instill a sense of racial inferiority in Africans.[41]

Obviously, biography as a printed genre struck a chord with readers and writers in West Africa, harmonising with established local discourses about heroism and leadership. In his own novel, Casely Hayford redeploys these biographical and praise traditions in an intriguing way, constructing an 'outstanding and instructive' hero who exemplifies the finest achievements of Africans in Africa and the USA. The hero of *Ethiopia Unbound*, Kwamankra, is a fictional amalgam of a series of real African leaders drawn from the turn of the century, including Edward Blyden and John Mensah Sarbah, alongside other great race-thinkers such as W. E. B. DuBois, Booker T. Washington and Casely Hayford himself. Above all others, the figure of Blyden towers over Kwamankra, who follows in his mentor's footsteps on particular issues, undertaking educational tours of black colleges in the United States and addressing large audiences on the subject of race emancipation. When Kwamankra is described as being 'foremost in bringing forward schemes to prevent the work of the [National] University becoming a mere foreign imitation',[42] he has stepped straight out of Blyden's mouth, embodying Blyden's educational ideals for West Africa.[43]

Evidence of Blyden's influence is furnished in a letter from Casely Hayford to the editor of the *Sierra Leone Weekly News*, dated 5 May 1908 and probably composed when the writing of *Ethiopia Unbound* was in full flow. In the letter, Casely Hayford says he has followed the series of articles by Blyden entitled 'African Life and Customs' with great interest.

Inspired by Blyden's effort to retrieve African traditions and to promote the concept of African personality, he writes:

When, in our modern way, we have demolished African strongholds, and, with the wantonness of an iconoclast, saved nothing to remind us of the artistic past and future possibilities of the people – nay, when we have laid out streets and encouraged shops to spring up mushroom-like here and there, we think we have solved the mystery of the gods, while all the time, the heart of the matter is not reached.[44]

Much of this letter is reprinted word for word in *Ethiopia Unbound* in a speech given by Kwamankra to the pan-Africanist conference in the Gold Coast in 1905: 'I have followed with keen interest the series of articles on "African Life and Customs" in the *Sierra Leone Weekly News* from the ever-instructive pen of Dr Blyden', Kwamankra states, three years premature for the real-time serialisation of Blyden's work. Kwamankra proceeds to quote extensively from Casely Hayford's letter to the *Sierra Leone Weekly News*, emphasising the need for 'racial development' and emancipation from 'foreign ideas'.[45] Such a translation across genres and time-scales illustrates the way in which Blyden's political ideology inspired Casely Hayford to write fiction, to create characters through whom he could demonstrate the effectiveness of Blyden's race-conscious philosophy.

Ethiopia Unbound is shaped in other fundamental ways by the sentiments contained in this letter. In the piece, Casely Hayford describes how, upon last meeting Blyden at the Royal Academy in London, the old man referred him to the picture of the wolf and the lamb: 'After we had both drunk in the beauty of portraiture for a while, he gravely remarked, "And a little child shall lead them – that is Africa". I was struck by the allusion and I still think there is a deal in the reflection.'[46]

The 'deal in the reflection' finds definite shape in the novel. *Ethiopia Unbound* reverberates with biblical allusions, especially the motif of the wolf and the lamb which is Africanised each time it is used and provides the final line of the novel. Blyden's quotation from the Book of Isaiah structures *Ethiopia Unbound* at a fundamental level. At different times both Kwamankra and his son are represented as the 'little child', the black messiah who embodies Blyden's version of the biblical quotation. On one occasion in the novel, Kwamankra transforms the 'wolf-lamb' quotation into a short folktale, labelled a 'tool' and narrated to his son to illustrate the bullying tactics of the colonial government;[47] at other times, the quotation is applied to contemporary political issues in order to illustrate the importance of achieving change by peaceful means. 'The wolf and the lamb story again, you see', says Kwamankra, to demonstrate his philosophy of peaceful transformation.[48]

Blyden overshadows the hero of *Ethiopia Unbound*. In the highly reflective chapters seventeen and eighteen, for example, Kwamankra lectures on Blyden and emancipation at a West African political conference: in his speech about Blyden, this Blydenesque character incorporates real articles published by Blyden in the *Sierra Leone Weekly News*, effectively lecturing upon 'himself' and 'his own' ideology using 'his own' voice.[49] By the end of this speech, Kwamankra has become totally possessed by the spirit of Blyden, calling upon Africans in Blyden's voice, 'to learn to unlearn all that foreign sophistry has encrusted upon the intelligence of the African'.[50]

Ethiopia Unbound is not a biography of Blyden, however, but a novel. Fiction enables the author to conflate his several role models into one and to reject their less agreeable ideas. Hence Blyden's belief in absolute racial differences and his promotion of racial segregation in the United States gets no mention in *Ethiopia Unbound*, cast aside in favour of the less biologistic but equally pan-African concept of African cultural integrity. Additionally, at strategic moments in the novel, separateness is abandoned altogether in favour of 'one broad divinity' and shared culture for the human race.[51] Casely Hayford thus incorporates his own lectures, beliefs and articles into the narrative alongside Blyden's, diluting the latter with the thoughts of the former.

This technique of conflating several role models allows Casely Hayford to create in Kwamankra an individual who is physically and intellectually flawless, leagues ahead of the mediocre white specimens shown in the novel to be running his country. Our first vision of him is of a man so 'carelessly' hyper-literate that he can skim through a copy of Marcus Aurelius's *Meditations* and comment with ease upon the parallels between classical Stoic philosophy, Christianity and the traditional African systems of thought from which, in his view, many European concepts derived.[52] Occurring at the centre of the colonial capital, off Tottenham Court Road in London WC1, this image of African literacy emphasises from the outset that the African protagonist has intellectual abilities far superior to the average Englishman. Indeed, the average Englishman who accompanies Kwamankra on this particular literary and etymological excursion is none other than Silas Whitely, a would-be Christian minister incapable of fathoming the mysteries of his own religion and immersed in a crisis of faith.[53]

Described as 'the scion of a spiritual sphere peculiar unto himself', a 'pagan' and an 'outsider', Kwamankra epitomises the concept of African Personality first promoted in West Africa by Blyden in the 1870s and 1880s.[54] *Extremely* erudite, *extremely* loving and humane, he represents the 'perfection of the black man', unaffected by – but thoroughly familiar with – European systems of knowledge.[55] Thus, in choosing to write fiction, Casely Hayford has chosen a form which offers unlimited possibilities in the 'realisation' of ideal and – in the case of most white colonial characters in the novel – impaired racial types.

None of the characters in *Ethiopia Unbound* can be situated within a realist framework, and it is unlikely that they were designed to be judged by such criteria. Functioning as 'ideas personified' rather than as 'flesh and blood', they 'are used generally as mouthpieces for expressing particular ideas'.[56] As we have seen, Kwamankra represents the ideal of the 'unspoilt cultured African'[57] who is proud to be a Fante-speaking 'pagan', connected by an unbreakable bond with non-colonised systems of knowledge.[58] By contrast, the English characters are shown to be morally decadent, physically weak and degenerate, incapable of holding to any moral principles and yet urging 'moral excellence' in others, 'with the gin bottle in the one hand, and the Bible in the other'.[59] The British Empire is shown to be the last gasp of a finished civilisation in the novel. Even the Reverend Whitely comments that, after reading about Osiris-worship in ancient Egypt, about Zoroaster and Buddha and Confucius, 'the more puzzled I have become as to the right of the people calling themselves Christians to a monopoly of divine light'.[60] White characters are conscious of the arrogance of labelling others 'heathen', but lack the vitality of the new black civilisation poised to take power at the start of the twentieth century.[61]

Numerous ethical fragments interrupt the narrative flow of *Ethiopia Unbound*. As the novel's subtitle promises, each chapter is a 'study' in racial oppression and emancipation. Kwamankra confesses to studying people as an 'intellectual pastime':[62] so too the novel features character studies of colonial administrators, white missionaries and magistrates, African missionaries, worshippers, leaders and schoolteachers. We meet the height of un-Christian racism in Reverend Whitely, whose support for racial segregation in both life and death – burying Europeans in a separate part of the graveyard from Africans – provides Casely Hayford with the means to expose the hypocrisy and racial prejudice amongst white Christians in the Gold Coast; we meet Kenny Bilcox, who describes progressive colonialists as 'a mere handful of white fools who are blind enough not to see where their bread is buttered';[63] and briefly we meet an African schoolmaster conducting a choir, who 'certainly looked a veritable "swell", but he also did look a veritable fool' in his 'elegantly cut-away black morning coat and beautifully blazed cuffs and collar, not to speak of patent leather shoes'.[64] These didactic character types are introduced to expose the false premises of western culture and Christianity.

On many occasions in the novel, Casely Hayford succumbs to 'the burning desire to give vent to certain definite ideas surging in him', particularly on the necessity for educational improvements in colonial schools and the value of indigenous languages, customs and clothing.[65] Many of these ideas derived from his active membership of the cultural nationalist ARPS, founded in 1897 with the aim of protecting African interests from the encroachments of Europeans with trading interests in the region. He had led ARPS delegations to London, carrying petitions and pleas for the customary authority of 'native institutions' to be recognised by the British; and he was a keen promoter of National Schools in the 1890s, which led to the founding of the fundraising company, 'Fanti Public Schools Ltd', and the opening of Mfantsipim School in 1904.[66] By 1919, however, much to the chagrin of certain powerful chiefs who had remained friendly with the colonial government and sympathetic to the demands of the ARPS,[67] he cofounded the NCBWA, arguing, amongst other things, that the educated African elite had a greater right to represent the people in government than the illiterate chiefs who were ill-versed in the complexities of western political systems. It is 'a mockery to send our *Omanhin*, as we know them, to go and sit in the council and to pretend to represent the people when they cannot follow what is going on there', he told an audience of young, educated men in 1926, for these chiefs 'are at present not competent to represent the people'.[68]

Casely Hayford's caricature of chiefs as 'illiterate' – and therefore unable to follow events – was unfair, but his language represents a typical intelligentsia-member's conception of the 'improving' potential of literacy, a conception often accompanied by a hostile reaction to the system of Indirect Rule which the colonial government was continuing to consolidate in the 1920s, having promoted it since the turn of the century. Elite anxieties about these reforms find expression in *Ethiopia Unbound* in the form of outright snobbery against non-educated classes.

'The salvation of the people depended upon education', the narrator comments.[69] Education is so crucial a concern of the novel that chapter 3 contains detailed syllabus recommendations, including teaching in African languages and the creation of a chair in African History. These ideals derive directly from the curriculum proposed by Blyden, upon becoming President of Liberia College in 1881. His inaugural address contained substantial ideas for a West African College, to be situated in the interior where 'race-individuality' could be nurtured, far away from coastal African culture with its racially self-deprecating 'apes' of European modernity.[70] Similarly, in his public speech within the novel, Kwamankra voices the same ideals and promises to 'take care to place the educational seminary in a region far beyond the reach of the influence of the coast'.[71]

In 'tone and outlook' *Ethiopia Unbound* has been described as 'too English to be African'.[72] Rather than relating to western narrative traditions alone, however, *Ethiopia Unbound* seems also to relate to established oral forms such as the folktale and song. Several *sanko* (sea-songs) and folktales are included, resonating with meaning and set in contrast with the 'wheezing sound' of the western forms performed by missionaries and converts. Explicitly incorporating local genres, Casely Hayford indulges in irony, mockery, hero-worship, praise and flattery. He also seems to be well-versed in the techniques of southern Ghanaian verbal traditions in which performers set up moral standards in stories and songs, encouraging audience members 'to relate to them, identify with them, contemplate them and be edified by them'.[73] Morally and politically educative character types take precedence over psychologically 'deep' individuals in the novel, especially in relation to the theme of marriage, and the novel as a whole is spiked with moments of autonomous story-telling, many of which begin 'once upon a time' and end with the listener inviting the teller to relate the meaning of the story to a contemporary situation.[74]

Ethiopia Unbound reveals some intriguing details about the way in which Casely Hayford conceived the role of the author and the function of fiction. Just as the narrative skill of *Moll Flanders* (1722), *Clarissa* (1748–49) and other pre-realist English novels was not undermined for readers by the infiltration of genres such as the Christian sermon and the domestic conduct book, so *Ethiopia Unbound* seems to derive from its own particular story-telling traditions in which emphasis is placed upon the ethical dimensions of narration. These traditions do not exclude Christian influences. As the foregoing discussion of biography implied, by 1911 Christianity had become a 'local tradition' in coastal Ghana, and even the most ardent, church-rejecting cultural nationalist would have been influenced to some degree by mainline Christianity, passing through or teaching in mission schools and having to form political and cultural counterpositions from the starting point provided by Christianity. Few written narratives in turn-of-the-century Ghana would not have been profoundly influenced by Christian moral discourses. Indeed, biblical references are explicit in *Ethiopia Unbound*, to the extent that one could argue that the Bible structures the entire novel.

Despite its earnest nationalism and classical erudition, this novel is no exception to the ethical rules which govern locally produced Ghanaian narratives: in its preoccupation with marriage, for example, and in its use of character types to demonstrate moral concerns, striking similarities connect Casely Hayford's novel with novels by later generations of Ghanaian popular novelists such as J. Benibengor Blay and E. K. Mickson. As with many later writers, within two chapters the theme of marriage has taken centre-stage as an ill-matched couple is introduced for readers to contemplate and assess. In chapter 2 we meet Tandor-Kuma and his wife, Ekuba, who sit together in a cold London room: the former has become a 'successful student' in England, while the latter, who weeps continually, is a nursemaid.[75] The narrator's voice interrupts this tableau, describing the moral dilemma facing the young man: 'now the circumstances were changed' for Tandor-Kuma, 'How did he, a professional man, used to all the luxuries of English life and habit, take back with him to start a career in Africa a nurse-maid? And what would he do, if asked to Government house?'[76] The wife knows what he is thinking: 'You press weak women in your service', she cries tragically, 'and when you have won their sympathy, for a dream you toss them away.'[77]

This marital dilemma-tale surfaces repeatedly in early Ghanaian narratives and newspaper columns.[78] On each occasion, the husband is faced with a difficult choice, having relied upon the wife's hard work, fidelity and financial assistance to educate himself out of her social class. Letters from newly educated husbands to the problem pages of Gold Coast newspapers express similar guilt and embarrassment about illiterate wives: married monogamously according to the Christian rule of 'till death do us part', these husbands feel trapped and desperate but, short of divorce, they are unable to find a workable way out of the problem.[79]

Casely Hayford finds the solution in an African alternative to Christian monogamy. As Kwamankra declares in a speech on African culture, western methods denationalise 'the African in marriage. . . He becomes a slave to foreign ways of life and thought.'[80] Thus, meeting again after many years apart, after Tandor-Kuma has married and had children by a junior wife, the troubled couple of chapter 2 realise their love for one another and enter a polygynous union. The husband's dilemma is resolved through the established system of polygyny which is promoted in the narrative as a peaceful alternative to monogamy, morally and culturally better suited to Africans than the Christian system.[81]

Having argued against the suitability of applying a realist interpretive framework to *Ethiopia Unbound*, it is necessary to note that the novel contains several sections of literary realism. Streets, passenger liners, churches, mines, gin-shops and items of clothing are all described with meticulous attention to detail as Casely Hayford paints vivid verbal pictures of the colonial society in which his hero moves. Having described the gin-sheds and scenes of drunkenness around the railway line, for instance, the narrator interjects with a moral judgement of alcohol: 'It is a terrible scourge, a veritable canker, eating its way slowly, yet surely, into the very vitals of the black people among whom this plague of modern civilisation is planted.'[82] A few pages later, Kwamankra ticks off Mr Bilcox about the profits reaped from imported gin by the very administrators who condemn local drunkenness.[83] In much the same manner as pre-realist English authors mingled realistic detail with didactic characters in order 'to preserve and maintain that air of probability which is necessary to be maintained in a story designed to represent real life',[84] so too Casely Hayford uses realism to a moral end in these sections, exposing the disparities between coloniser and colonised.

The realist sections of *Ethiopia Unbound* address town-dwellers' dissatisfactions with the colonial administration: 'Now, if you want to see Sekondi at its best and the water question at its worst', declares the narrator in chapter 5, 'you must approach the town in the month of March on one of Messrs. Elder Dempster's boats. . . As you round off Tacoradi Bay, you see the mother of Gold Coast civilisation enveloped in a sheet of overhanging clouds charged with electricity.'[85] Lacking clean water supplies and adequate harbour facilities, 'Sekondi at its best' is revealed to be a down-trodden statement of colonial neglect. The underdeveloped 'metropolis' is introduced to the visitor by the narrator, who displays all the vantage points with a cutting ironic logic. Scenes such as these give rise to a moral insistence that the colonial government should undertake specific social and political reforms, including the supply of clean water to town-dwellers, the development of harbours, the improvement of railways and the provision of higher education institutions to serve the expanding population of literate Africans.

Thus, realist narrative is put to a particular use on each occasion. Having presented a problem in stark detail, Casely Hayford offers practical proposals for change. Ethical positions are pasted into the novel, facilitated each time by the realist narrative. The narrative mode, in consequence, may be described as *ethical realist*, for there is no apparent conflict between mundane detail and moral message. Casely Hayford's politics mesh perfectly with his poetics, and the fictional universe gives him the space to critique servile, imitative Africans and drunken, racist colonial officials.[86]

Ethiopia Unbound reveals a great deal about the literary conventions governing local creative output in the early years of the twentieth century. Combining pan-African politics with a cultural nationalism directed towards the retrieval and conservation of 'native institutions' and 'traditional' culture in West Africa, Casely Hayford calls out to Africans from within the pages of his novel: 'In the name of African nationality the thinker would, through the medium of *Ethiopia Unbound*, greet members of the race everywhere throughout the world.'[87] Curiously, this 'greeting' is also in the medium of English and yet, in the very first chapter, Kwamankra finds the English language incapable of carrying complex concepts such as God. The language is too diffuse, spiritually 'drifting' too much to be useful.[88]

Kwamankra's discontent with English is 'a delicious piece of irony' according to Margaret Nkrumah for the way in which it contravenes colonial educational beliefs that African languages were too shallow for the expression of intricate or modern ideas.[89] Nevertheless, Casely Hayford has to face the problem, in this English-language novel, of how to use English without being clothed in it like the African schoolmaster with his mimicking gestures and misfitting suit. It is strangely contradictory that the author should promote African languages, customs and institutions in the master's voice, and yet aim, through his writing, to generate '*men* – no effete mongrel product of foreign systems'.[90] The solution to this contradiction seems to lie in the tone taken by Casely Hayford towards the English language, for the narrative moves towards irony at each encounter between Europe and Africa. Words like 'elegant' and 'beautiful' are used to opposite effect throughout the novel, implying the existence of African alternatives to these cultural standards. By using English concepts and aesthetic ideals against themselves – in describing the mincing African schoolmaster as 'elegant' and 'beautiful', for example – Casely Hayford implies that his own foundations lie elsewhere, in the aesthetic and ethical realm of 'the other'.

Through the different types of irony deployed in the novel, Casely Hayford opens up fissures in the English language and retains his position 'without' it. Irony is one of the few discursive modes available to the truly *self*-conscious African who is, nevertheless, situated within the colonial language and culture. Positioned thus, Kwamankra understands English (and Englishness) fully, employs it when necessary, but remains aloof and other: he speaks from a separate cultural and linguistic sphere from where his ironic interjections are made possible and from where he reveals the African alternatives to British law, religion and government. Without irony, the 'other' would become a mimic, aping the colonial language rather than innovating from within it.[91]

The ambiguous status of *Ethiopia Unbound* as a novel arises because the book is episodic, 'loosely structured' and makes for 'heavy moralistic reading'.[92] In these and other features, it fails to abide by the terms of a twentieth-century realist tradition which demands a lack of authorial polemics in a novel, continuity of plot, the development and resolution of conflict, fidelity to social realities, psychological interiority in protagonists and a full, empathetic exploration of character. *Ethiopia Unbound* contravenes these principles unashamedly. Neither fully fictional nor wholly non-fictional, the narrative is barely held together by the hero, and for the duration of its 214 pages the reader remains suspended in a discursive space located somewhere between political treatise and Akan-Christian parable. Its 'Ethiopian'[93] content is indeed 'unbound', for the front and back covers barely contain the chaotic mixture of genres, episodes and cipher-like characters which circulate within its pages.

Ethiopia Unbound deserves to be dusted down and opened up for reappraisal and analysis. Casely Hayford found in the novel a flexible, digressive genre through which he could express high religious and philosophical ideals alongside proposals for constitutional reforms and changes in conjugal relations. *Ethiopia Unbound* is the meeting point for what, according to a realist mindset, are incompatible discourses: didactic folktales coexist with political speeches, reprinted in full from the West African press; Christian-style parables and classical Greek references give way to newspaper cuttings about Japan's distinctive political system and analyses of 'Negro education' systems in Africa and the United States. Also, the novel is tightly packed with folksongs and references to African drums, dances and rhythms, all of which are translated in to the English-language text to demonstrate the resilience of past traditions and to enhance the cultural nationalist message. Casely Hayford seems to have been inspired in his creative enterprise by

diverse non-realist narrative models, all of which – whether Christian, classical or non-western – are ethically motivated.

Writing at a time when excessive novel-reading was considered to be
damaging, Casely Hayford was under no aesthetic pressure to write what
western-trained critics might label the 'true novel', and he expressed no
anxieties about the generic ambiguity of his final product. Similarly, the
earliest West African readers and reviewers of *Ethiopia Unbound* seem to
have been unconcerned about its fragmented structure and didactic tone.
'A remarkable book has recently appeared here, written by an African on
purely African lines from the African's standpoint', wrote one Sierra
Leonean reviewer in November 1911.[94] This reviewer summarises the way
that 'Mr Hayford proceeds to *construct* the social system as it is and *as it
may possibly be* on the same Native lines developing normally into proper
Native Schools and a University in the heart of the Country, pointing and
leading to further progress and literary heights not yet anywhere attained
by the educated African'.[95] This reader has been impressed by the bold
idealism of *Ethiopia Unbound*, its 'construction' of future social possibilities for West Africans. The significant point is that much subsequent
Ghanaian fiction has remained true to this mold. These narratives, produced by authors resident in the homeland, are 'untrue' in the same sense
as *Ethiopia Unbound*, pleasing readers with their ideas and ideals but earning criticism for their 'didactic tone', underdeveloped (but over-idealised)
characters and 'stiff' prose.[96]

Notes

1 Priebe, 1986: 828; Dako, 1998: xi. Both contenders for the position of 'first'
  novel ignore *Guanya Pau*, the novel written by Liberian author Joseph J. Walters
  in 1891, and *Marita, or the Folly of Love* by 'A. Native', published in 1886–87.

2 Cited by Ugonna, 1977: 160.

3 Nkrumah, 1993: 57–8.

4 *Ibid.*, 3.

5 Obiechina, 1975: 13.

6 Richardson, [1747–48] 1985: 36: author's emphasis. Richardson is dissem-
  bling to some extent, reiterating an already familiar formula about the moral
  purpose of fiction and yet writing a story which contains many titillating
  scenes without a clear moral purpose.

7 See Edsman, 1979.

8 Casely Hayford became a nominated member of the Legislative Council in
  September 1916; he became the elected municipal member for Sekondi in
  1927, three years before his death.

9 The NCBWA, of which Casely Hayford was vice-president under the Hon. T. Hutton Mills, was 'founded on the loyalty and faith of a people under British Rule' and its primary objective was to achieve 'universal liberties' such as representation for the tax-paying class of commoners (*SLWN*, 13 January 1923). 'The only way is not the way of violence', Casely Hayford told delegates at the second session of the NCBWA, held in Freetown in February 1923: he continued, 'I am called upon to remind you that the policy of the NCBWA "is to maintain strictly and inviolate the connection of the British West African Dependencies with the British Empire"' (*SLWN*, 24 February 1923: 9). This instinct to reform caused Casely Hayford to fall out of favour with his ARPS colleagues when he appealed for support of the Native Administration Ordinance of 1927 (see Ugonna, 1966).

10 See Ugonna, 1977.

11 The eclectic 'jigsaw mode' of *Ethiopia Unbound* is reminiscent of other similarly assembled art forms along the West Coast of Africa (see Barber, 2000; Cole, 1997, 2001).

12 Nkrumah, 1993: 57.

13 See *Gold Coast Native Institutions* (1903) for an example of Casely Hayford's constructions of the past.

14 Casely Hayford, [1911] 1966: 1.

15 *Ibid.*, 2.

16 *Ibid.*

17 *Ibid.*, 107.

18 *Ibid.*, 21.

19 *Ibid.*, 15.

20 *Ibid.*, 16.

21 Contrast this with government examination papers of 1911–18: in subjects such as history and literature, no African material is included on the syllabus at this time. The transnational nature of Casely Hayford's political project is revealed by the inclusion of Hausa and Yoruba on his school syllabus. As chapter 3 revealed, however, when in the mid-1920s Governor Guggisburg took up Casely Hayford's lead and introduced schooling in African languages, a local argument broke out which did not die down for twenty years.

22 Casely Hayford, [1911] 1966: 18.

23 *SLWN*, 30 December 1911: 5.

24 Casely Hayford, [1911] 1966: 207.

25 *Ibid.*, 207.

26 See Ugonna, 1977.

27 Casely Hayford, [1911] 1966: 45.

28 *Ibid.*, 45.

29 *Ibid.*, 51.

30 *Ibid.*, 53–4.

31 *Ibid.*, 62. Comically, the spirit realm is entered through medical anaesthetic not through state of possession.

32 *Ibid.*, 42–3.

33 Smiles, [1859] 1997: 5.
34 *Ibid.*
35 *Ibid.*, 303–4.
36 Anon., 1932: 37–9.
37 The influential Phelps-Stokes Fund report, *Education in Africa* (1922), advocated 'the use of biographies of great personalities, especially those of African origin', which they felt would be effective in the 'character training' of Africans (Jones, 1922: 27–8). Interpreting the popularity of biographies from the other end of the political spectrum, Kofi Baku (1987) notes, 'writing popular or glorified biographies was an integral part of the protest culture evolved by the westernised Africans to assert their worth, and to inspire others to greater achievements' (p. 89).
38 Sampson, 1937: 41–2.
39 *Ibid.*, 44–5.
40 *SLWN*, 25 April 1903: 3.
41 *Ibid.* Blyden's comments on good and bad reading materials sparked a debate in subsequent editions of the *Sierra Leone Weekly News* about the extent to which biographies of white heroes could function as role models for West African readers (see also Blyden, [1887] 1967: 71–92). Unusually, on this occasion the current went against Blyden, with biographies of white and black heroes being applauded as useful reading material: one letter-writer commented in Smilesean fashion, 'The genius of any Race – white or black – is the common property of humanity' (*SLWN*, 2 May 1903: 3); 'men of genius', agreed another correspondent, are not the exclusive property of any race or nation, for relevant local lessons can be drawn from the lives of diverse historical heroes (*ibid.*, 4).
42 Casely Hayford, [1911] 1966: 197
43 See Blyden, [1887] 1967.
44 *SLWN*, 23 March 1908: 2.
45 Casely Hayford, [1911] 1966: 183.
46 *SLWN*, 23 March 1908: 3.
47 Casely Hayford, [1911] 1966: 112–16.
48 *Ibid.*, 118. *Ethiopia Unbound* is replete with biblical quotations of this nature, used each time to nationalist ends, demonstrating the ease with which the Bible provided early nationalists in the colonies with a moral-cum-political discourse to insist that colonialists 'set my people free' (see Hastings, 1997; Sanneh, 1995).
49 Blyden was still alive when *Ethiopia Unbound* was published, so the novel functions in large part as a praise narrative to the author's acknowledged hero.
50 Casely Hayford, [1911] 1966: 164.
51 See *ibid.*, 25–30, 41.
52 *Ibid.*, 3–5.
53 The metropolitan centre figures as a location for the expression of African intellectual brilliance in other early Ghanaian narratives, such as Mabel Dove's *Adventures of the Black Girl in her Search for Mr. Shaw* (1934) (see Newell, 2000).

54 Casely Hayford, [1911] 1966: 2–3.
55 Nkrumah, 1993: 53.
56 Ugonna, 1977: 163; Nkrumah, 1993.
57 Casely Hayford, [1911] 1966: 193.
58 The 'unspoilt African' is offered as a 'third way' between the 'scholar' and the 'noble savage' in a speech given by Kwamankra in the novel ([1911] 1966: 193).
59 Casely Hayford, [1911] 1966: 69.
60 *Ibid.*, 26.
61 Casely Hayford's philosophy of Africanness, in which 'pure' Africans take the moral and physical high-ground over Caucasians, makes use of *fin de siècle* European theories of decadence and degeneration. Throughout the first years of the twentieth century, the *Sierra Leone Weekly News* overflows with concerns about the racial degeneration of Creoles compared with the natives of the interior who were seen to possess virility and an intact, unpolluted black culture. In addition, there are strong Nietzschean overtones in *Ethiopia Unbound*, with its *Übermensch* set over against the degenerate culture.
62 Casely Hayford, [1911] 1966: 22.
63 *Ibid.*, 78.
64 *Ibid.*, 73.
65 Angmor, 1996.
66 See Nkrumah, 1993.
67 In a speech at the Optimism Club in Sekondi, Casely Hayford described how the first political action of the new NCBWA in 1920 was to send a delegation to London to petition for the same franchise that Sierra Leone and Nigeria enjoyed. By the time the delegation reached London, however, a cablegram from Nana Ofori Atta had overtaken them accusing them of misrepresenting the population (*SLWN*, 7 August 1926: 10).
68 *SLWN*, 7 August 1926: 11.
69 Casely Hayford, [1911] 1966: 15.
70 Blyden, [1887] 1967: 71–92.
71 Casely Hayford, [1911] 1966: 194.
72 Nkrumah, 1993: 74.
73 See Agovi, n.d.: 28.
74 Eg., Casely Hayford, [1911] 1966: 87, 134, 144.
75 *Ibid.*, 13.
76 *Ibid.*
77 *Ibid.*, 13–14.
78 See Blay, 1945; Amarteifio, [1967] 1985.
79 See Jahoda, 1959.
80 Casely Hayford, [1911] 1966: 192–3.
81 *Ibid.*, 141–2. Contrasting this troublesome union, Kwamankra and Mansa exemplify the ideal marriage, 'congenial. . . pleasant and spontaneous' ([1911] 1966: 33). The great political leader's 'dear little wife' is constantly by his side 'to cheer and to comfort him' (p. 37). Mansa is just as fictive as Kwamankra,

but she is an ultra-feminine model of good wifeliness, showing African readers how to establish 'a sweet little home all of their own, with plenty of flowers, and sunshine, and love, and God's blessing' (*ibid.*).

82 *Ibid.*, 147.
83 *Ibid.*, 155.
84 Richardson, [1747–48] 1985: 1499.
85 Casely Hayford, [1911] 1966: 66.
86 Ugonna, 1977; see also Nkrumah, 1993.
87 Casely Hayford, [1911] 1966: 167.
88 *Ibid.*, 7–8.
89 Nkrumah, 1993: 54. A qualifier to this belief is that most Christian missionaries and educationists accepted the importance of teaching concepts such as
   sin and redemption in the African's first language. The mother-tongue was
   believed to touch the soul in ways that were impossible through a second language (Meyer, 1999).
90 Casely Hayford, [1911] 1966: 197.
91 See Bhabha, 1994. It is doubtful whether colonised populations actually experienced 'otherness' at the ontological level described by some theorists for, as
   Casely Hayford writes in *Ethiopia Unbound*, the Sphinx was not 'a puzzle unto
   itself': it had 'one soul, one ideal' ([1911] 1966: 181).
92 Priebe, 1988: 10.
93 'Ethiopian' was a label commonly applied by Africans to themselves, and 'cultural nationalist' organisations such as the 'Ethiopian Progressive Association'
   flourished in the political climate of the early twentieth century (see Panford,
   1996). Ethiopia had retained independence for thousands of years, seeing off
   the Italians at the Battle of Adowa in 1895 and thus forming, in the minds of
   African nationalists elsewhere, an island of independence in a continent otherwise completely colonised by the Europeans. Unsurprisingly, then, Ethiopia
   became both metaphor and model for a pan-African political movement
   stretching from local political organisations to the United States, all of whom
   identified with Ethiopia as the cradle of civilisation. It is necessary to note,
   however, that Ethiopia was invoked in different ways through the colonial
   period and its connotations were particularly transformed in West Africa by
   the impact of Garveyism (see Hill, 1986).
94 *SLWN*, 11 November 1911: 2.
95 *Ibid.*; emphasis added.
96 Senanu, 1972; Priebe, 1986.

8 'Been-tos' and 'never-beens':
Kobina Sekyi's satires of Fante society

It is never to the credit of any West African to strive manfully to become Anglo-African, Europeanised or Anglicised in anything. A Black Whiteman is a creature, a freak, a monstrosity. (Attoh-Ahuma, *The Gold Coast Nation and National Consciousness*)

Many of the Gold Coast's earliest creative writers were also the colony's leading cultural nationalists and pan-Africanist thinkers, actively involved in the project to construct, or 'invent', traditions that would confer dignity and race-pride upon local populations in the context of colonialism and global racial oppression.[1] This cadre from the coastal 'lawyer-merchant' class acted as filters for the interpretation of pan-African and pan-West African ideologies at the turn of the twentieth century, and they wrote history books with titles such as *Fanti National Constitution, Gold Coast Native Institutions, The Gold Coast Nation and National Consciousness*.[2] Selecting aspects from the past to promote in the present, these intellectuals, in the words of Kofi Baku, 'produced a corpus of "bias history" (or an authorised version of their past)' by invoking a near-perfect African tradition.[3]

Ideologically motivated by the project to legitimate and retrieve the past, and to retrieve with it a sense of racial pride, authors such as J. E. Casely Hayford (1866–1930) and Kobina Sekyi (1892–1956) turned with ease to creative writing, making use of the imaginative and moralistic potential of fiction to achieve their cultural goals. This chapter explores the ways in which, through drama and prose fiction, Kobina Sekyi continued the educated elite's nationalist literary project to 'invent a tradition' for the Gold Coast, making 'tradition' and the past serve his own particular political agenda.[4] An idealised but lost African past is referred to frequently in his writings, functioning as a pivot for bitterly satirical comparisons with the present. By invoking a golden age of Africanness, Sekyi is able to indict the local effects of colonialism with the full weight of 'the past' at his fingertips.

Sekyi's satirical technique involves a series of ideological risks and paradoxes, however, for his lost African worlds seem to be both idyllic and real, static and dynamic, timeless and recent. In particular, the representations of rural Africans in his writings conjure up the image of a 'noble savage' drawn from a European philosophical tradition.[5] The 'noble savage' recurred in abolitionist literature in the United States, in which a golden age of liberty and plenitude was set against the present;[6] it was also widely invoked by colonial policy-makers to justify their imposition of Indirect Rule in West Africa. In his own way, Sekyi also made use of this construction, setting it over against the 'freaks' and 'monstrosities' of his anglicised culture. Paradoxes such as this reveal the conservative side of Sekyi's writings, for in promoting old and rural values he shows no comprehension of the socio-economic reasons which prompted an entire class of non-'noble savages' – of the kind encountered in chapter 1 – to abandon their ancestral customs and embrace the colonial, 'literate' lifestyle.

Both Casely Hayford and his protégé, Sekyi, were leading members of the ARPS, an organisation based in Cape Coast. Both men responded to the increasing exclusion of educated Africans from political and economic power-structures in the late nineteenth century by writing about the past, defending what Sekyi termed 'the great and glorious traditions of our ancestors and the peerless social and political institutions which our ancestors perfected long ago, and which it is our duty to preserve from the inroads of European irresponsibility as regards things non-European'.[7] In their non-fictions these authors wrote their own social class into the past in the role of spokesmen for the chiefs, 'linguists' at court and scribes, and in different ways their fictions continued this project on the plane of ideals.

Sekyi became a convert to tradition – a kind of 'born-again African' – during his time as a student in London. The racial prejudice he experienced in the metropolis increased his anti-colonial feelings and led him to criticise the way in which anglicised coastal Africans had sacrificed their cultural identities. Hakim Adi notes in his study of West African students in Britain in the 1900s, 'they became much more aware of their colonial status during their sojourn in Britain, as well as the hypocrisy of colonial rule'.[8] Whatever the sources of Sekyi's cultural nationalist principles, his commitment to the original ARPS manifesto endured from 1918, the year of his permanent return to West Africa from Britain, through to 1949, when he initiated a rapprochement with chiefs on the Joint Provincial Council on the issue of native administration.[9] In the meantime, all around him in the economically turbulent 1920s and 1930s, his close political allies seemed to be compromising by accepting seats in government and accom-modating policies such as Indirect Rule. ARPS colleagues such as Casely Hayford entered the Legislative Council and worked from within to reform the system while Sekyi chose to remain excluded from – and ardently opposed to – colonial rule for the duration of his political career.

Throughout his life Sekyi was pledged to the founding principles of the Aborigines' Society, especially its commitment to rejuvenate 'the laws, Customs and Institutions of the country'.[10] Isolated in the old colonial capital, Cape Coast, he remained robust in his argument that the British intrusion into West Africa had disrupted a pre-colonial golden age in which, amongst other things, native authority was egalitarian and com-moners had the power to elect and destool chiefs through the state coun-cils and *Asafo* companies.[11] As leader of the ARPS in the 1930s and 1940s, he continued to insist that 'the Society is composed of the Chiefs them-selves', by which he meant, firstly, that the chiefs' legitimate representa-tives were 'certain literate natives' such as himself, and secondly, that their institutions should remain autonomous from government.[12] This belief in the role of 'certain literate natives' as mediators and spokesmen for the chiefs pervaded the ARPS. As with Casely Hayford, Sekyi took a dim view of chiefs entering the Legislative Council, not only on grounds of custom – chiefs were supposed to speak through linguists and not to make their voices heard at assemblies – but also on grounds of literacy. The educated elite believed firmly that 'at present there is not a sufficient number of Head Chiefs capable of intelligently and effectively taking part in the debates and the proceedings of the Legislative Council'.[13]

After the First World War, the effort to reinstate institutions from a bygone era retreated in the imaginations of Accra-based nationalists such as Casely Hayford, for whom idealist cultural politics were supplanted by more immediate and pragmatic struggles, such as the achievement of municipal representation, legislative reform and increased educational opportunities for Africans.[14] Meanwhile, the 'Sage of Cape Coast', as Sekyi was known, refused to accept the marginalisation of the ARPS and held out in his home-town, writing vehemently anti-colonial newspaper articles and presiding over an organisation that was increasingly regarded by the gov-ernment as anachronistic and unrepresentative of the chiefs.[15] By the early 1930s, Sekyi was *persona non grata* with colonial officials: the Governor would, as a matter of course, decline requests to meet up with ARPS repre-sentatives, and district commissioners boasted of the defeat of Sekyi by the pro-Indirect Rule chiefs. 'The Chiefs are now the masters and the very members of the Aborigines are subject to Native Stools and Tribunals', wrote one district commissioner triumphantly in February 1932.[16] 'Only a few of Sekyi's adherents remain in the Society', he continued, 'and they appear to do nothing but oppose all Government measures.'[17]

Sekyi's sense of an African golden age existing prior to colonialism profoundly informed his writing. In newspaper articles, his faith in a glorious ancestral past gave rise to 'a language which both exposed Government officials to public ridicule and impressed his admirers with his fearless nature when dealing with men in high office'.[18] In his creative writing, the ideal gave rise to the comic-satirical mode adopted in *The Blinkards* (1915) and the cynical-satirical mode of *The Anglo-Fanti* (1918).

The Blinkards

In *The Blinkards* satire is used as a continuation of the 'attack-attack-attack method' that characterised Sekyi's newspaper articles.[19] More than a simple comedy of manners, *The Blinkards* parades a long line of monstrous African imitators before the audience. Set in Cape Coast in 'the present', the play unmasks the social effects of the British presence on the West Coast of Africa, exposing the pathological nature of the colonial relationship. A certain class of people is shown to have lost all sense of history and ethnic identity, preferring to mimic European dress codes and manners rather than to speak the mother-tongue and eat local foodstuffs. Mrs Borofosem, for instance, has gleaned her Englishness from a week or so spent in 'Seabourne, in Blankshire', a working-class seaside resort where she purchased her lorgnette and learnt to shake hands using only the fingertips.[20] She speaks and acts with fraudulent authority, for her version of aristocratic English etiquette is revealed to have been gleaned from working-class sources, particularly the suburban 'Mrs Gush' who taught Mrs Borofosem (whose name means 'Englishness') all that she knows about manners.[21] Similarly, the consequences of 'bad reading' by newly educated Africans are explored in the seduction scene between the clerk, Mr Okadu, and the trainee Englishwoman, Miss Tsiba: to attract her love-object, Miss Tsiba plans to drop her handkerchief in the manner of 'the book I read last night till morning'.[22] Luckily for her, Mr Okadu has read the same popular novel and he knows, from the actions of the romantic hero, to propose marriage immediately. 'The chief woman in the book, she drop her handkerchief', he comments, and 'the chief man in the book pick it up and give it to the girl. Then they fall in love at first sight. Then they get engaged.'[23]

Through scenes such as these, Sekyi shows how the worst British popular literature has been taken to be realistic by semi-educated local readers, who justify their violation of all customary practices with the outrageous comment, 'it's the English way'.[24]

Mrs Borofosem's cigar-smoking, English-speaking husband diagnoses the problem at the outset of the play: 'we are born into a world of imitators, worse luck', he says, 'They see a thing done in England or by somebody white; then they say we must do the same thing in Africa.'[25] 'My parents set out deliberately to make me as much like a European as possible', he continues, 'They would have bleached my skin if they could.'[26] Alienated, confused and self-conscious, Mr Borofosem is trapped in an imitative lifestyle of his wife's making, clearly emasculated by the cultural forces at work in his world. The hilarity of *The Blinkards* derives from its satirical exposure of these low-class African mimics of low-class English culture. Their efforts at anglicisation are shown to have failed on every count.

Coastal Africans are shown in *The Blinkards* to have abandoned what is represented as a social ideal. Miss Tsiba's mother, Na Sompa, and her grandmother, Nana Katawerwa, exemplify the rural utopia and adhere to traditional ways of life. The tragic demise of Fante life is performed through these female characters for, astounded at the rapid engagement of Miss Tsiba to Mr Okadu, Na Sompa dies from shock at 'the English manner' in which the affair is conducted.[27] Meanwhile, the old grandmother expresses outrage at the young couple's multiple violations of local customs and insists that the young bride depart to the village to perform her mother's funeral rites.[28] This removal of Miss Tsiba to a rural location allows Sekyi to set a scene in the village. The 'unsullied Africa' represented by the grandmother and the old fishermen in the village is invoked as a corrective to westernisation and as a comment on the degenerate, morally corrupt present. In this way the coastal Fante community is exposed with reference to virtues from a time and a place that are being obliterated by the process of historical change.

Ironically, the image of Africa untouched by western civilisation which the rural folk represent seems to derive directly from an eighteenth-century European tradition exemplified by Rousseau and the German idealists.[29] This romantic philosophy gave rise to an image of the 'noble savage', evolving naturally in rural areas without intervention from outsiders or city-dwellers. Persisting into the twentieth century, the idea of the 'noble savage' was set in a binary relationship with hybrids, mulattoes and other supposedly impure, racially degenerate types.[30] *The Blinkards* thus seems to be imbued with some of the very systems of knowledge that are openly rejected in the play. Similar constructions of native purity, unsullied by western concepts, led the British to impose the policy of Indirect Rule in their African colonies.[31] Lasting until the late 1940s in the Gold Coast, this policy was informed by the philosophy of romantic primitivism, for a key figure in official government rhetoric was the 'authentic' African, set over against the cultural fraud. For instance, in setting up the Provincial Councils in 1925, Governor Guggisberg intended that the chiefly class would 'meet together to defend and *preserve* their native constitutions, institutions and customs'.[32] At the same time as 'preserving' customs and institutions, of course, Guggisberg argued that it was imperialism's mission to produce competent new leaders: 'to *create*. . . leaders is an implied part of Britain's recently self-imposed task of tutelage and development' he wrote, for 'there cannot be a moment's doubt as to their incapacity to-day to stand by themselves.'[33] Thus Guggisberg both defended and transformed African traditions, separating them off from the forces of modernisation which had created an army of 'dangerous', 'denationalised' Africans out of touch with their past.[34]

While the government's image of the authentic African was constructed differently from the traditional African invoked by Sekyi, we need to note that both discourses revolve around the scornful rejection of Africans living non-'traditional' lifestyles. Eric Hobsbawm makes the obvious point that, in Britain's colonies, 'elite resistance to the west remained westernizing even when it opposed wholesale westernization on grounds of religion, morality, ideology or political pragmatism'.[35] Thus western-trained lawyers such as Mahatma Gandhi operated according to ideologies that made perfect sense to their colonial oppressors but would not have been easily comprehensible to traditionalists in their own countries.[36] In Sekyi's case, one ideological consequence of this epistemological baggage is that he operates within a binary model in which – with the exception of members of his own highly educated class – the only alternative to being a 'noble savage' is to be a fraud, a denationalised mimic of English culture.

It is important not to conflate the radical conservatism of Sekyi with the conservatism of reformist administrators such as Governor Guggisberg.[37] In Sekyi's case, as Jones-Quartey notes, 'the more European philosophy he read, the more African he became in his arguments for the restoration of an Akan-Fante state system.[38] Both Guggisberg and Sekyi seem, however, to speak from a shared platform involving the preservation of a golden age of 'pre-colonial values' – constructed differently in each case – to the exclusion of ambitious new social groups. 'The "educated native"', Sekyi wrote in 1931, repeating sentiments he first aired at the NCBWA conference in 1920, 'is the most potent enemy of real progress among Africans in West Africa', for such a person lives by means of 'the deleterious foreign substances and ideas which have been introduced'.[39] There is 'a new type of African in Africa', he continued, 'European educated and subservient and ignorant of ancestral Africans' heritage'.[40]

By no means new, Sekyi's attitudes date from the mid-nineteenth century when, with increasing fervour in European memoirs and accounts of West Africa, newly literate Africans were represented as imposters and mimics, illegitimate heirs to positions that had been, until the 1890s, occupied by the African elite.[41] Many decades before the formal imposition of Indirect Rule, Brodie Cruickshank (1853) wrote that African clerks and their educated peers possessed 'an exaggerated idea of their superiority over others. With all the self-sufficiency of ignorance, they conceived that they had surmounted the barrier which divided the uninstructed African from the enlightened European.'[42]

Coinciding with the formal consolidation of the British Empire, theories of black mimicry opened up an ideological space for the suppression of educated commoners in the colonies.[43] Newly literate Africans tended to be regarded by administrators as imposters who were stranded between cultures and likely to regress into savagery at the drop of their bowler hats. The figure of the 'scholar' was invoked by dominant power groups for seventy years or so, updated and upgraded with the passing years, revised to suit contemporary political controversies such as the promotion of an Africanised education system and Native Administration in the 1920s. The longevity and emotional power of this figure is intriguing, for the 'scholar' seems to trouble the European's self-identification as 'literate man' and to disturb the colonial right to rule in Africa. As T. K. Utchay pointed out in 1938, 'they say that education has spoilt him [the West African] and that he is worse to deal with after he has been educated. Is it not because after his education he is better prepared to defend his own interests and refuses to be bullied?'[44] Unbulliable and ambitious, these lower-class 'scholars' violated both cultural nationalist and imperial ideologies, and newly literate Africans became the easy target of satirical abuse by both 'superior' classes.

Concerns about the links between literacy and African insubordination were not confined to the European community. During the high-times of the African professional elite, in the 1870s, the Fante African-owned *Gold Coast Times* expressed consternation about the lifestyles of semi-educated 'scholars'. A reader's letter printed in the November 1877 contains the familiar complaint, carried over from Cruickshank's time, that, 'Before our school boys are able to read or write with any degree of accuracy, they fancy themselves "educated". . . . To be gentlemen they fancy they must wear good clothes and put on costly ornaments.'[45] Sekyi's social milieu is summed up by this reader's letter to the *Gold Coast Times*. Born in 1892 into the elite 'merchant-lawyer' class and educated in Britain, Sekyi probably shared more *class* attitudes with well-educated colonialists than he would have cared to admit, and in *The Blinkards* he derides the same section of the population that successive colonial governments sought to squeeze from positions of power.

Writing from the 'other' side of the colonial divide, local commentators such as Sekyi reveal the extent of elite African revulsion for the up-and-coming commoner. 'Scholars' such as Mr Okadu, the clerk in *The Blinkards*, exemplify the ambitions of these 'never-beens' who want to be educated in English manners and to enter elite society. Okadu chants, 'All native ways are silly, repulsive, unrefined./ All customs superstitions, that rule the savage mind.'[46] In representing Mr Okadu thus, Sekyi is defending his own superior class position and privilege against intruders, labelled 'freaks', 'imitators' and 'apes' by other members of the elite.[47] Perhaps such defensiveness was an economic necessity during the period when the policy of Indirect Rule was formalised. Employment opportunities for educated Africans decreased dramatically after 1900: between 1919 and 1927, for example, only twenty-seven Africans were employed in the higher ranks of the civil service; Africans were excluded from lucrative business deals, and competition was intense for junior clerical posts.[48]

A similar 'authenticity versus counterfeit' model was used on a regular basis by colonial commentators in the early twentieth century in their bids to belittle the newly educated African, and to justify the exclusion of 'scholars' from political processes in favour of the fully fledged African, the 'native chief'. Semi-educated servants in government houses would be described by their mistresses inscribing 'Custard Birds' and 'Potatoes in trowsies' on menu cards instead of 'Birds Custard' and 'Jacket Potatoes'.[49] The 'half-educated native – not "civilised" in the same sense as the native barristers and doctors' was found to be 'most amusing' but also most 'irritating' for the way he would mimic English manners and 'insist in talking English to his countrymen'.[50]

Governor Guggisberg's wife, Decima Moore, illustrates the ruling class's fluctuation between lofty amusement and irritation at the African mimic in her memoir, *We Two in West Africa* (1909). Published six years before Sekyi completed *The Blinkards* and a full decade before Guggisberg became Governor of the Gold Coast, the book contains an extended satirical dramatisation of an encounter between two semi-educated men at a railway station in Ghana. 'Wearing an air of conscious superiority', both men are over-dressed in European attire and keen to display their 'newly found language'.[51] Moore establishes a distance between herself and her 'partially educated' subjects by naming them 'Bowler Hat' and 'Gaiters' and by using stage directions to emphasise their affected manners: 'It was a perfect piece of acting, so I will give it as a play', she writes.[52] 'Ah – it is you!' cries Bowler Hat at the sight of his friend; 'Ah – it is you', parrots the other.[53] 'Good morning' is repeated by both characters, as an admiring crowd of 'half-clad brethren' gather to witness these native scholars: 'I am glad to see you', they echo several times, continuing, 'Are you well?' and 'It is a good day.'[54] A near fight results from one phrase, when Gaiters, who works at the station, angers Bowler Hat by repeating his 'I go Tarkwa.'[55] Having resolved the problem and established that Gaiters is staying put, Bowler Hat waves goodbye as the train steams away to the sound of their repeated hellos, offered in place of farewells.

There are many similarities between Sekyi's satire of 'scholars' and Moore's short satirical dramatisation, for in much the same manner as the colonial commentators, Sekyi derides the inability of newly educated Africans to master English grammar and pronunciation. As with Moore's caricatures, in *The Blinkards* Mrs Borofosem makes continual grammatical mistakes and slides into pidgin English whenever she becomes overexcited. Sekyi also ridicules the way in which 'never-beens' – the 'half-clad brethren' of Moore's piece – confer full cultural authority upon 'been-tos', seeking advice from ill-informed cretins on topics such as English manners and pronunciation. Sekyi also ridicules these people's reading choices, and he criticises their efforts to improve their English through literary societies. In consequence, just as Moore belittles her targets, Sekyi debunks any claims on the part of this class to social and political authority.

A key difference separates elite African commentators from the colonialist writers: this relates to the former group's preoccupation with *degrees* of African literacy. As with Casely Hayford in *Ethiopia Unbound*, in Sekyi's writing an 'unspoilt cultured African' is inserted into the binary moral division between 'noble savage' and 'mimic' (or, to preserve the cultural nationalists' bias, between 'illiterate chief' and 'semi-literate scholar'). Reminiscent of Kwamankra in *Ethiopia Unbound*, Mr Onyimdzi in *The Blinkards* exemplifies the ARPS ideal for highly educated Africans: he is a hyper-literate, foreign-trained native who is the natural representative of illiterate chiefs, being the product of colonial education systems while remaining an opponent of westernisation in his own culture. Fluent in both English and Fante, he bridges the divide between custom and colonialism; he refuses to speak English or to wear Eureopan clothes outside of the workplace, and declares 'I will have some fun with that numbskull' when Mr Okadu begs him to 'teach me to be English'.[56] Heroes such as Onyimdzi thus play out the political ideals of the professional elite, set over against the demands for more English culture from undiscriminating 'never-beens'.

What connects the African elite's response to that of the colonial ruling class is that, far from appreciating the ways in which English literacy was being appropriated and used locally by non-elite Africans, these commentators tended to view the 'scholar' in terms of the failure of mission schools to graft western 'civilisation' onto essentially tribal individuals who had cut dangerously loose their customary ties. The new literate class, composed of clerks, teachers, middlemen and catechists, was seen to have cultural affiliations and economic aspirations that were not at all natural, that illustrated the dangerous side effects of an English education system in the colonies.

Sekyi dramatises the dangerous local consequences of the imported education system in his representation of the 'Cosmopolitan Club', a literary society based in Cape Coast. Ripe for ridicule, the club members portrayed in the play suffer from grossly inflated self-images, and their pompous, ungrammatical English remains entertaining to this day. 'The manifestations of incredible merrimentations has displayed in this capacious hall due to wedding matrimonial jollification', announces the president of the literary club at Mr Okadu's wedding to Miss Nsiba.[57] Sweating profusely and exhausted, he sits down at the end of his speech and asks comically, 'What did I say? Did I speak well?'[58] Another club member continues in this mode, expressing 'joyful lachrimosity' at the marriage and praising the 'bride and bridesmaids of amazing pulchritudity'.[59] Rejecting rural rules of behaviour, these young 'scholars' in the Cosmopolitan Club have turned to imported reading matter, choosing to read 'how to' books with titles such as *Don't* for advice on 'civilised' clothing, foodstuffs, relationships and marriage. Sekyi shows that domestic conduct books are all the rage with club members and satirises this misuse of literacy: 'The

Librarian has ordered two dozen copies of *Don't* and three dozen copies of *How to Dance*', club members are informed, 'When we have learnt all by heart, we will make further additions to our bibliotecha.'[60]

To give its full title, *Don't: A Manual of Mistakes and Improprieties More or Less Prevalent in Conduct and Speech*, was written by 'Censor' in the late nineteenth century and by 1912 it was published in London, Melbourne and Toronto for distribution to readerships throughout Britain and the colonies.[61] The pamphlet probably attracted great interest among newly educated readers in Britain's West African colonies, and it was advertised in bookshops throughout the region (see Plate XI). Inheriting the mantle from William Cobbett's *Advice to Young Men* (1830) and the plethora of popular 'domestic conduct' books that followed in its wake, *Don't* includes sections on public behaviour and dress codes, as well as sections 'Affectionately Addressed to Womankind', 'For Husbands' and 'For Young People'.

Attacking 'vulgar' behaviour throughout, Censor lists the most common forms of tastelessness to affect suburban English society and he prescribes rules for refining one's manners. Readers learn that 'it is the very soul of vulgarity' for men to 'appear at table or in any company' while in a dressing-gown and slippers.[62] 'Don't wear trinkets, shirt-pins, finger-rings, or anything that is solely ornamental', readers are informed;[63] 'Don't speak ungrammatically. Study books of grammar, and the writings of the best authors';[64] 'Don't pronounce incorrectly. . . If in doubt, consult the dictionaries';[65] 'Don't be too fond of superlatives';[66] 'Don't confine your reading exclusively to novels. An excess of this kind of reading is the great vice of womankind.'[67] For 'never-beens' who wished to learn about English decorum, this book held all the secrets of English drawing-rooms, pantries and wardrobes.

While Sekyi satirises African readers of *Don't* in *The Blinkards* by portraying the constant consultation of dictionaries by semi-educated characters and their rigid conformity to foreign rules of politeness, he actually *upholds* many of Censor's prescriptions about inappropriate clothing and plain speech. Hence our first view of Mr and Mrs Borofosem is of a woman wearing a 'loose European underdress gown' and a man in pyjamas and slippers.[68] Indeed, the entire Borofosem household epitomises the 'vulgar' classes described in *Don't*, and the comedy depends upon the audience's recognition of these improprieties. In satirising the effects of a blind subservience to the counsel of English etiquette books, with their lengthy instructions on the avoidance of vulgarity, the entire play itself becomes a kind of instruction manual, a set of cultural 'don'ts' for Fantes.

Based on a rejection of the Englishness promoted in *Don't*, the play participates keenly in the debates about good and bad reading matter that raged in West Africa in the early twentieth century. *The Blinkards* exposes the role of English literacy in forming the attitudes of anglicised Fantes, for their only means of access to English culture – alongside African 'been-tos' – are imported popular novels and etiquette books. The play can thus be regarded as an Africanised version of an English domestic conduct book: it upholds the distaste for the 'vulgar' classes manifested in *Don't*, while indicating its own, Africanised domestic code.

If Sekyi's satire of literary and social clubs is aimed at a moral end, naming and shaming local organisations in order to achieve their reformation and improvement, how is it that the first performance of *The Blinkards*

BOOKS FOR THE MILLION.

PRICE 3D. EACH.

Card Players' Hand Book,
Christian Names,
Egyptian Circle of Fortune,
Home Pastimes,
How to Obtain A Situation,
Ladies' Guide to Etiquette,
Ladies' Letter Writer,
Letter Writers' Assistant,
Modern Reciter,
Napoleon's Book of Fate,
Raphael's Chart of Destiny,
Rules for Every Day Life,
Tales for Boys and Girls,
Wishing Cards,

DON'T, (new and enlarged edition). A Manual of Mistakes and Improprieties more or less prevalent in Conduct and Speech. Price 9d.

RAPHAEL'S BOOK OF DREAMS, and BOOK OF FATE, at 1s. 6d. each.

The Life and Prophecies of Mother Shipton. Beautifully Illustrated. Price 1s. 3d.

IN VARIOUS BINDINGS & PRICES:—

Wesley's Hymn and New Supplement,
Methodist Sunday-School Hymn Books,
Public Prayers and Services,
Public Prayers and Wesley's Hymns (combined),
Bible, Public Prayers, and
Wesley's Hymns (combined).

T. A. KING & Co.,—OPPOSITE POST OFFICE.

Plate XI 'Books for the Million!' Advertisement for T. A. King's store in Lagos, including a revised, enlarged edition of *Don't*, in the *Mirror*, 1888: fp

in 1916 was by members of the Cosmopolitan Club in Cape Coast?[69] How could Sekyi's moral censure succeed when his actors were members of the very organisation which seems to epitomise the vice of mimicry in the play? Was the play perhaps less morally 'corrective' and more unashamedly comical than critics have assumed?

The relationship between the first cast of *The Blinkards* and the play's satirical target reveals the truth behind the comment that satires tend to have a 'double audience', for 'no reader, however foppish, avaricious or venal, will see himself in the satiric mirror. Satire, almost by definition, is about other people.'[70] The extreme nature of Sekyi's satire would have positioned most audience members beyond identification with the characters, for targets such as Mrs Borofosem and members of the literary club are laughable precisely for their *excessive* travesty of western values and fashions. They are exaggerated and grotesque characters, lacking the taste and decorum which characterise Lawyer Onyimdze and members of his highly educated social group. This latter, elite group were the actual members of the Cosmopolitan Club in Cape Coast, and they constituted the play's first actors and audience, a fact which exposes the class-conscious nature of Sekyi's satire. If moral correction and education were its goals, spectators would have recognised its targets beyond the club-room, in Fante society 'out there'. The critique contained in *The Blinkards* relates to those half-educated Africans who whole-heartedly supported the colonial education system. Recognising the problem and agreeing to the moral censure of these groups, the audience would probably have responded by ridiculing, exposing and shaming the target.

The apparent contradiction involved in the Cosmopolitan Club sending up their own institution is thus explained by the status of the real Club members as highly elite. Unlike the literary club which is portrayed in the play, the Cosmopolitan Club was established in Cape Coast by members of the professional class. In his satire of literary and debating clubs, then, Sekyi's writing is neither reformist nor transformative. In fact, in this instance it appears to be elitist and superior, poking fun at the newly educated 'scholar' class who were busily setting up their own clubs, practising their English language and asserting their own literary tastes and aspirations.

As with the bulk of Ghana's locally produced fiction prior to independence, one of the central themes in Sekyi's creative writing is marriage. Following the Marriage Ordinance of 1884, which transformed the status of those women who undertook 'legal' and church marriages, a great deal of Ghanaian creative writing centred upon the effects of the new law upon gender relations. The Marriage Ordinance impacted upon some, but by no means all, Ghanaian women:[71] however, to writers of early novels such as *Marita: Or the Folly of Love*[72] the Ordinance was shown to increase female disrespect towards husbands by making it impossible to divorce a wife except on grounds of adultery. The Ordinance lurked in the background of many tales by other creative writers, including Sekyi, who found a theme in the widely held perception that the Ordinance increased female disobedience in the household.[73] Focusing on personal relationships but responding to political changes, the narratives produced around these legal shifts manifested male authors' uneasiness with the intrusion of the British colonial state into local domestic and sexual arrangements that had developed over the decades according to customary codes. As one rural fisherman comments in *The Blinkards*, 'Wonders never cease! What has marriage to do with the Government?'[74] The consolidation of the colonial state and the concurrent socio-economic 'emasculation' of elite men is thus played out in this cultural nationalist literature on the level of images (and nightmare scenarios) of household gender relations.

Sekyi opposed the Christian orientated legislation of 1884, which had been introduced eight years before his birth; in later years he attacked the Marriage Ordinance of 1922 which further recognised the domestic rights of women in monogamous unions.[75] It is hardly surprising, therefore, that he turned to 'topical satire' to 'safeguard the morality of the nation' by exposing the extent to which the state had upset the balance and introduced chaos into nuanced traditional values.[76] His satires function as 'a way to assess blame'[77] and, interestingly, in his writing moral blame does not lie with the colonial authorities; nor does it lie with male members of Ghana's literary and social clubs. Rather, blame is laid squarely at the feet of African women, who are shown to have suffered from excessive anglicisation and to have benefited the most from the adoption of a Christian marital ideology. In *The Blinkards* Sekyi's most extreme satirical censure is aimed at female characters whose behaviour comically exceeds the bounds of acceptability. Women are paraded before the audience in various degrees of denationalisation: they function both as targets of social satire and as vehicles for the expression of extreme pro-British colonial values.

Careful not to promote accidentally any of the western values he criticises, Sekyi creates in Mrs Borofosem an embodiment of the 'worst' type of British feminism. In her poem about the delights of England, recited to a group of admiring African girls, she chants:

I'm glad I've been to England
And learned to rule my spouse:
For there the wives are bold, and
Command in every house.[78]

In the character of Mrs Borofosem, we witness the dire consequences of non-traditional values, for women such as this epitomise the breakdown of morality in Fante society as a result of western education.

Significantly, whilst Mrs Borofosem takes a young girl into her household for training, she does not appear to have any children of her own. Her apparent sterility reinforces our image of her as a travesty of African femininity, a violation of the fertile 'Mother Africa' trope which recurs in male cultural nationalist discourse.[79] Monstrously comic in her transgression of Fante gender codes, this stereotypical termagant and leader of local female taste is set over against the image of the unspoilt rural woman represented by Miss Tsiba's mother, Na Sompa, and her grandmother, Nana Katawerwa. Sekyi thus creates potent symbols of the cultural extremes of English vice and Fante virtue in his women characters, for female characters voice the values which Sekyi opposes in *The Blinkards* and they also embody the 'traditional' cultural values which are endorsed in the play.

In an article entitled 'Education with Particular Reference to a West African University', first delivered as a speech at the NCBWA conference in 1920, Sekyi made the following rather violent observations about female education. The Gold Coast school system, he said, 'should be to fit our women to share and supplement our views and aspirations and still remain women, and not to evolve [into] the hideous and unsexed abortions which the so-called higher education of women in Europe has produced'.[80] In the light of these sentiments, it is hardly surprising that Mr Onyimdze, the hero of *The Blinkards*, cries, 'No thanks! I do not want any such thing as a wife', when asked if he will be marrying into his own social class.[81] An explanation of this vehement rejection can be found in Sekyi's article on education, which continues, 'consider. . . how our young women are growing shameless and becoming demoralised in every sense of the term';[82] he concludes by pressing for the reinstatement of a system of education based upon the family and the home.[83]

Mrs Borofosem and her young trainee, Miss Tsiba, are the ultimate in female 'shamelessness' and 'demoralisation', for Mrs Borofosem has inculcated into her ward sexual values which challenge masculine domestic authority and diametrically oppose Fante gender roles.[84] Over against their illegitimate power, Fante femininity is preserved as an untouchable ideal in Sekyi's creative writing, labelled a 'unique African pride', even by the most anglicised African man: 'The Fanti ideal of womanhood is not reflected in the young ladies of [t]his age', reflects the narrator of Sekyi's novella, *The Anglo-Fanti*, for 'although all these young ladies have acquired in some degree the modern accomplishments of reading, writing, playing the piano or the harmonium, etc., yet most of them have had little time in which. . . to make any acquaintance with the manifold problems of housekeeping and with their solution.'[85] Fantasising about the perfect wife, the protagonist of *The Anglo-Fanti* imagines 'that he may get engaged to a very young girl and attach her to some illiterate female relative to be brought up to suit his tastes'.[86] Set against these ideals, women such as Mrs Borofosem and Miss Tsiba exhibit a new urban assertiveness which usurps masculine authority both inside and outside the household.

In *The Blinkards* Mr Onyimdze is hailed as a cultural hero at the end of the play. Change is shown to be possible in Fante society through the success of this heroic figure who helps 'a heathen woman, Nana Katawerwa, to triumph over the church in court' and to dissolve Miss Tsiba's marriage.[87] Even Mrs Borofosem is shown wearing native dress in the final scene: 'I wonder why I feel so comfy?', she muses while promising to speak Fante to local Africans.[88] Her husband voices the moral of the play, ending the performance with a speech upon the validity of inherited customs.[89] Albeit elitist and superior in tone, then, this satire functions in a potentially transformative manner, for the satirised characters are set over against an idealised, non-satirised hero who converts the fools back to a traditional morality at the end of the play.

The Anglo-Fanti

By the time Sekyi came to write *The Anglo-Fanti*, his satirical attitude had become far more cynical and disgusted. Satire regularly gives way to polemics in this novella, and the comedy of *The Blinkards* gives way to a direct critique of the way in which the coastal, christianised classes have perpetuated the myth of English cultural superiority. Fante society is portrayed as totally diseased, and unlike Mr Onyimdze, the hero of *The Anglo-Fanti* becomes a tragic victim of local cultural processes. Narrated in the present tense, the story charts the life of Kwesi Onyidzin, an elite Fante Everyman, from boyhood through to youth, manhood and

death.[90] 'A healthy black boy' in the opening scene, Kwesi's social intercourse is regulated by his culturally degenerate family, who rename him
Archibald Edward and indoctrinate him with a belief in 'the superiority
in every respect of everything European over everything African'.[91] At
the start of the tale, in a wonderful rendition of the Lord's Prayer, Fante
children in the infant class recite, 'Ahfallah, wee-chart, in heaven.
Hallaway, be, thah-name. Thaheheelankam', and so on, 'the rest of the
prayer being similarly adapted, after the Fanti boy's fashion. . . because
he does not understand a word of the prayer'.[92] By the middle of the
tale, however, the hero has lost the ability to comprehend Fante idiom,
and by the end of the narrative he is broken and isolated, stranded on
the outskirts of his community.[93]

The difference of tone between the comical-satirical play and this cynical-satirical novella may be explained by Sekyi's heightened sense of bitterness towards the elite coastal community after his return home from
Britain. A sense of cultural crisis pervades the text and, in the absence of
lower-class mimics to act as comic foils to the hero, Sekyi's bitterness
becomes more urgently focused upon the values and lifestyles of his *own*
class. Without losing his emphasis upon the necessity to 'meet the contemporary crisis by reinvigorating the past',[94] Sekyi turns his critical gaze
upon the elite, finding there a tragic victim so riddled with identity conflicts that he dies from his own contradictions.

Sekyi's novella has been described as 'more or less his version of
Casely Hayford's *Ethiopia Unbound*' for the way in which it critiques
Christian and 'Ordinance' marriages and rejects English education in
favour of an Africanised system.[95] In other ways too, the narrative echoes
Casely Hayford's novel, particularly in its satirical representation of
anglicised Fante mimics dressed up like British gentlemen and reading
the 'wrong' type of literature. However, Sekyi lacks Casely Hayford's
optimistic, utopian imagination. His creative writing dramatises in an
extreme and painful manner the social consequences of the African Fall.
The snake to enter the Fante garden is that of English Christian culture,
pointing out bare shoulders and savage customs here, bare feet and primitive languages there, causing the educated section of the coastal population to abandon their past and adopt woollen European suits, collars,
buttons, stockings, bonnets and ties in place of simple local cloth and
sandals.[96] Additionally, *The Anglo-Fanti* is more domestic and intimate
than *Ethiopia Unbound*, revealing the psychological damage caused by the
assimilation of Victorian English culture by coastal Africans. Englishness

is shown not to be universally meaningful or adoptable, but culturally relative and specific to its place of origin. This is a central theme of the narrative, facilitating the contrast between the mimic's cultural shallowness and the local's depth of understanding.

Throughout the story, Sekyi uses the present tense in combination with speculative terms such as 'probably' and 'perhaps'. In this way, he emphasises the point that anglicised Fantes have embarked upon a developmental path which could have been different at any stage along the way. All the major 'ages of man' – youth, manhood, marriage, paternity and citizenship – are distorted or corrupted in the narrative.[97] A process of nurture is clearly described in a tone which indicates that Kwesi's tragic life need not have ended in death. The young boy has values, desires and ambitions implanted in his mind so that, 'Putting together all he has heard and seen of things. . . [he] comes to the conclusion that certain things are worth having, for example, money and respect'.[98]

Sekyi's favourite bugbear, the etiquette book *Don't*, surfaces in this narrative as it did in *The Blinkards*, exemplifying the effects of bad reading upon anglicised Africans. The narrator comments, 'Strange conceptions of behaviour proper to Europeans. . . are gathered from the many books on European life put forth in Europe by European authors. Kwesi and his companions are convinced that European life is ideal.'[99] They give breakfasts at which they rehearse 'etiquette as prescribed in books such as *Don't*' and, as in *The Blinkards*, they form clubs for the refinement of 'rules and manners of Good Society'.[100]

The conventional view of satire is that it has a corrective function and the author's strongly held values are asserted through the exposure of mankind's 'follies and vices'.[101] Writing is thus 'an instrument of social change', for a normative structure is confirmed by the satirist, set over against deviations from it by the satirical targets; a clear 'positive norm' is upheld and 'the way to reform' is laid bare.[102] In *The Anglo-Fanti*, however, with its colonial setting, Western mankind's follies and vices are shown to be so attractive to Fante mankind and so deadly to African culture that the hero, Kwesi, who returns as a 'born–again African' from his education in Britain, dies from the contradictions caused by the norms of his age. The strength of the *wrong* normative values in the coastal community renders him an isolated outsider, quirky and quixotic like Mr Onyimdze in *The Blinkards*. In fact, Kwesi is the victim of others' satire within the text, ridiculed and baited by his family and community as they assert a hegemonic Englishness at every stage of his life. In wearing Fante clothes, for example, he is seen by his family to be 'exposing himself to ridicule' and by his friends to be 'different from all who before him have returned form England as professional men'.[103]

On an individual level Kwesi fails to respond to the 'ridicule' of his family just as, on a larger scale, Fante society is likely to fail to respond to the corrective censure of Sekyi's satire. The 'corrective' function of satire is troubled in *The Anglo-Fanti*. Two competing 'normative' structures are shown to exist in coastal African society – the European and the Fante – and in spite of the title, Sekyi shows that it is not possible to 'hyphenate' identities in this colonial setting. It is not possible to combine Fante and English cultural influences into a positive 'Anglo-Fante' social model.[104] Rather, each cultural identity is the other's 'satiric antithesis' in a death-dealing dialectic with no resolution.[105]

The heroes in Sekyi's narratives have been cited by some critics as biographical source material on a writer whose life-story remains sealed from public view. 'Whereas he saw himself as lawyer Onyimdzi in *The Blinkards*, he assumed the character of Kwesi Onyidzin in the *Anglo-Fanti*', writes Baku.[106] Certainly, in the manner of Onyimdzi and Onyidzin, Sekyi inhabited a society where the wearing of 'native cloth' was considered by many Africans to indicate a state of barbaric unenlightenment. Bravely, Sekyi insisted upon wearing *kente* cloth when he was outside the law courts, and he poured scorn upon Africans who chose to spend the hot days in woollen suits, socks and neck-ties.[107]

Apart from these similarities, we cannot simply look to the unyielding heroes of *The Blinkards* and *The Anglo-Fanti* for a mirror image of the author. Satire is not a mimetic discourse, urging external truths upon the reader; nor does a retrievable authorial 'I' loom large, either within or beyond the satirical text.[108] Lawyer Onyimdzi and Kwesi Onyidzin are ideal heroes, and they are most unlike Sekyi on several practical levels: for instance, Sekyi loved European wines, foods and literatures; despite his writings on African education, he sent his children to England to be trained; he got married in a Methodist Church, wearing a formal European suit (albeit under duress); perhaps most incriminating of all, in the 1920s and 1930s he sought mining concessions from local chiefs on behalf of himself and London firms, supporting the interests of European speculators in the Gold Coast.[109] Additionally, in his creative writing Sekyi uses such an excessive style to ridicule and expose anglicisation in his society that one cannot simply extract biographical truths from the dense layers of satirical representation.

Sekyi does not satirise a pre-existing reality. First he constructs reality, creating a vision of mimics and scholars; next he satirises the reality he has posited.[110] The moral prescription he recommends – the exclusion of low-class scholars and female 'been-tos' from positions of authority – is thus a response to a particular representation of the up-and-coming classes. Actively constructing its targets, Sekyi's satire does not refer to a pre-existing, off-page world. In the light of this, at most Onyimdzi and Onyidzin can be seen as 'authorial figures positioned (liminally) outside of conventional morality'.[111] Rather than reading Sekyi's biography into the culturally puritanical heroes, then, we should respect the textuality of these fictions in which life is represented in terms of extremes.

If Sekyi's biography exists at all in this work, we have to distinguish it from the exaggerations and binary logic of his representations. Certainly, his nationalist ideals are incarnated in the isolated heroes, but if we find Sekyi there, it is also possible to recognise him in extreme mimics such as Mrs Borofosem and Mr Okadu. Here it is possible to find autobiographical commentary in the form of self-satire. It is well known that in his youth Sekyi uncritically adopted the Victorian dress codes and values which are scorned in both *The Blinkards* and *The Anglo-Fanti*. He was 'brought up as an Anglo-African' and remained what he called an 'Anglomaniac' until his cultural rebirth as a Fante while in Britain.[112] Until this rude awakening in London, everything English was admirable to the young Sekyi, who refused to wear African cloth at Mfantsipim School despite the head-teacher's encouragement.[113] Thus, in *The Blinkards*, when Mr Okadu is shown chanting, 'I despise the native that wears the native dress – / The badge that marks the bushman, who never will progress',[114] he is echoing, in an exaggerated form, ultra-anglicised opinions from Sekyi's own past.

Sekyi has been described as stubborn, uncompromising and an 'extreme Africanist'.[115] Satire was the perfect form to carry his moralistic tirades against colonial, coastal society. Scornful in his social life and satirical in his creative life, Sekyi asserted in his writings that cultural interventions by the West generated immorality and a diseased type of hybridity in the social organism. As Onyimdzi says in *The Blinkards*, 'social hybrids, born into one race, and brought up to live like members of another race' are doomed to failure and psychosis.[116] In place of hybridity and in the face of the apparent failure of Anglo-Fantes to 'hyphenate' their identities, Sekyi upheld a communalistic vision of African society: he was convinced that morality and social progress could only be achieved through a process of 'natural' (that is, autonomous) evolution.[117] From a firm base in custom, Sekyi believed African societies would be able to select the most useful western technologies and discard the rest as superfluous material.[118]

This chapter has suggested that Sekyi's creative writing was probably less successful in achieving its socially transformative goals than in reasserting the superiority of an elite, male subject-position. Additionally, his discourse of purity and alterity and his rejection of hybridity allow little room for manoeuvre for cultural 'in-betweeners' who had not mastered the colonial language nor visited the metropolis for professional training. These educated, economically aspirant scholars – who were anything but simple mimics of Englishness – were borrowers and innovators of English cultural and literary forms. Their bombastic, 'fine', English did not necessarily signify the desire to imitate colonial culture. Perhaps the ultimate irony affecting Sekyi's satires and the writings of the 'golden age' nationalists before him was that, as Baku points out, 'their publications became sources of reference for the Government in support of colonial administrative policies which alienated rather than incorporated them', to such an extent that publications by ARPS stalwarts such as Mensah Sarbah would be cited in the Legislative Council and in judgements favouring the Provincial Councils of chiefs.[119] In the final analysis, then, Sekyi's creative writing treads a fine line between effective, corrective satire and complicity with the systems he opposed in his writings.

Notes

1 See Jenkins, 1990.

2 Sarbah, 1898; Casely Hayford, 1903; Attoh-Ahuma, 1911.

3 Baku, 1987: 64.

4 Sekyi was also a poet. Sections from his long poem, 'The Sojourner' are included in *The Anglo-Fanti*; extracts from this and other poems by Sekyi can be found in the appendices of Kofi Baku's D.Phil. thesis, 'An Intellectual in Nationalist Politics' (1987).

5 See Appiah, 1992.

6 See Langley, 1973: 35.

7 Cited in Langley, 1973: 100.

8 Adi 1998: 3; see also Osei-Nyame, 1999. It is also possible that Sekyi joined African cultural organisations such as the Ethiopian Association while in London, and attended plays by didactic and discursive dramatists such as George Bernard Shaw. A popular myth about the source of Sekyi's anti-British sentiment stems from his experience in 1915, when a German U-boat

torpedoed the ship carrying him back to London after a period of study in the Gold Coast: cast overboard, Sekyi reached the lifeboat only to be told by the helmsman that he did not deserve to live when so many white passengers had been killed (see e.g. Langley, 1970: 18; Nkrumah, 1993). This story has been discounted by Baku (1987), citing the work of Ray Jenkins who provides convincing evidence that Sekyi was rescued without prejudice and went on to publish accounts of the incident in which he praised the crew member who saved his life (pp. 101–4).

9 NAG(CC), ACC. 80/64, 1949.

10 NAG(CC), ACC. 2/64, 1907: 3.

11 See Baku, 1987.

12 *GCT*, 9–16 April 1932: fp.

13 NAG(CC), ACC. 80/64, 1922–39: 4.

14 The intricate political history leading up to this shift away from the ARPS cannot be covered here: for detailed studies, see Alexander Baron Holmes's Ph.D. thesis, 'Economic and Political Organizations in the Gold Coast, 1920–1945' (1972) and R. L. Stone's Ph.D. thesis, 'Colonial Administration and Rural Politics in South-Central Ghana, 1919–51' (1974).

15 Jones-Quartey, 1967: 75.

16 NAG(CC), ADM 12/5/157, February 1932: 13–14.

17 *Ibid.* The government's negative attitude toward Sekyi and his Cape Coast allies is revealed in remarkable detail in the confidential diaries kept by district commissioners (especially those kept by Mr C. E. Skene who did not disguise the extent of his abhorrence for Sekyi) (see NAG(CC), ADM 12/5/157, April 1932: 12). Sekyi's lifelong belief in the original ARPS constitution, drawn up and signed in 1907, left him vulnerable to accusations of intransigence and 'Cape Coast chauvinism' (de Graft Johnson, 1928: 71; Holmes, 1972: 468). Guilty of these accusations, perhaps, but steadfast in his rejection of British jurisdiction, he never stood for election to the Legislative Council and refused to compromise his ideals, earning the open hatred of colonial administrators in the Central Province where his influence was wide. The District Commissioner of Central Province wrote in exasperation, 'The Aborigines Society have prevailed on the foolish people of Asebu and Attandaso to make their *omanhin* sign a declaration that they will never attend a Provincial Council again' (NAG(CC), ADM 12/5/157, February 1932: 12–13). Furious at the success of Sekyi's ongoing propaganda campaign against native administration in the early 1930s, he continued, 'I propose to ask Your Excellency to suppress the Society as far as public meetings go' (*ibid.*).

18 Baku, 1987: 83.

19 Jones-Quartey, 1967: 76.

20 Sekyi, [1915] 1974: 31.

21 *Ibid.*, 19.

22 *Ibid.*, 50.

23 *Ibid.*, 67.

24 These characters were very common in early Ghanaian concert parties, particularly the three stock types, the 'Lady', the 'Gent' and the 'Houseboy' (see Cole, 1997). The 'Lady' is described by Catherine Cole as 'an educated Fante woman with Western affectations', who wears hat, gloves, earrings and a frock; her husband, the 'Gent', is 'an educated Fante man who. . . would revert to Fante abuse when he became angry or agitated'; and the 'Houseboy' is a disruptive 'trickster figure' (p. 367).

25 Sekyi, [1915] 1974: 8–9.

26 *Ibid.*, 9.

27 *Ibid.*, 28.

28 *Ibid.*, 120–2.

29 See Baku, 1987: 115–18.

30 See Young, 1995.

31 See Kimble, 1963.

32 NAG(CC), ADM 23/1/692, 24 November 1926: 2; emphasis added.

33 Guggisberg, 1924: 14; emphasis added.

34 *Ibid.*, 14–17.

35 Hobsbawm, 1987: 77.

36 *Ibid.*

37 See Langley, 1970.

38 Jones-Quartey, 1967: 74.

39 *GCT*, 14 November 1931: 6.

40 Cited by Langley, 1970: 14. The conservatism of Sekyi's standpoint is illuminated by the more accommodating views of other ARPS representatives in the 1910s and 1920s. In a collection of articles published in 1928, J. W de Graft Johnson insisted, 'It is a common mistake to define the "educated African" as the Negro in coat and trousers, speaking English and imitating Western manners' (p. 2). He condemns the 'malicious propaganda about the educated African' and insists that these natives have never lost their 'African psychology' (pp. 50, 47): indeed, a 'renaissance is occurring among educated Africans', coming to the continent through literature and ideologies reconnecting them with their racial distinctiveness (p. 2).

41 See Kimble, 1963.

42 Cruickshank, 1853: 65.

43 See Kimble, 1963: 87–92. For excellent etymological discussion of hybridity and for a history of racial science in the nineteenth century, see Robert Young's *Colonial Desire* (1995).

44 Utchay, [1934] 1970: 435.

45 *GCT*, 17 November 1877: 2.

46 Sekyi, [1915] 1974: 45.

47 See Attoh-Ahuma, 1911.

48 Drah, 1971: xv; Jenkins, 1990.

49 Moore and Guggisberg, 1909: 60.

50 *Ibid.*, 90.

51 *Ibid.*

52 *Ibid.*
53 *Ibid.*, 91.
54 *Ibid.*
55 *Ibid.*
56 Sekyi, [1915] 1974: 27–8.
57 *Ibid.*, 115.
58 *Ibid.*
59 *Ibid.*, 117. Ironically, Sekyi's own writing style has been described as abstruse and pompous: in the words of Ayo Langley, he wrote 'notoriously long sentences and "ponderous" vitriol against colonial bureaucrats and "black Englishmen"' (1971: xx). Thus there is a possibility that, in this humorous representation of the Cosmopolitan Club, Sekyi is self-consciously parodying his own style of English (see below for a brief discussion of Sekyi as a self-satirist). Sekyi did not reject literary and debating clubs outright, for he was himself 'in popular demand to address the educated community in town wherever he went' (xxi) and he lectured regularly at young men's clubs.
60 *Ibid.*, 109.
61 Precise readership figures are unavailable for *Don't*, but publication details inside the front cover of the 1912 edition reveal that it went into many editions, remaining popular until the early 1950s. The back pages contain lists of related material in The Manners Series, offering 'both entertaining and instructive. . . handbooks on Etiquette in all its phases', including *Concerning Marriage* by Rev E. J. Hardy, and the comicly titled *How to be Happy Though Married* (1912: n.pag.).
62 Censor, 1912: 17.
63 *Ibid.*
64 *Ibid.*, 63.
65 *Ibid.*
66 *Ibid.*, 35.
67 *Ibid.*, 54.
68 *Ibid.*, 4, 7.
69 See Langley, 1971; Baku, 1987.
70 Browning, 1983: 2.
71 See Gocking, 1999.
72 'A. Native' (pseud.), 1886.
73 See Langley, 1971.
74 Sekyi, [1915] 1974: 132.
75 Baku, 1987.
76 See Markley, 1995: 111.
77 *Ibid.*
78 Sekyi, [1915] 1974: 51.
79 See Stratton, 1994.
80 Cited by Langley, 1970: 14.
81 Sekyi, [1915] 1974: 33.
82 *Ibid.*

83 *Ibid.*

84 It is important to note the role played by the 'trickster' houseboy, Nyamekye, in *The Blinkards*: at the end of the play, Nyamekye enters the room drunk, dressed up as Mr Borofosem. Reeling, pulling ornaments from the piano, he calls Mrs Borofosem 'duckie' and tries to kiss her. This 'comic' sexual assault seems to echo the force of moral justice which has prevailed in the play, for Mr Onyimdze has won the case against Christian, anglicised society and, in so doing, he has won the case against Mrs Borofosem's western mode of femininity.

85 *West Africa*, 14 September 1918: 548.

86 *Ibid.*

87 Sekyi, [1915] 1974: 137.

88 *Ibid.*, 157.

89 *Ibid.*, 173.

90 Kwadwo Osei-Nyame (1999) notes that the protagonist's surname translates as 'one-without-a-name', thus drawing readers' attention to 'the ideological practices of colonialism which devalue all things African or deny the African subjectivity' (p. 138).

91 *West Africa*, 25 May 1918: 274.

92 *Ibid.*, 8 June 1918: 304.

93 *Ibid.*, 28 September 1918: 594.

94 Langley, 1970: 10.

95 Baku, 1987: 43.

96 See also Casely Hayford, [1911] 1966. The organic 'garden' metaphor is not out of place, here, for Sekyi's journalistic writing and speeches were filled with references to colonial society as a diseased organism needing to be rerooted in a non-hybridised ancestral soil (Baku, 1987). He wrote in an article, 'the fault with those in Africa and elsewhere who are at present striving might and main to emulate Europe is that they are copying the habits of a diseased state of society' (cited by Langley, 1970: 26).

97 William Cobbett's *Advice to Young Men and (Incidentally) to Young Women* (1830) contains sections addressed to each of these groups. Crucially, in the 'ages of man' model which Sekyi deploys in this story, the protagonist does not reach 'paternity' or 'citizenship' status; instead, his marriage to a Christian, anglicised 'frock lady' precipitates the failure of his life-cycle and causes his premature death.

98 *West Africa*, 13 July 1918: 396.

99 *Ibid.*, 3 August 1918: 454.

100 *Ibid.*

101 DePorte, 1983: 85.

102 Riley, 1995: 206.

103 *West Africa*, 7 September 1918: 542.

104 Salman Rushdie celebrates hyphenated identities as ideal for the post-colonial migrant, whose identity is hotchpotch and hybrid, combining 'East-West' in a joyful tangle of languages and cultures (1991).

105 See Zimbardo, 1995.
106 Baku, 1987: 94; see also Sekyi, 1973.
107 Jones-Quartey, 1967: 74.
108 Zimbardo, 1995: 24.
109 Baku, 1987: 110–11; Baron Holmes, 1972.
110 See Riley, 1995.
111 Alliker Rabb, 1995: 127.
112 Langley, 1971: xv.
113 *Ibid.*
114 Sekyi, [1915] 1974: 45.
115 Jones-Quartey, 1967: 75.
116 Sekyi, [1915] 1974: 35.
117 See Baku, 1987. One can discern the influence of Marcus Garvey's separatist pan-African ideology, here (see Langley, 1973). The political model for Sekyi's cultural assertiveness was that of Japan which, in 1905, defeated the Russians in the war over Manchuria and, by the 1910s, was seen by anti-colonial nationalists to be successfully applying the best of European science to its society and economy without losing its traditional cultural identity (see Baku, 1987).
118 Langley, 1970.
119 Baku, 1987: 30.

9 R. E. Obeng's *Eighteenpence*: the first Ghanaian novel?

According to J. B. Danquah in his foreword to the first edition of *Eighteenpence* (1943), this is 'an immensely important book', marking 'a new epoch' of realistic and non-derivative literature in the Gold Coast.[1] In Danquah's view this new work of fiction is 'a true novel in the sense of [being] a fictitious prose tale concerned with the more sensitive passions of the human heart'.[2] Since the appearance of this flattering foreword, R. E. Obeng's *Eighteenpence* has been hailed by many literary critics as Ghana's earliest novel, to be contrasted with *Ethiopia Unbound* for the way in which it creates a coherent fictional universe, uninterrupted by politics or overt polemics.[3]

For sixty years, *Eighteenpence* has been regarded as 'the first true West African novel in English'.[4] This oft-repeated claim ignores the vibrant reading and writing culture existing in Ghana throughout the colonial period, explored in previous chapters: for this reason, my discussion of the nation's supposed first novel has been reserved for the final chapter of this book. When 'true' fiction is defined in terms of literary realism, nearly all of the narratives discussed so far will fail the litmus test, turning the wrong colour for fiction because they include swathes of political, moralistic or parabolic discourse. Ironically, this failure includes *Eighteenpence* itself, for several post-colonial commentators have viewed Obeng's novel as an example of the popular, didactic folktale genre with roots in the oral tradition. Thus Charles Angmor regards *Eighteenpence* as a non-realistic 'moral fable', influenced by 'the folktale tradition';[5] for Emmanuel Obiechina, despite its achievements the novel remains 'too simple, almost simplistic, to be read as a novel. Indeed, it is more like a popular moral tale than a novel.'[6] Both of these critics have perceived that *Eighteenpence* is a non-realist narrative and, in consequence, they deny its identity as a novel. On the other side of the scholarly divide, efforts to redeem the text's status as Ghana's earliest novel in English involve a series of denials of preceding publications.

Rather than engaging directly with the terms of this 'either–or' debate, this chapter will confer on Obeng's novel a different set of labels.

The following pages will explore the status of *Eighteenpence* as the first full-length novel to have been produced by a 'never-been', by a member of the class of aspirant, newly educated 'scholars' who emerged in the Gold Coast in the 1920s and set up literary and debating clubs throughout the south of the colony.[7]

Whereas Casely Hayford and Kobina Sekyi were born into prominent, established coastal families and gained professional qualifications in Britain, Richard Emmanuel Obeng (1877–1951) never travelled out of the Gold Coast: he was a Basel Mission-trained catechist and schoolteacher from Kwawu[8] who spent his professional life as a teacher in the local education service; he worked in numerous humble mission schools around the country before joining the Government Teaching Service, where he remained until his retirement.[9]

Obeng was fairly wealthy by local standards: he had a pension from the Colonial Service and inhabited a 'storey house' in Abetifi Christian Quarters, built with the large sum of money he inherited from his mother, Akua Kru. He was no newspaper proprietor, however, no 'merchant-lawyer', no elite nationalist with substantial financial backing; rather, he was a Kwawu 'scholar' who enrolled in school against his family's wishes and survived on his teacher's salary, pension and maternal inheritance, out of which he tried to pay for the production of *Eighteenpence*.[10]

The unique feature of *Eighteenpence*, compared with the other full-length novels and plays discussed in this book, is the author's status as a member of the newly educated 'scholar' class. Obeng's emergence onto the literary scene in the late 1930s indicates a complex, significant shift in the currents of Ghanaian literary culture, brought about by the rapid changes in educational policy since the mid-1920s. As Guggisberg's policy of mass primary education yielded increasing numbers of new literates in search of simple, relevant reading matter, so too in the late 1930s and early 1940s ambitious, newly educated African journalists, clerks and teachers started to produce short novelettes and pamphlets with titles such as *Sorrows of a Jealous Wife* and *Be Content with Your Lot*. By the mid-1940s, popular novelists such as J. Benibengor Blay were earning a living from the sale of their work in Ghana, hawking pamphlets from door to door and selling entire print runs within weeks of a popular title's release.[11] Obeng's *Eighteenpence* was the first full-length contribution to this expanding pool of non-elite Ghanaian literature. Sales must have been good, for in addition to *Eighteenpence* he also wrote a collection of detective stories, *Issa Busanga*, as well as a popular novel entitled *Triple Tragedy*, neither of which survives today.[12]

Taken together, the spurt of new novelists in the late 1930s reveals the way in which English literacy was taken up confidently and deployed by 'scholars' for their own purposes. Having debated hot moral issues in their literary and social clubs, having read their essays aloud to fellow club members, having composed extensive commentaries on works of English literature and philosophy, the more talented club-men now tried their hands at creative writing. They released popular novelettes about love, jealousy and conjugal fidelity, picking up themes which had been circulating around Ghanaian literature since the turn of the century. *Eighteenpence* forms part of this popular canon, particularly in its depiction of Konaduwa, the troublesome wife, and also in its attention to Akrofi, the social 'nobody' desperate 'to ascend to that rung in life in which one is expected to be a happy man – marriage'.[13] In addition, from the 'eighteenpence' of the title onwards, the author manifests an intense consciousness of money, accounting for every penny spent, lost and gained by the protagonists. No previous novel pays such detailed attention to the prices paid for goods and the cash earned from cocoa sales and wage labour.

Unlike ambitious young authors such as J. Benibengor Blay, who made a living from writing, and unlike Kobina Sekyi, who found time for creative writing as a youth while studying in London, it was only when Obeng retired in 1937 that he was able to find time to compose novels and history books.[14] One of the reasons he picked up his pen, it seems, was to ward off the risk of 'vegetating' as a pensioner: 'As I do not like to be vegetated', he informed the Director of Education in 1943, shortly after the publication of *Eighteenpence*, 'I am writing *Stories from the Gold Coast History*, which, subject to your kind and respected approval, is intended to be used as a Historical Reader' in local schools.[15] As this statement reveals, a second important motive for Obeng's writing activities was pedagogical: he intends this latter book to be read by local schoolchildren, hoping perhaps to educate them in their own national history; thirdly, as the editor's note to another of Obeng's histories reveals, he aimed to provide examples of 'courage, fidelity, and self-sacrifice' to local readers, writing inspirational moral texts for use in the classroom.[16]

Self-conscious and modest about his literary abilities, but prolific in the sheer quantity of his output in Twi and English, Obeng frequently sent his manuscripts to European officials 'for perusal, correction of the English and criticism'.[17] The extent of foreign intervention in his manuscripts is revealed in the case of *Eighteenpence*, where the author allowed his British publisher to edit out the novel's many references to latrines, defecating, urinating and spitting, and to transform culturally specific words such as 'cloth' into words invoking the native's semi-nakedness, such as 'loin-cloth'.[18] Obeng's eloquent 'Gold Coast English' has also been revised in the first edition, published by Arthur H. Stockwell: the editor at Stockwell's eliminated Obeng's 'inappropriate similes', 'euphemistic out-pourings' and 'elaborate sentence structures that give the impression of hyper-correctness'.[19] Ironically, these very 'corrections' seem to give rise to Danquah's comment that, 'with superb ease R. E. Obeng tells his story in a mode of King's English that would live for long years'.[20]

At its most basic level, *Eighteenpence* is the story of a poverty-stricken farmer who starts out as a debt-slave for the sum of eighteen pence and ends up an immensely wealthy man with pots of gold at his fingertips. The nar-rative is less linear than implied by this summary, however, for it is encrusted with episodes centred upon the themes of obedience, citizenship, justice, legitimate wealth, marriage and the abuse of chiefly power. J. B. Danquah states in his foreword that something other than plot emerges as the 'chief merit' of Obeng's novel, for, 'the outstanding quality of *Eighteenpence* is its emotional treatment of certain commonplace situations in Gold Coast life, with indications of what [the] future improvements in these situations might be'.[21] Through the use of example and counterexample, providential rewards, punishments and direct advice, Obeng trusts his readers to heed these 'indications' and imbibe 'future improvements' from the narrative.

As with many of the short stories appearing in Gold Coast newspa-pers during the colonial period, *Eighteenpence* is a moral tale which is loaded with scenes of explicit advice-giving, particularly on the issues of marriage and modern farming methods. In the manner of the discursive newspaper serials discussed earlier in this book, in which readers' opin-ions are solicited on the issues raised by the story, Obeng sets moral choices into the novel, inviting readers to make judgements of the char-acters. During one scene of marital tension, for example, the husband states, 'There is nothing which is more pleasant to a man than to see his wife serving him. . . I therefore candidly advise the women here assem-bled that they must never be ashamed when they are performing domes-tic duties for their husbands.'[22] Readers must choose whether or not to be similarly 'advised' in their own married lives. In another, more exten-sive exploration of what makes a good wife, Obeng follows his hero's search for the best girl to marry, concluding, after many pages of story advice and discussion between characters, that an unattractive but hard-working woman is preferable to the beautiful shrew who cannot mend shirts or cook puddings: 'if the shirt and pudding qualifications be absent', says the wise old man who oversees this scene, 'then woe to the unhappy man and woe to the unhappy woman.'[23] At other times in the novel, Obeng offers agricultural advice in simple language, to such an extent that the novel serves as a practical handbook for farmers, containing a great deal of information on the preparation of seedlings, the use of pesticides, tilling, draining and planting the land.

One fascinating aspect of *Eighteenpence* is the presence of Konaduwa in the first half of the novel. Konaduwa is probably the most disruptive, quarrelsome and litigious woman of Ghanaian literature to date. Interestingly, J. B. Danquah and other, more recent male commentators seem to have repressed all references to this anti-social female whose story dominates the first eleven chapters. Focusing instead upon Akrofi, they describe a hero who is 'prepared to work his fingers to the bone, even to enslave himself in order to make a living';[24] they describe how, in the morally just realm of this novel, providence rewards Akrofi with unimaginable wealth and a 'happy home adorned with a good wife and three really lovely daughters'.[25] In contrast to Akrofi's 'good wife', Konaduwa is amoral and incapable of obedience to masculine authority. She 'shower[s] abusive words' and 'noisy quarrel[s]' on all authority figures, from her husband to her mother-in-law, from the *Omanhene* to the District Commissioner: 'I am not at all afraid', she tells them all.[26] Crises escalate whenever Konaduwa is in the vicinity. In all her words she breaks customary rules of courtesy, insulting and libelling individuals with every breath.

Is Konaduwa a rural version of 'bad wives' such as Mrs Borofosem, the terrible termagant in *The Blinkards*? Kari Dako notes that the female characters in *Eighteenpence* reveal Obeng's uneasy relationship with women: as with Sekyi's representation of assertive femininity, Konaduwa is a 'strong steamroller of a woman who describes herself androgynously as a "masculine woman" and who overcomes all and everything in her path'.[27] To this extent, she shares the gender-violating defiance of Mrs Borofosem. Unlike Sekyi's character, however, there also seems to be a feminist dimension to Konaduwa's insubordination, for she is presented as the radical challenger of patriarchal institutions, both judicial and conjugal, customary and colonial. 'You cannot hush me', she tells her antagonists while dismantling their carefully constructed systems of power.[28]

Contrasting Mrs Borofosem, who has sold out to European culture and adopted a western mode of femininity, Konaduwa sets the two different

political and judicial systems against one another. Preferring neither customary nor colonial authority, she exposes the partiality towards men of *both*
systems of 'justice' and the patriarchal underpinnings of values such as
'truth'. When ordered to appear before the native tribunal, for example, she
argues with 'blazing audacity' that her judges stand to profit from her fine:
'I find that I am like a cockroach who has fallen amongst a multitude of
fowls', she tells the elders, refusing to continue with her case unless it is
transferred to the District Commissioner's court.[29] Standing in the colonial
court a few pages later, her disappointment in the colonial system is
expressed with reference to the very elders she has rejected: 'I never knew
that you did not know how to try cases', she tells the District Commissioner,
'In my town, when two men get a case, they all make their statements. Then
the Elders question them, and fix a point which is to be proved by the wit-
nesses; but there is nothing of this sort at this court. I prefer to go back to be
tried by the Elders of my State.'[30] Back before the Elders, she declares, 'If I
should have been punished, why did not the District Commissioner see to
it?. . . there is a court much higher than this, to which I will appeal.'[31]

Assertive women are not unusual in Akan society, and they surface regularly as characters in popular literature: unlike their socially real counterparts, however, in a great deal of literature characters such as Konaduwa
represent the capacity of women to usurp men's 'legitimate' domestic and
social authority. In Obeng's novel, the assertive woman is both troublesome
and troubling to men, but she also signifies a broader challenge: as Dako
suggests, Konaduwa's gender enables her to 'speak what no man dares', to
expose the vested interests of the chiefs by pointing out what they stand
to gain from her own, and others', trials.[32] This illiterate rural woman pen-
etrates multifarious different court systems in the Gold Coast, crossing
colonial and customary boundaries, testing out and rejecting each system
through which she passes. She is the deconstructive element in men's
structures of power, for with each court appearance she challenges the *form*
of each case rather than engaging with its *content*; she avoids punishment
by questioning court procedure and escaping through the loopholes which
she exposes in each system.[33]

Given Konaduwa's subversive, deconstructive presence in the narrative, a feminist perspective is attractive and pertinent. To achieve a fuller
reading of the novel, however, it is also necessary to filter Konaduwa
through the network of Akan beliefs about disorder and chaos within
which Obeng operated.[34] A compulsive liar who is incapable of obeying
court orders, Konaduwa places the concept of truth under erasure and

incarnates the Akan principal of chaos. She personifies what Tom McCaskie describes as 'irruptive and anarchic nature', waiting to overwhelm man's fragile cultural systems.[35] Like a female version of Kwaku Ananse, the 'trickster' who disrupts human society in Akan folktales, often her refusal to heed authority is inexplicable, even to herself. Konaduwa is labelled 'mad' and 'demented' by members of her community and also by the colonialists she encounters: she is confusing and incomprehensible to those around her who seek to establish the whole truth and restore order to society.[36] She accepts the label in the end, admitting that her subversive, anti-social behaviour has no origin, no actual injustice at its source: 'She sighed deeply, and from a kind of mental depletion, exclaimed that in fact she did not know what induced her to do and say all these.'[37]

The sense of disorder inscribed in this character makes it necessary to modify our feminist interpretation of Konaduwa's troubling presence by attending to more culturally specific concepts of order and chaos in Kwawu. Nevertheless, gender remains a crucial signifier in the narrative, for as a woman Konaduwa is beyond the reach of the masculine judicial systems she has sabotaged. She seems to incarnate the political turbulence caused by the conflict between colonial and customary cultural practices. 'You don't seem to have heard of me', she boasts to the Kwawu elders: 'I outmatched the District Commissioner at Asiakwa. He sent me to Accra in hand-cuffs, but I came back scot free.'[38] Men in positions of power express confusion about how to deal with this 'masculine woman',[39] who baffles both the customary tribunal and the colonial court. She terrorises their systems while remaining beyond their reach, leaving them powerless to implement their own judicial processes. In the end, she is allowed to go 'scot free' on the grounds that she is a woman: 'she is but a woman', one sub-chief says in judgement, 'and as you all know, a woman who has had a fit of jealousy can do anything';[40] the consensus amongst the chiefs and elders of the customary court is that she is the weaker vessel, and because 'she is a woman, we must not persecute her'.[41]

Konaduwa's final pacification remains provisional, for the end of disorder comes on her own terms, with her promise to keep the peace and to be a good wife to her new husband. The narrator comments conclusively, 'Konaduwa became the best wife and a very good mother and housekeeper; and as the fairy-tale puts it, they lived happily ever after'.[42] Given her history of bad words and false accusations, however, readers cannot be assured that she will not resurface in the narrative to disturb the peace once more with her highly charged oral 'madness'. Indeed, a sinister version of

her appears in the form of Akrofi's wicked uncle, Dawoanom, who manifests similar anti-social behaviour, destroys everything in his path and
drives his nephew out of town. Described as quarrelsome and disorderly,
Dawoanom is Konaduwa's masculine double, a force for chaos which is far
more malevolent and destructive because, as a man, he works from a position of power *within* society from which he can usurp Akrofi's power and
property.[43]

Kari Dako is the only critic to have commented upon the way in which,
against Obeng's intention to create a moral fable centred upon Akrofi,
Konaduwa 'hi-jacks the story and becomes the main character', at least for
the first seventy-five pages.[44] In consequence, a certain ambivalence
attaches to Akrofi for the remainder of the story.[45] With the suppression
of the chaotic element, Akrofi rises to prominence in the second part of
the novel, representing all that Konaduwa is not, including political order,
rationality, truth-telling, the achievement of justice and civil stability.
Whilst the trickish woman does not resurface in person for the remainder
of the narrative, her spectre hovers over Akrofi's numerous court cases,
subtly commenting upon and destabilising the legitimacy of his claims. In
particular, Akrofi's victory in the colonial High Court is coloured by the
spirit of Konaduwa, for she has shown truth to be negotiable and context-
dependent.

The court scenes in the second part of the novel cannot fail to recall
how chaos prevailed when Konaduwa set colonial and customary systems
against one another. At times Akrofi uses the same disruptive strategies as
Konaduwa, such as when he refuses to allow his case to be tried by the
chiefly tribunal and insists that it pass to the District Commissioner's
court.[46] These similarities introduce the possibility that Akrofi's utopian
stand on behalf of the commoner will prove to be a similar kind of 'madness' to that of Konaduwa, who reverberates softly through these court
scenes. In consequence, Akrofi fails to attain full 'hero' status, for his challenges to the Kwawu chieftaincy are shown to be potentially anarchic.

What prevents the conflation of Akrofi with Konaduwa is the presence
of a transcendental principle of justice in the novel. Thus when Akrofi dis-
covers the first pot of gold on his farm, the narrator comments, 'Mother
Earth had indeed repaid Akrofi amply for his industry!'[47] Fortune, not
luck, holds pride of place in this universe, rewarding the hero for his hard
work and moral probity. Similarly, in the High Court scene, when Akrofi
contests the *Omanhene's* claim to this treasure-chest, providence wins the
case for the commoner. In earthly, judicial terms, the validity of Akrofi's

claim against the *Omanhene* is ambiguous, for there is no precedent for his actions in Kwawu. Indeed, Akrofi 'knew that according to the custom of the country, anybody finding a treasure-trove was to send it full to the Ohene of his town, who in turn would send it to the Omanhene'.[48] In moral terms, however, Akan providence is rewarding the hero for his honourable lifestyle. The judgement of the 'Chief Justice of the Gold Coast Colony and its Dependencies' supports this transcendental force and the treasure chest is awarded to Akrofi.

The benevolent presence of providence is reinforced by Akrofi's discovery of a second substantial pot of gold in the final scene of the novel. Thus the commoner-hero is rewarded a second time. Morally worthwhile and upright, Akrofi has found a way of leashing the bounteous earth to his power, harvesting the wealth that has been withheld from his murderous uncle, Dawoanom, by the same providential force.[49]

Given this 'rags to riches' plot, some critics have dismissed *Eighteenpence* on the grounds of its simplicity, claiming that the entire novel functions simply to 'vindicat[e] the virtue of labour and the reward of an honest life';[50] it contains 'numerous artistic flaws', according to Richard Priebe;[51] 'it is a thinly fictionalized didactic treatise on the theme of rags to riches', complains Emmanuel Obiechina, in whose view it is a potential novel rather than a fully realised achievement.[52] The prevailing assessment amongst these scholars is that *Eighteenpence* is didactic in the manner of a folktale, and as a result it is rather flawed as a novelistic achievement.[53] *Eighteenpence* contains a range of complex issues, however, particularly relating to the political and economic history of Kwawu in the inter-war period.

In many places, the plot and characters of Obeng's novel are riddled with themes and dilemmas which require close attention to local history in order to be understood. Destoolments of chiefs were widespread in southern Ghana between 1900 and the 1950s.[54] Between the 1900s and 1930s, Kwawu State was riddled with political instability. The colonial policy of Indirect Rule between 1883 and 1927 recognised the chiefs and ignored the commoners' associations, thus generating abuses of authority amongst the region's 'natural rulers'; this in turn led to the reorganisation of *asafo* companies who, in the name of the common people, marched on the chiefs and demanded destoolments.[55] The *asafo* of towns and villages in Kwawu united under the umbrella of the *Asafo Kyenku* (the United *Asafo*), an organisation run by the younger generation, which, much to the chagrin of the *omanhene* and elders, became increasingly active between the 1910s and 1930s.[56] In southern Ghana as a whole, ninety-four paramount chiefs were destooled between 1910 and 1924, and between 1928 and 1943 a further forty-two chiefs were removed.[57] Between 1915 and 1918 – the period in which *Eighteenpence* is set – the United *Asafo* in Kwawu forced the paramount chief to accept and sign 'a comprehensive set of rules regulating political and economic affairs in the State'.[58] Commoners were collectively asserting their new-found status against the chiefs, remolding and reconstructing the 'traditional' system to bring about a more inclusive, democratic order. By 1917 the Kwawu *asafo* had produced a charter (the Asafo Rules, or the Magna Carta of Kwawu) to protect their interests.[59] Amongst other things, the Rules prohibited 'judicial extortion', regulated the fees and fines charged by tribunals, controlled the prices of foodstuffs in local markets, and regulated the practice of swearing a fetish oath to demonstrate innocence in court.[60] Many points of the 1917 charter are echoed and endorsed by Obeng in *Eighteenpence*.

Alongside these stool-conflicts, the 1910s and 1920s were marked by a proliferation of land disputes and litigation cases, as wing-chiefs challenged the boundary claims of others, and as members of tribunals contested the private sale of stool-lands by individual chiefs.[61] In the face of vastly inflated fees and fines in the native tribunals after 1905, citizens would prefer to take cases to the District Commissioner's court; and on some occasions *asafo* companies enforced total boycotts of the tribunals, halting proceedings for many months.[62] Denied political representation, educated men led the new *asafo* organisations in offensives against corrupt chiefs; all along, they attracted the attention of the colonial authorities who, for the duration of the twentieth century, had been formulating and refining the policy of Indirect Rule in a manner that favoured the chiefs over and above the commoners' formal groups.

Economic factors fuelled what Francis Agbodeka describes, rather dramatically, as 'a general state of rebellion against the authority of the chiefs and elders'.[63] The state of flux between 1900 and the 1930s arose, at least in part, from the economic effects of the cocoa industry upon social relations between chiefs, elders, farmers, and male and female agricultural labourers.[64] The production of cocoa after 1900 created opportunities for enterprising commoners, who became wealthy as 'middlemen, brokers, transport agents, building and timber contractors'.[65] Increasing numbers of farmers accumulated cocoa-wealth from their lucrative cash-crop, and they were loath to pay the large taxes demanded by the chiefs, preferring to use their reserves to educate their children and make status-enhancing investments. In matters of private accumulation and taxation, then, this new socio-economic group tended to be hostile towards the duties imposed on them by the chiefs.[66]

It is vital to take account of these historical factors if we wish to comprehend *Eighteenpence*, for the narrative rehearses the demands of Kwawu *asafo* during this period, exploring the legitimacy of the private individual's assertion of political and civil rights. Set during the most turbulent period of Kwawu history, the narrative is saturated with court cases, many of which serve to expose chiefly abuses of their customary powers. Akrofi's final victory in the High Court exemplifies the manner in which confident, cocoa-wealthy commoners bypassed the customary courts and asserted their individual property rights in the colonial courts.

Eighteenpence does not simply *reflect* the political and economic history of Kwawu in the inter-war period; it contains a vision loaded with the hopes, values and political tensions of the period in which it was composed and published.[67] The novel is part of the complex social history of the 1940s and 1950s, and its construction of the Kwawu past reverberates with contemporary concerns: for instance, court reform was a burning issue in the 1940s, and several commissions of enquiry were set up in this decade to investigate the Native Tribunals, opening with the Blackall Commission in 1943, which led to reforms in 1944 and finally to the replacement of Native Tribunals with magistrate courts under the first Nkrumah government in the 1950s. The well-ordered society imagined in *Eighteenpence* derives directly from the public debates generated by these commissions of enquiry and Obeng's 'real-time' stands over and dictates the utopian dream-time of the novel.

Eighteenpence does not unambiguously support one system over another, however, for the chiefs are not rejected in the name of the commoner; nor are they criticised in favour of British colonialism. Ample evidence of Obeng's loyalty to chiefly authority can be found in the ordered utopia established by Akrofi towards the end of *Eighteenpence*. Akrofi's new settlement contains a mixture of colonial and customary ideals: thus, the school he establishes is a rural version of Achimota, the leading government school of Obeng's day and the house he builds for his family is in a colonial style; yet the new settlement is administered on customary lines, for Akrofi is 'now looked upon as the *chief of that town*', approached by citizens to settle disputes.[68] Obeng has created a version of 'traditional' Kwawu society which is purged of chaotic elements and abuses of power, 'modernised' to conform to European standards of civil society and ruled over by a democratic commoner-chief, assisted by his 'Queen Mother' wife.[69] Firmly based in a dynamic, democratic conception of power, the novel clearly asserts the commoner's right to participate in political processes. Obeng seems to be arguing that political positions should be available to industrious, progressive men such as Akrofi, for, according to the narrator, 'it was obvious that the central power of Akrofi's personal magnetism, which held together all what he possessed was nothing but industry which brought fortune in its train'.[70]

Given Obeng's status as a schoolteacher responsible for imparting literacy skills, it is interesting to note that Akrofi is represented as both illiterate *and* progressive. This combination was not unusual, especially among Kwawu traders, who would pay for the education of younger members of the family and build themselves Eureopan-style houses. In addition to this real social practice, Obeng seems to be generating in his hero a powerful vision of the 'scholar-farmer', described by Carl Christian Reindorf as the leader of future African states.[71] Akrofi is portrayed as a modern democrat who is conscious of his illiteracy, not because it keeps him in a state of mental bondage, but because of its pragmatic value, its capacity to make his modern life easier to maintain. Writing is regarded by Akrofi as a useful technology, as a time-saving device rather than a force to rescue him from what the missionaries labelled 'inferiority and frustration', 'despair and helplessness'.[72] Faced with a failing cocoa crop, for instance, Akrofi needs to consult the Curator at Aburi Botanical Gardens, but he has no time for the overland trip and 'unfortunately, he could not write', so he cannot send a letter requesting advice from the expert, nor, it seems, is there a local letter-writer to hand.[73]

Apart from the actual fact of his illiteracy, Akrofi manifests all the signs of the modern, 'literate' lifestyle. The presence of such a progressive 'illiterate' – or non-literate – moderniser contests the prevailing view amongst educationists that unschooled Africans have existed 'in a state of destitution for thousands of years. . . doomed to poverty, oppression, and fear until they are rescued from illiteracy'.[74] Obeng suggests a link between Akrofi's illiteracy and his gullibility to the wiles of others: thus, on several occasions the hero's generous, gentle nature is exploited by those who know he cannot read or write. For instance, the new headmaster at Akrofi's rural school masquerades as a literate and claims an enormous salary, but is in fact a semi-literate who teaches the eager children to babble 'Broken English' and to write meaningless lines on their slates.[75] 'As Akrofi was himself an illiterate, he was easily deceived', the narrator comments of this scene.[76] However, at no point in *Eighteenpence* is it suggested that the hero's illiteracy is linked with poverty, degradation, fear or oppression. By *not* engaging with the colonial side of the literacy debate, *Eighteenpence* critiques these Eurocentric prejudices against 'illiterates'. Indeed, Akrofi's non-literate modernity includes 'a very nice type of European house', made from cement blocks, with a large, colourful hall, 'a beautiful Axminster carpet' and wide doors and windows painted 'French grey'.[77]

Previous chapters have suggested that for hyper-literate nationalists such as Casely Hayford and Sekyi, as well as for the majority of Christian and colonial educationists in West Africa, illiteracy was regarded as a disability, symbolising the backwardness and 'darkness' from which Africans must emerge in order to compete with Europeans on an equal footing. The supposedly debilitating nature of illiteracy is not dwelt upon in *Eighteenpence*. Rather, Obeng exposes the politics of the binary division between 'oral' and 'written', 'illiterate' and 'literate' in colonial Ghana. In his detailed presentations of customary court cases, for example, he demonstrates the manner in which 'oral' methods of establishing truth have been displaced by the use of documents as evidence. Concepts of truth are shown to have shifted away from discussion, persuasion, eloquence and collectively agreed precedent, towards the objective materiality of the written contract, produced as evidence in court. For instance, it is clear that the 'truth' Akrofi asserts in the High Court by producing documents proving his purchase of the farm goes against all existing customs and conventions relating to the discovery of treasure on stool-land.[78] While there is no clear division between oral and written in the customary court, where documents serve as evidence alongside oral recollection, truth is shown to be established differently in each system.[79] Whereas negotiated, consensual settlement is emphasised in the customary court, the colonial court ascertains truth by establishing objective facts. Neither system is necessarily superior to the other. In juxtaposing the two judicial systems, Obeng shows how cases will be dismissed for different reasons from the different courts: in so doing, he exposes the provisional, relative nature of truth.

Ultimately, Obeng seems to privilege the written document, the private contract which can be produced in court to support an individual's truth-claim. Having won his case in the British courts, Akrofi gives thanks for the existence of writing, for 'he knew full well, though illiterate himself, that he owed his present good fortune to education. It was the document. . . that had saved him from the deep mire of infamy.'[80] Writing is shown to have 'saved' the commoner, for Akrofi's individual property rights are enshrined in the legal document produced against the chiefs in court. Such a bias towards written texts is hardly surprising, for as we have seen, Obeng typifies the category of men who participated in Ghanaian literary and debating societies in the inter-war period – the very group satirically debunked by Sekyi in *The Blinkards* – and his novel expresses many of the socio-economic concerns and dreams of this 'club class' in Ghana.

Akrofi is the product of a Basel Mission-trained man's imagination, and the author's educational values and notions of rural modernity would have been informed by official propaganda, teachers' journals, missionary publications, policy documents and newspaper debates about changes to the syllabus. Despite his illiteracy, in many ways Akrofi is the vehicle for these educational ideals to readers. He particularly resembles the masculine image of the village schoolteacher promoted in missionary and colonial publications in the 1920s and 1930s: 'Teachers in African villages are the chief agency through which new ideas can reach the people', stated the Advisory Committee on Education in the Colonies in 1935;[81] 'the village teacher has often to stand alone', they continue, 'confronting conservatism and ignorance and trying to maintain standards of life and behaviour different from those prevailing in the community'.[82] 'People must be able to see improvements in his garden', insists an article in the Christian *International Review of Missions*:[83] 'the teacher's home must serve as a model for the community where he is living, since a large part of his task to supply those essential elements in education which are seen in satisfactory home conditions.'[84] All in all, educationists looked to the village teacher for evidence of 'the demonstration his home life affords of the lessons he is attempting to inculcate'.[85] As we have seen, Obeng inscribes many of these official ideals into Akrofi, particularly in portraying him as a model farmer and householder – both implicitly masculine constructs – who has implemented western agricultural techniques and building styles.[86] Despite his apparent illiteracy, then, this hero personifies colonial and Christian hopes for the newly literate rural African man in the 1920s and 1930s.

Obeng takes these ideals one stage further by defining the school curriculum. As with Casely Hayford's *Ethiopia Unbound*, published thirty years earlier, *Eighteenpence* contains details of a model syllabus for Gold Coast youngsters. Focusing upon the primary sector and rural schools, Obeng seems to be utilising his novel to react to official educational policy in the 1920s and 1930s, especially the influential Phelps-Stokes Fund report, *Education in Africa* (1922), and Governor Guggisberg's *The Keystone* (1924), both of which emphasised the necessity for 'character training' and 'industrial training' in Africa alongside literacy skills. In support of these influential documents, the syllabus at Akrofi's school includes the training of children in trades and the inculcation of 'good behaviour'.[87] In addition to this approving incorporation of the official line, the author's gruelling early experiences as a teacher in the mission sector and his low pay as a government employee probably contributed to the representation of Akrofi as an educational philanthropist who pays high salaries to his new teachers, retains staff for long periods without transfers, and ensures teachers' and pupils' loyalty by arbitrating in disputes. In this way, personal experience is condensed into Obeng's narrative alongside reactions to government policy shifts since the 1920s.

In the absence of readership figures for *Eighteenpence*, it is difficult to describe either the make-up of Obeng's audience or the popularity of his novel in the 1940s: how many Gold Coasters actually purchased the novel when it was released in 1943? From which social groups did Obeng attract the most readers? Did he intend the narrative to be consumed by foreign or local readers? Kari Dako has unearthed a fascinating 'Memorandum of Agreement' from Obeng's first British publisher, dated 8 July 1938, in which Arthur H. Stockwell agrees to print one thousand copies of *Eighteenpence*.[88] Obeng paid a total of £78 for this publication, the arrival of which was delayed until 1943 by the outbreak of the Second World War; a second edition of two thousand copies cost Obeng £256.10.0 in 1950, published this time with Willmer Brothers in Britain and despatched to Obeng for distribution.[89]

Obeng's relative wealth is indicated by the reasonably high print-runs, the evidence of a second edition and the author's responsibility for advertising and marketing his book. There must also have been a reasonable demand for *Eighteenpence* within the Gold Coast, meriting the second edition. 'Many were the encouraging congratulations which I have received from well known persona and schoolmasters', Obeng writes in his autobiographical notes.[90] It is probable, then, that the novel was disseminated through Obeng's own social networks of schoolteachers, catechists and educationists, as well as amongst the coastal and colonial elite in Ghana. It is likely that the issues raised in the novel – particularly concerning the ideal wife, order in society and private accumulation – would have appealed to primary-schooled commoners as much as to the professional classes. This probability is supported by Danquah in his foreword to the first edition. Here we find details of the types of reader to whom *Eighteenpence* will appeal (and for whom it will assist) the most. The class-crossing, career-crossing nature of the list reveals a great deal about Obeng's projected readership:

The farmer, the trader, the police constable, the schoolteacher, the
lawyer, the chief, the judicial and political officer, even our young
daughters. . . Nay, even the husbands and wives [and]. . . women who
have to share their husbands with other women – each one of these
typical men and women in the Gold Coast will find a picture of himself
or herself in this book, for better or for worse.[91]

'And yet the book is not didactic', Danquah insists, for it 'teaches without
seeming to teach; it flows, without seeming to flow.'[92]

Danquah's list of likely readers goes against the opinion of scholars
such as Margaret Nkrumah, for whom *Eighteenpence* is an instance of 'elite
nationalist' writing which is 'directed towards foreign audiences or the
educated and partly alienated indigenous elite, not the masses'.[93] The content of *Eighteenpence*, the fact that the protagonist is 'a "nobody" in traditional terms'[94] and the social status of its author indicate that Obeng gets
closer to the elusive 'masses' of colonial Ghana than any of the writers discussed in previous chapters. Obeng was no 'elite nationalist': as this chapter has argued, he was one of the few authors of the early 1940s *not* to have
been a member of the highly educated coastal elite, and his writing conveys many of the political and economic ideals of the Gold Coast 'club
class' of the 1920s and 1930s.

With aesthetic roots in the late nineteenth century and intellectual
stimulus provided by the club culture of the inter-war years, *Eighteenpence*
is the perfect text with which to close this study of literary currents in colonial Ghana. It symbolises the rise of the mission-educated 'scholar' – a
figure who represented a very particular set of socio-economic aspirations,
intellectual activites and gender values, negotiated through his classroom
experience – to the status of local novelist. It also marks the beginning of
a new stream of narratives within Ghana, popular in content and ethical
in tone. It is an inspirational text, according to Danquah, 'a possible fore-
runner of many great works – let us hope – by Mr Obeng and by other
Gold Coast men and women who should be proud to follow the trail he has
blazed'.[95] The novel combines ethical commentary with realist narrative,
inviting debate on subjects as diverse as marriage, the education syllabus,
literacy, justice, wealth and citizenship. Many of these issues surfaced in
the locally authored literature of preceding decades, and core themes such
as marriage, wealth and citizenship surface repeatedly in the popular fiction produced in Ghana since the late 1930s. Rather than representing a
radical break from existing literary practices in Ghana, then, this 'first true

novel' calls upon an established tradition of discursive writing and combines old themes with concerns of the moment in a complex and strikingly new intervention in Gold Coast literary culture.

Notes

1 Danquah, [1943] 1971: vii.
2 *Ibid*. J. B. Danquah wrote numerous forewords to locally produced novels and pamphlets, and he played a vital role in promoting local literary production in the 1930s and 1940s.
3 Dako, 1998.
4 Priebe, 1986: 828.
5 Angmor, 1996: 39.
6 Obiechina, 1975: 13–14.
7 It is tempting to use the word 'commoner' to describe Obeng, for he was not a chief nor, until his retirement, did he hold formalised political office in the customary court. The term is too broad and problematic to be useful in this context, however, for it serves only to indicate a person's relationship to chiefly office: it says nothing about the differences in social status, wealth, age and gender among 'commoners', nor does it describe their multifarious alliances and identities (Miescher, personal communication). Many 'commoners' became wealthy and influential during the cocoa boom of the early twentieth century, a period when new commercial opportunities enriched the Kwawu trader (see Garlick, 1967). Given his occupational pension, large house and substantial maternal inheritance, Obeng was far more than the average commoner. 'Scholar' (or *akrakyefo*) is a more useful category than 'commoner': it demarcates the economic and cultural differences between people with no formal education and those, such as Obeng, with a Standard VII certificate, school experience and exposure to the missionary project (see Miescher, 2001b).
8 The Twi spelling, 'Kwawu', has been used throughout this chapter in place of the anglicised 'Kwahu'.
9 See Dako, 1998: xiii.
10 Obeng, 1998: xxi–xxxv. Kari Dako has evidence that Obeng borrowed money within the family to fund the publication of his books (personal communication).
11 See Newell, 2000.
12 Dako, 1998.
13 Obeng, [1943] 1998: 1.
14 *Ibid*., xxxiv.
15 NAG, RG 3/1/225, 1 November 1943.
16 Obeng, 1952: n.pag.
17 NAG, RG 3/1/225, 1 November 1943.
18 Kari Dako's annotated new edition of the novel restores many of the excised references and publishes Obeng's autobiographical fragments for the first time.

19 Dako, 1998: xiii.
20 Obeng, [1943] 1971: ix.
21 Danquah, [1943] 1971: viii
22 Obeng, [1943] 1971: 81.
23 *Ibid.*, 92.
24 Danquah, [1943] 1971: viii.
25 *Ibid.*
26 Obeng, [1943] 1998: 7–8; 53.
27 Dako, 1998: xv.
28 Cited by Dako, *ibid.*
29 Obeng, [1943] 1998: 23.
30 *Ibid.*, 38.
31 *Ibid.*, 49.
32 Dako, 1998: xvii.
33 Konaduwa's use of all available judicial systems fits well with the historical evidence from colonial Ghana. As Allman and Tashjian (2000) argue, people of subordinate status, such as commoner women, would take their cases to the British courts, using the colonial forum as a means of challenging their lowly social position: 'women, in particular, seemed inclined to contest various forms of exploitation in the early British courts, either as complainants or defendants' (p. 22).
34 See Akyeampong and Obeng, 1995.
35 Cited by Akyeampong and Obeng, 1995: 484.
36 See Obeng, [1943] 1998: 30.
37 *Ibid.*, 67.
38 *Ibid.*, 49.
39 *Ibid.*
40 *Ibid.*, 67.
41 *Ibid.*, 68.
42 *Ibid.*, 75.
43 *Ibid.*, 149.
44 Dako, 1998: xvi.
45 *Ibid.*
46 Obeng, [1943] 1998: 116.
47 *Ibid.*, 110.
48 *Ibid.*, 115.
49 The moral economy of wealth is a significant topic, explored in a great deal of recent anthropological and historical work (see Barber, [1981] 1997; Meyer, 1999; Guyer, 1995; McCaskie, 1995; Wilks, 1993).
50 Angmor, 1996: 39.
51 Priebe, 1986: 828.
52 Obiechina, 1975: 13–14.
53 One might question the simplicity attributed to Akan folktales in these accounts.
54 See Li, 1995.

55 See Simensen, 1975. The 'asafo company' in southern Ghana is a kinetic, mutable form of organisation which responds and adapts to social and political transformations. The best definition of asafo in colonial Ghana can be found in Anshan Li's (1995) article, 'Asafo and Destoolment in Colonial Southern Ghana, 1900–1953'. Li describes how the word asafo has multiple meanings in any single case, and also how the asafo company takes on different forms in different regions and changes over time. Traditionally, the asafo company was the 'warrior organisation' among the Akan of southern Ghana, and most towns and villages possessed companies. Each company was organised patriarchally and distinguished by its own flag, songs, drums, horns and paraphernalia. Crucially, asafo 'had the right to criticize all acts of the executive [i.e. within the customary state] and was regarded as representative of the common people' (Li, 1995: 332). Li shows how these companies underwent great changes under colonial rule: despite the fact that they represented commoners' interests, they 'received no recognition from the colonial government' (p. 331). The colonial government favoured the chiefs in its policies and failed to recognise formally organised commoner interest groups within the state. Unified but unrepresented in state affairs, asafo companies thus became increasingly involved in destoolments of chiefs. An extensive bibliography on asafo is provided in the footnotes to Li's article (see also Stone, 1974).

56 Li, 1995: 335.

57 Agbodeka, 1972: 49.

58 Simensen, 1975b: 383.

59 Li, 1995: 341.

60 Simensen, 1975b: 384: Li, 1995.

61 Simensen, 1975a: 400.

62 Agbodeka, 1972; Simensen, 1975a and b.

63 Agbodeka, 1972: 73.

64 Mischer, personal communication; Austin, 1993; Garlick, 1967.

65 Agbodeka, 1972: 48.

66 See Arhin, 1986.

67 I am indebted to Stephan Miescher for his perceptive reading of the first draft of this chapter; the paragraph that follows derives entirely from his comments.

68 Obeng, [1943] 1998: 134; emphasis added.

69 Kari Dako (1998) is far more ambivalent in her interpretation of this 'utopia': she notes that Akrofi takes up the position of 'lord and master' in his colonial-style plantation, ruling over a foreign workforce in the manner of a European settler. 'This modern utopia is an upside down world', she continues, for 'the Omanhene loses a case in an alien court to a person who has the slur of indebtedness and slavery attached to him' (p. xix; see also Dako, 1994). This alternative perspective is valid and persuasive, but it goes against the grain of the narrative, in which Akrofi is shown to rule his workers in the manner of a democratic chief, paying generous wages to them, feeding them, schooling their children and building houses for them.

70 Obeng, [1943] 1998: 137.
71 See Jenkins, 1985: 357.
72 Laubach, 1948: 13, 119. This attitude was prevalent amongst colonial educationists and educated Africans, particularly on the coast.
73 Obeng, [1943] 1998: 96.
74 Laubach, 1948: 1–2.
75 Obeng, [1943] 1998: 131–2.
76 *Ibid.*, 131.
77 *Ibid.*, 136–7; see Miescher, 2001a and b. In this Akrofi closely resembles the Asante *akonkofo* described by Kwame Arhin (1986). At the turn of the twentieth century these influential but nonliterate 'rich men, gentlemen' returned to Asante from their trading activities on the coast having adopted 'the coastal version of the British way of life', including architectural designs, dress styles, the desire to educate their children and a belief 'that the British presence would guarantee protection against exactions by traditional authorities' (Arhin, 1986: 26–8).
78 See Obeng, [1943] 1998: 118.
79 See Miescher, 1997.
80 Obeng, [1943] 1998: 129.
81 NAG, CSO 18/1/33: 2.
82 *Ibid*, p. 12.
83 Anon., 1929b: 235.
84 *Ibid.*, 236.
85 *Ibid.*
86 Obeng, [1943] 1998: 84–90.
87 See *ibid.*, 130–4.
88 Dako, 1998: xi.
89 *Ibid.*
90 Obeng, [1943] 1998: xxxv.
91 Danquah, [1943] 1971: viii.
92 *Ibid.*
93 Nkrumah, 1993: 12.
94 Dako, 1999: 11–12.
95 Danquah, [1943] 1971: vii.

Conclusion:
the production of a West African aesthetic

'The object of all writing', Mabel Dove commented in 1933, is 'to curb certain moral tendencies in us and make our society beautiful, pure and perfect.'[1] 'All writing should aim at being instructive', she wrote on another occasion, adding that it should also 'be a model in style'.[2] This literary aesthetic would have been familiar to Ghanaian readers in the 1930s, most of whom had been taught to read in mission schools, supplied with 'good' Christian literature from local bookshops and trained from birth to extrapolate socially relevant meanings from stories and figurative folktales.

Literate locals were lively participants in the business of reading from the very first moments of large-scale literary activity in colonial Ghana, with the production of newspapers in the late nineteenth century. In the decades since then, readers involved themselves in newspaper debates and, when the first local popular novels appeared on the streets in the late 1930s, readers were thoroughly acclimatised to the practice of writing letters to authors, commenting on characters and plots, and demanding explanations when stories failed to meet their expectations. Through such interventions, West African readers exposed the fallacy, prevalent amongst many missionaries and educationists before independence, that texts formed part of a 'loose canon', autonomous from the societies in which they circulated.

This book has charted the multifarious ways in which African readers refused to be the passive recipients of a literacy controlled from above. Readers appropriated the English language and adapted it to suit their own attitudes about literacy and interpretation. So forceful were Ghanaian readers' appropriations that a long-running struggle over English usage took place in the colony, and for much of the early twentieth century the native speaker of English was involved in a confrontation with the 'native' speaker of English, particularly over the issue of the latter's long-windedness.

Education Department reports, school inspectors' reports and the diaries of governors' wives were riddled with complaints against what became known as 'Gold Coast English', a euphemism for the 'unmitigated evil' of the African 'scholar's' bombastic style.[3] Yet for many primary-schooled, low-status Africans in British West Africa in the first half of the century, the mark of 'education' was a command of the English vocabulary, and to substitute simple for complex words would have been to compromise the expression of mental culture and 'civilisation'. In the face of official opposition, local English-speakers stuck to their own evaluative criteria: aware of the official position and yet defensive of their own, students felt that pomposity was 'a harmless fault common with most of us'.[4] Indeed, when they praised novels such as *Alice's Adventures in Wonderland*, they couldn't help but appreciate the heroine's 'readiness to show off her knowledge at the first opportunity'.[5]

Of course, no homogeneous literary values separate Africans from Europeans. Highly educated members of the African elite did not express themselves in the florid English of the lower orders: the most elaborate English stemmed from the least educated social class, the 'scholars', who were socially and economically differentiated from the elite and occupied a different place within the colourful spectrum of 'West African English' styles.

The inspectorate of the Education Department insisted repeatedly that 'teachers and pupils need to realise that long words, flowery diction and hackneyed quotation do not constitute good writing'.[6] Official efforts to reform this type of English in the 1920s included the introduction of four-year teacher-training courses, a national teachers' journal and a register of qualified teachers: at all points in the teacher-training process, emphasis was placed upon 'simplicity of words, absence of official language, and avoidance of quotations and figures of speech designed only to give an impression of great learning or piety'.[7] 'Simplified', graded versions of English literary classics were published by Longmans and Oxford University Press in the UK and incorporated into the syllabus of British West African schools; and school inspectors in the region insisted upon 'simplicity and correctness of speech' in English classes, combined with 'better pronunciation'.[8] Simultaneously, the vernacular was introduced as the compulsory medium of education in the first three grades of elementary school in order to eliminate the apparent problem of semi-literate school-leavers speaking meaningless English to illiterate peers in order to gain prestige within the uneducated community.

The British reaction against 'Gold Coast English' was chiefly of an aesthetic and ideological order – aimed once again at the suppression of social upstarts such as 'scholars' – but it was masked as the discussion of correct and incorrect English usage. For example, when asked to describe the visit of a bald colonial official to the Wesleyan Elementary School in Adum, Ashanti, the young Joe Appiah wrote, 'The chief commissioner has no follicles on the cutaneous apex of his cranial structure.'[9] The young scholar was perhaps attempting to avoid a direct – in Akan terms, discourteous – reference to the senior man's affliction. In addition, as he confesses when confronted by the English reverend overseeing the class, 'I want my teacher to know that I am studying hard. . . [T]his is good English, as spoken by the famous Dr. Johnson who made the English dictionary.'[10] Reverend Sanders disagrees, insisting that the wordy phrase is in fact *bad* English which should be replaced with the simple formulation, 'The chief commissioner is bald.'[11] However, when the boy's classmates hear the offending sentence read out aloud as an example of poor style, they shout, '*Brofo, Brofo* (English, English)', and Appiah knows he has won their approval, for '*Brofo, Brofo*' is called by schoolchildren 'when what is spoken in English sounds nice to them, regardless of its meaning'.[12]

This stand-off between the Akan schoolchild and the English educator exemplifies the positions that were adopted in the struggle over English usage in colonial Ghana. As Reverend Sanders explains to young Appiah, 'people must be able to understand what you say *or it is of no use*'.[13] The essential features of Appiah's eloquence in English are 'long words, flowery diction and hackneyed quotation',[14] precisely the 'useless' elements which educationists sought to eliminate from West African speech in the 1920s and 1930s. The style of English which is rejected and corrected by Reverend Sanders is the antithesis of the terse, functional language preferred by colonial officials. Yet Appiah was following a prestigious tradition, for the great Dr Aggrey himself 'was usually discursive and often florid in style' and, much to the frustration of many of the Europeans in his audiences, he 'clearly loved the roll of long, sonorous words – often used deliberately to impress people'.[15]

Ghanaian students knew that they were supposed to express themselves with simplicity and clarity in English, but the temptation to be 'fine' arose, ironically, even in the process of describing the foreigner's ideal. 'To cultivate a pure and simple style enlivened by lively wit and felicitous combinations of words one should devote his days and nights to the study of this book', wrote one student in 1935 in praise of Samuel Smiles' *Self-Help*.[16] Simultaneously expressing and violating the rule of simplicity, this student conveys the tensions that emerged in the 1930s between educational policy and classroom practice. Indeed, sentences such as this are cited by officials in order to suggest 'that the introduction of such publications as the New Method Readers came none too soon'.[17]

As with many other West African societies, the Akans were 'a people normally decorous in speech and conduct' with clearly defined ideas about what constituted eloquence, and it seems as if locals had taken up the colonial language and instilled it with their own values of elegance and beauty.[18] In this connection, it is important to emphasise that the majority of teachers in Gold Coast elementary schools were Africans, themselves educated and trained by African teachers and catechists in the mission school system which dominated West Africa until the 1940s. The role of mission-schooled African teachers is easily neglected in studies of literacy and literature in Ghana, especially given the impression of European pedagogic control conveyed by material in the archives: numerous European-authored documents – official reports, educational journals, memoirs, 'New Method Readers' and personal diaries – survive to the detriment of African classroom material. Yet pupils' primary influence would have been their teachers, from whom they would have inherited particular styles and modes of English speech alongside a distinctive reading culture and distinctive representations of literacy.[19]

In recognition of this silent majority of teachers, the Director of the Education Department comments in 1931 that 'Much has yet to be done before *teachers and pupils alike* are persuaded that the pompous style which some describe as "fine English" is not only inappropriate but ridiculous'.[20] However, what emerges from the survival of 'fine English' at the classroom level, in the face of decades of official efforts to remould and transform it, is a signal that throughout the colonial period there existed an enduring and competing set of assumptions held locally by Africans about the significance of literacy in the colonial language.

Despite the systematic transformations to the education system in the mid-1920s, African literary culture in the late 1930s closely resembled that of the 1910s. Local writers continued to pour forth complex sentences in a sumptuous language which challenged English aesthetic norms. In one of many 'libellous' newspaper articles, for example, the outspoken and troublesome secretary of the West African Youth League, I. T. A. Wallace Johnson, described the activities of the Sierra Leonean politician Herbert Christian Bankole-Bright in the following terms: 'Death due to Political diarrhoea and the collapse of the White House Demoniacal Maniac while diligently oscillating the Political Pendulum of the Microscopic Coons suspected in the Big Cigars and the body politic.'[21] When the case came up for trial in 1939, the editor of the *Gold Coast Times* deciphered the libellous meaning of Wallace-Johnson's sentence, explaining to readers that the implication was 'that the said Herbert Christian Bankole-Bright is a demoniacal maniac'.[22] The case attracted coverage in all of the Gold Coast newspapers and at no point was critical comment passed on Wallace-Johnson's incomprehensible prose.

What is striking about Wallace-Johnson's turn of phrase is his revelry in the *sound* of polysyllabic words and his assertion of political authority through the use of such 'eloquence' in English. The existence of local expressive and interpretive standards seem to have made such a claim to authority possible. His expressive mode conforms to the West African aesthetic described and practised by Dr Aggrey: 'with my people, it is not so much *what* you say as *how* you say it, and *who* does the saying'.[23] What is also striking in this instance is the fact that a libel trial was brought at all. Evidently Wallace-Johnson's victim, Bankole-Bright, felt the message to be sufficiently clear and insulting to merit an expensive, public court case, a decision which is not questioned in the Gold Coast press.

Beside the local aesthetic conventions which were generated around English, the English language has a history in West Africa which can be traced back to the British administration in the era of bureaucratic expansion, when Africans were educated for low-grade Civil Service posts. As I hope to have shown in this book, any literary aesthetic to have emerged in Ghana during the colonial period is embedded in the country's complex colonial history. Thus, if we turn to the 'dictation' section of the Civil Service Examination conducted by the Gold Coast Government in April 1904, we find a clue to the sources of African students' enthusiasm for complex English sentences. A typical sentence in the passage set for transcription runs, 'I should not do these gentlemen justice if I did not take some opportunity to declare that they always showed the utmost readiness to carry into execution, in the most effectual manner, every measure I thought proper to take.'[24] To stand any chance of gaining salaried employment in the clerical, white-collar workforce, students would have spent many months attempting to master formal English of this type. Wallace-Johnson's ebullient language shines out in comparison with this dull dictation passage.

African trainee teachers were subjected to similar tests to prospective civil servants: the 'dictation' passage of the teachers' certificate in 1906 begins, 'The effect of the mortification of the domestic affections upon the general character was probably very pernicious'.[25] In the new Education Rules of 1915, 'recitation' was included alongside dictation as an examination topic, and students were required 'to repeat 100 lines of Shakespeare or any other standard English author'.[26] Quotations from difficult works of English literature and the ability to write long words were thus the bedrock of the student's knowledge. Official complaints in the 1920s and 1930s about 'flowery' and 'hackneyed' English therefore exhibit a lack of responsibility for the failings (or achievements) of the previous system.

Alongside the highly 'literary' syllabus that prevailed in British West Africa before 1925, a certain degree of coercion was involved in encouraging students to learn the colonial language. Lionel Greaves recollects that, in 1922, 'it was quite common to find small children in the "Infants I" standing on their desks with a heavy wooden block tied around their necks, carrying the words: "I must not speak the vernacular".'[27] The 'extreme Englishness'[28] of this system persisted until 1925, when western educationists and missionaries – struck by the realisation that 'what he takes into his brain by means of a European language remains foreign to his mental make-up'[29] – started to stress vernacular creativity and simple English comprehension above 'imitation and "bluff"', and parrot-cries and catch-words and clichés and mere chatter and verbiage'.[30] To remedy this evil, students in Standards I to III were to be taught in African languages while, in Standards IV to VII, the reading of full-length literary classics was to be replaced with 'simplified' readers published especially for students in the colonies.

Official efforts to remove the 'follicles on the cutaneous apex' of the English language and to render it bald again are at the pedagogic core of the *New Method Readers* (Longmans), the *Simplified English Series* (Longmans), the *African Life Readers* (Ginn and Co) and the *Stories Retold Series* (Oxford University Press). The *New Method Readers* were in use at many schools to enhance the acquisition of 'correct speech' and 'the capacity for writing simple English correctly'.[31] Containing word-drills, word-lists, word-counts and simplifications of words such as 'glare' and 'fondle' to 'see' and 'touch', the editors of these new series were confident that 'It is possible to "translate" any story of action into a vocabulary of less than 2000 words' suitable for the 'bilingual foreigner'.[32]

Drastic abridgements of original narratives such as *The Coral Island*, *Silas Marner* and *Kidnapped* appeared in the early 1930s alongside dramatised versions of *Tom Brown's Schooldays* and *A Tale of Two Cities*. Additionally, books such as Anthony Praga's *Great Books Retold as Short Stories* were advertised in the local press, containing reductions of the Brontes, Disraeli, Scott, Dickens and Thackeray for 'busy people with a love of the classics and no time to read them'.[33] Also available were simplified versions of texts which had already been simplified from their originals, such as the Lambs' *Tales from Shakespeare*.[34]

At the helm of local opposition to these educational reforms was Dr J. B. Danquah, an influential newspaperman in the 1930s and leader of the Gold Coast Youth Conference, who found his passion for the English language compromised by the graded readers produced for African classrooms. 'Whatever merit it may have, a "simplified" system can never be said to offer a "broad" preference', he wrote, for in such a system 'there could be nothing else to choose from but the limited number of 1,779 words which the Standard V boy is supposed to know from the Primer and Readers I to VI.'[35]

The primary problem for Danquah was that foreigners held the educational reins, particularly at Achimota School. Europeans had diagnosed a condition they called 'detribalisation', or 'denationalisation', in educated English-speaking Africans, and they were attempting to halt it by formulating language policies and publishing texts which, in Danquah's view, halted the 'organic' growth of English and vernacular literatures in the colony and limited the 'broad choice' of reading matter that was previously available to students.[36] From positions of authority in schools and government departments, foreigners interfered in the development of English and vernacular literatures by controlling orthographies, dictating the syllabus, determining teaching methods and commissioning text-books.[37] To this end, vernacular literature was labelled 'genuine literature' by the Colonial Office, over against the English classics, and collections of proverbs and folklore were promoted above other genres of literature.[38]

In an angry memorandum to the Acting Principal of Achimota, Danquah stated, 'the artificial restriction of the scope of English in the school system yields a mechanical and not an organic taste for English.'[39] An unambiguous European 'reader response' accompanies these complaints about educational policy. Scrawled in the margins of Danquah's memorandum are comments which condemn the document: 'Internal policy cannot be dictated by laymen' writes the reader, probably Charles Kingsley Williams in whose papers the memo was found.[40] 'Rubbish' is written in red ink a few pages later, in response to Danquah's proposed 'remedy to improve English and the taste for reading' by 'scrap[ping] the "simplified" studies' and substituting 'the study of English as a living and an organic language and not an "experiment" or mechanical contrivance of limited parts'.[41]

An intriguing feature of this argument between Danquah and the staff at Achimota is that it closely echoes the stand-off between Joseph Appiah and Reverend Sanders in the Wesleyan Elementary School. For the leading intellectual as much as the African schoolchild, it seems, 'English' meant anything but simplicity and sparsity of speech. The tenacity of this African countercurrent shows the manner in which local expressive conventions were persisting and developing in the face of European opposition, and it is necessary to take such conventions into consideration if we are to appreciate the appeal of what Appiah describes as the sound of 'good English. . . regardless of meaning'.[42]

Danquah's ideal for the growth of 'organic' West African English can be seen to be flourishing in the local publishing sector, in which newspapers and privately published titles circulated outside the bounds of the school syllabus. He went out of his way to promote books which challenged the educationists' concept of 'good' English style. For example, in his review of *Marriage Problems in the Gold Coast* (1938), a book published privately by David Heman-Ackah, Danquah quotes a single sentence of dense verbiage:

Besides recognising the necessity for instituting an effective and rigid campaign against the incursion of sensuality as a malady fatal to our social organism and a menace to our moral and spiritual growth, those of us who are supposed to be race-leaders, and are therefore principally influential in the development of the country towards prosperity and nationhood, realise that some substantial and relentless efforts must needs be made by the different religious denominations working among us and the various Native States towards the modification of the Akan system of inheritance as enunciated and practised by our ancestors and which has long been customary in this country.[43]

In the sentence, clarity of meaning has been completely subordinated to the author's revelry in the English language itself. As with Wallace-Johnson's libellous prose and Joseph Appiah's sumptuous descriptions of baldness, Heman-Ackah's stylistic decisions tend towards the 'elegant' end of the scale; he seems to be delighting in the English language, treating words as resources to play with and inventing compounds to further stretch his vocabulary. 'Are you out of breath, dear reader?' Danquah asks at the end of his quotation.[44] In posing this question, he acknowledges the educationists' position in the debate about simplicity. Filling in the opposition's side before developing his own, he adds, 'You may think the style [of this book] is merely baboo English, that it is not style as such, not really English, but just a string of meaningless words'[45]

Heman-Ackah's book is deployed by Danquah in order to develop a strongly argued Africanist counterposition in the debate about English style. It is here, in the African nationalist's review of the African-authored, locally published book, that it becomes possible to see the production of a West African aesthetic space: 'There it is, absolutely Native, Gold Coast bred, racy, unquestionably distinctive, not common place, nor simplified or basic', Danquah writes.[46] The book has been produced by an 'elementary school product' who loves 'English as a beautiful work of art' and was 'lucky to have an African schoolteacher who was a thorough master of English'.[47] The author, then, is a living exemplar of Danquah's ideal for an 'organic', localised literature in the English language, developed and communicated by African schoolteachers: this is a literature which is 'agreeable, refreshing, luxurious, almost voluptuous in its rich generosity and departure from the merely banal'.[48] The same might be said of Appiah and Wallace-Johnson and the many other West African English-speakers who failed, over a period of more than thirty years, to respond to official criticisms of their writing styles.

The persistence of this style in the face of attempts to eliminate it indicates that local writers were deliberately subverting 'British English' and the colonial system it symbolised, insisting upon their own literary ideals. Possibly influenced by the wordy, race-conscious material coming into the Gold Coast from the United States and certainly influenced by the writing style of local political heroes, local authors and readers translated plain English into 'fine' English 'and, in the process, asserted their credentials as what Heman-Ackah termed 'race-leaders. . . principally influential in the development of the country towards prosperity and nationhood'.[49]

Examples of overt subversion of British English are not difficult to find. On the eve of Governor Shenton Thomas's detested Sedition Ordinance of 1934, the *Times of West Africa* published this brilliantly 'bombastic' and parodic rejection of colonialism and Christianity:

Foresightedness is our shepherd; we shall not be easily persuaded. It maketh us to protest against machinations to jeopardise our interests. It vivifies our soul and leadeth us into the paths of our rights and liberty for its integrity's sake. Yea, though we are destined to suffer under a Shentonian Administration, we will not fear any evil or the pernicious bills and their introducers, for rationalism is with us [etc.].[50]

This anti-colonial rendering of Psalm 23 reveals the way in which educated West Africans appropriated the English language and decolonised it, subverting British English from within by producing texts filled with loquacious alternatives to the short, direct sentences and barked orders preferred by officials.[51]

European educationists frequently noted Ghanaian readers' 'failure' to extract the essential meanings from particular texts. 'When discussing a book' Claude de Mestral writes, 'one is often conscious that many of the essential points have not been grasped, or have been understood in a different way from that intended by the writer, usually a westerner'.[52] Similarly, in a survey of university students' comprehension of English literature in the late 1940s, P. Gurrey concludes that there was a frequent 'misunderstanding [of] the purport and intention of the writer', and complains about 'the prevalent habit of attending to some meaning suggested by a word or phrase, but which bore little relation to the passage'.[53] Viewed from a different perspective, however, this *inability* to 'understand everything they read' points, once again, to the persistence of a local reading culture and a residual set of aesthetic conventions affecting Ghanaians' interpretations of English literature. Such apparent failures of comprehension point to the emergence of a distinctive reading culture in the colonial period.

This book has described the complex, diverse ways in which 'British West African' authors and readers responded, not only to colonial and missionary notions of African literacy, but also to the debates about education, marriage, literature and language taking place in West Africa between the 1900s and the 1940s. The inception of creative writing in the region closely parallels the emergence of a vociferous English-language press, itself an integral part of the trans-Atlantic and paracolonial networks which grew up alongside the British colonial presence in West Africa.

Local newspapers from the colonial period provide a consistent source of information about West African reading culture and the changing lifestyles of the educated minority, particularly in Ghana where editors and journalists adopted the role of preachers and opinion-makers rather than reporters, treating their profession as a kind of 'calling' in which they moralised about society through short stories and set up discussions involving readers. Offering 'eloquent sermon[s]' alongside news items,[54] Ghanaian newspapers contain rich seams of information relating to literacy and readers, for debates and wars of words were staged regularly in editorials and letters pages. Editors and columnists played a critical role in facilitating public discussions, and they encouraged a vibrant reading culture in the country. 'Send in your candid opinions and views on great questions', editors declared at regular intervals;[55] 'We shall be happy to place as much space in this journal as we possibly can, at the disposal of contributors'.[56] In response to these calls, the literate community offered themselves as arbiters of 'national problems' in a largely illiterate country.

Over the decades, Ghanaian readers benefited from the atmosphere of discursive freedom nurtured by the African-owned press, writing to editors and participating in debates about Syrian traders, polygyny, cocoa prices, male unemployment, marriage and cinema-going amongst youths. Newspaper editors deliberately encouraged 'protracted controversy',[57] and their appeals for readers to become involved in ethical debates neatly capture the issues that I have addressed in this book. Participating in a literary culture in which written interventions were the norm, in the five or six decades prior to independence West African readers seem to have evolved a set of complex literary values for themselves, centred upon the 'literary activism' encouraged by the newspapers of the period.

The African reading culture which emerged in colonial Ghana was anything but silent and solipsistic, as in European models of post-Enlightenment reading culture. Reader participation reaped high praise in editorials: 'We cannot help sympathising with the efforts of these public spirited contributors to save the country from the impending moral collapse', wrote the editor of the *African Morning Post* in the midst of one fierce debate about the moral decadence of church singing bands.[58]

As with the readers, the Ghanaian authors featured in this book participated in these newspaper debates, taking sides in discussions of ethical topics. Writing for 'native' rather than metropolitan readerships, they produced didactic, idealistic tales which revolved around the central themes of love and marriage. Narrative preoccupations did of course emerge and shift during the four decades covered by this book: but perhaps the most surprising feature to emerge from the material presented here is the remarkable aesthetic cohesion linking the earliest narratives by 'been-to' authors such as J. E. Casely Hayford and Kobina Sekyi with later novels by 'never-beens' such as R. E. Obeng. In most of the narratives discussed in this book, the printed text allows authors to generate moral guidelines on the topics of marriage, money and romantic affairs. In so doing, these novelists attempted to arouse readers to transform their personal worlds for the better; they tried to assert control over one of the few areas of life in the colony that it was possible for readers positively to transform; in the long term, by intervening in the institution of marriage, they also sought to prevent the nation from falling into disarray. As 'Marjorie Mensah' warned in 1935, 'a national calamity' will hit the Gold Coast if female promiscuity is allowed to continue, for local girls are the mothers of tomorrow, responsible for the moral training of their children.[59] Predictions such as this generated at least one powerful full-length play in the 1930s, *A Woman in Jade*, and a great deal of popular fiction in the 1940s, 1950s and 1960s, aimed at morally correcting the behaviour of young women in the Gold Coast.

Literacy meant different things to different social groups in colonial West Africa, but it also created a meaningful, shared reference point for the broad spectrum of readers who jostled for positions in the modern state. In order to get a sense of the power of the concept of literacy (and its real social and economic effects), this book has attempted to reconstruct some of the attitudes towards reading held by West Africans in the early years of the twentieth century. Literate Africans were a vociferous group with diverse personal and political ambitions. Taken en masse, they caused problems for the colonial administration throughout British West Africa, but their shifting political allegiances and internal divisions prevent an easy homogenisation of the category of 'West African reader'. In the Gold Coast, for example, diverse readerships emerged during the colonial period. Some individuals, particularly the lawyers from the coast, born into established, wealthy families, used reading and writing to seek political leadership roles; meanwhile others – such as the early non-elite authors and members of literary clubs – sought primarily to educate themselves and to set their local communities upon the path of 'self-development'.

Nevertheless, Ghanaian readers possess a solid, distinctive reading culture of their own. Contemporary concepts of literary value probably derive from the notions of 'good' reading set in place during more than a century of missionary literary activity in the country, combined with the narrative conventions of a lively folktale tradition and the concepts of 'literary activism' and 'ethical reading' which were generated in the African-owned press. Surprisingly little differentiates contemporary readers' expectations from the aesthetic values expressed by young readers in the 1930s. Just as *Advice to Young Men* helped one reader in 1935 to 'know how to play the game of life' and just as *Alice in Wonderland* was praised in the same year for the way the heroine 'became obedient when she was reduced to a small strip of a girl',[60] so too Ghanaian readers in the late 1990s continue to insist upon the morally instructive nature of fiction. In the words of one young man, authors should 'write powerful messages in their novels, about the essence of moral upright-ness in a society, thus critically spelling out the norms of morals in the society'.[61] 'Writers should always write novels that will uplift the image of morality by creating morally sound heroes', agrees a student from Cape Coast, expressing a unanimous sentiment amongst contemporary Ghanaian readers.[62] International West African authors may have broken away from this heritage, but literary activism and ethical reading remain the popular interpretive modes at the local level. In a remarkable instance of continuity, to this day Ghana remains a country where locally pub-lished authors fulfil readers' demands for up-to-date moral guidance, and where readers operate within a finely tuned reading culture passed down and refined through the decades.

Notes

1 *TWA*, 16 March 1933: 2.
2 *TWA*, 27 February 1935: 2.
3 Gold Coast Government, 1923: 385.
4 NAG, CSO 18/1/144, 1933.
5 *Ibid.*
6 Gold Coast Government, 1929–30: 32.
7 Anon., 1928: 19.
8 Gold Coast Government, 1930–31: 38.
9 Appiah, 1990: 15.
10 *Ibid.*, 16–17.
11 *Ibid.*, 17.
12 *Ibid.*
13 Appiah, 1990: 16–17; emphasis added.
14 Gold Coast Government, 1929–30: 32.
15 Smith, 1929: 6–7.
16 NAG, CSO 18/1/144: n.pag.
17 *Ibid.*
18 Rattray, 1927–28: 6.
19 The significance of the African teacher did not pass unnoticed by education-ists, particularly in the missionary sector: many pamphlets were published between the 1930s and 1950s containing practical advice on teaching meth-ods and moral advice about the teacher's position as a role model in the com-munity (e.g. Jowitt, 1932, 1934; Austin, 1956).
20 Gold Coast Government, 1930–31: 38; emphasis added.
21 Cited in *GCT*, 18 February 1939: 11.

22 *Ibid.*
23 Cited in Smith, 1929: v.
24 Gold Coast Government, 1904b: 129.
25 Gold Coast Government, 1906: 35.
26 Gold Coast Government, 1915: 63.
27 RHL, MSS.Afr.s.1755: 3.
28 *Ibid.*
29 Baudert, 1931: 526.
30 Kingsley Williams, 1937: 4–5.
31 Neill and Kingsley Williams, 1937: 25.
32 Kingsley Williams, 1931: 5.
33 *NDT*, 7 January 1933: 12.
34 Kingsley Williams' abridgement of this latter text appeared in 1933, containing a rendering of Charles and Mary Lamb's version of *The Tempest* which represents the plot thus: 'There was a certain island in the sea, on which there lived only an old man, whose name was Prospero, and his daughter Miranda, a very beautiful young lady' (p. 9). Caliban is not described as an inhabitant but as 'an ugly monster', hated by Ariel whom Prospero has 'freed' through his magic (*ibid.*). This unsubtle fairytale rendering of *The Tempest* bears out J. B. Danquah's complaint against 'reduced' books of this type, that they compromise the 'rich flexibility and mellow classicity' of English literature and stifle an interest in the nuanced meanings available in the language (*AMP*, 14 October 1937: 2).
35 RHL, MSS.Brit.Emp.s.282: 5.
36 See *AMP*, 5–9 October 1937: 2.
37 See Danquah, *AMP*, 11–16 October 1937.
38 See Colonial Office, 1943: 33.
39 RHL, MSS.Brit.Emp.s.282, October 1939: 4. The Prince of Wales College at Achimota was Guggisberg's pet scheme, founded in 1924 and offering a prototype for African language teaching in other schools.
40 *Ibid.*
41 *Ibid.*, 4–5.
42 Appiah, 1990.
43 *AMP*, 9 July 1938: 12.
44 *Ibid.*, 2.
45 *Ibid.* Note Danquah's intriguing use of the word 'baboo'. Clearly, verbosity is not simply a West African 'problem' but a trans-colonial one with Indian precedents. It seems that the educated 'natives' in anglophone colonies stretching from Cairo to Bombay were expressing a sense of excitement and discovery as they played with the resources provided by the English language.
46 *Ibid.*
47 *Ibid.*
48 *Ibid.*
49 *Ibid.*
50 *TWA*, 23 April 1934: 2.

51 Even the schoolboys at Achimota composed vernacular plays in the 1930s in which 'The European was invariably depicted as a stiff wooden figure, furiously angry, barking out incomprehensible orders and incapable of listening patiently' (Ward, 1991: 175).

52 De Mestral, 1959: 7.

53 Gurrey, 1949: 23.

54 *GCT*, 14 September 1929: 2.

55 *AMP*, 7 July 1938: 3.

56 *AMP*, 12 July 1938: 2.

57 *Ibid.*

58 *Ibid.*

59 *TWA*, 10 January 1935: 2.

60 NAG, CSO 18/1/144.

61 Questionnaire, July 1997.

62 Questionnaire, January 1998.

Bibliography

Archival material

Locations and classmarks have been indicated for archival material.

National Archives of Ghana, Accra (NAG)

CSO 18/1/33. Colonial Office. 1935. *Memorandum on the Education of African Communities*. London: HMSO.

CSO 18/1/83. *New Script for Languages Spoken on the Gold Coast*.

CSO 18/1/144. Methodist Book Depot. 1935–36. *Essay Competitions: Report on an Essay Competition Held in the Gold Coast in Dec/Jan 1935/36*.

CSO 18/6/93. Gold Coast Education Department. 1933. *Report on the Work of the Teacher Training Classes of Achimota College*.

CSO 18/6/94. Gold Coast Education Department. 1934. *Report on the Training Classes, Achimota*.

CSO 18/6/96. Gold Coast Education Department. 1930. *Inspection of Achimota Training College for Teachers*.

RG 3/1/15. Gold Coast Education Department. 1953–57. *Books Recommended for Primary Schools*.

RG 3/1/144. Sister Angela of Our Lady of the Apostles Training College, Cape Coast, 24 November 1931. *Handbook of Suggestions for Gold Coast Teachers*.

RG 3/1/168. School Literature Committee. 1931–33. 'Letter from J. C. de Graft Johnson, Assistant Secretary for Native Affairs, 26 April 1932, to Director of Education'.

RG 3/1/175. Gold Coast Education Department. 1930. *New English Paper for Standard VII Examination*.

RG 3/1/225. R. E. Obeng. *Stories from Ghana History by Mr R. E. Obeng*.

RG 3/1/315. G.S.R.A. *Appeal to the Patriotic Ga Man and Woman*. April/May 1945.

National Archives of Ghana, Cape Coast (NAG[CC])

ACC 2/64. 1907. *Constitution of the Gold Coast A.R.P.S., 1907*.

ACC 80/64. 1922–39. *Gold Coast A.R.P.S. Correspondence File No. 3*.

ACC 80/64. 1949. *The Gold Coast A.R.P.S. Correspondence File No. 8*.

ACC 383/64. *Letters to and from W. E. G. Sekyi, 1938*.

ADM 12/5/157. 1932. *Confidential Diaries of the Honourable Commissioner, Central Province (C. E. Skene)*.

ADM 23/1/463. *Native Languages and Literature*.

ADM 23/1/692. 1926. *Propaganda Work by the Gold Coast A.R.P.S. against the Provincial Councils of Chiefs*.

ADM 23/1/726. *Confidential Diaries, Saltpond District, 1936–1940*.

Ofori-Atta, Nana. 1931. 'Memo to Hon. Commissioner, Eastern Province, Koforidua'.

Power, G. 1933. 'Memo to the Hon. Colonial Secretary from Gerald Power, Director of Education, Gold Coast', in *Native Languages and Literature*.

Methodist Missionary Archives at the School of Oriental and African Studies (SOAS, MMS)

SOAS, MMS.257 (box). Methodist Missionary Society Sub-Committee on African Literature. 1924–50:

1929a, 'Visit of Rev A. E. Southon to Gold Coast, December'.

1929b, 'Russell Roseveare's report'.

1930, 'London Committee, minutes of July 10th'.

1932, 'A brief history of the Wesleyan Methodist Book Depot, 1882–1932'.

1933, 'Balance sheet statement'.

1939, 'Report on the Methodist Book Depot'.

1943, 'Secondary Education for Girls: report of the commission appointed by the synod of the Methodist Church of the Gold Coast, January'.

1944, 'Wesley Girls' High School, Cape Coast, June'.

1950a, 'Statement by the Book Steward – Gold Coast Book Depots'.

1950b, 'Balance sheet statement'.

1950c, 'Book supplies in the Gold Coast'.

Rhodes House Library, University of Oxford (RHL)

1934. 'The Entry of Seditious Literature into the Gold Coast'.

Chapman, D. A. n.d. 'Changing patterns of reading: the West African Library Association annual lecture'.

Danquah, J. B. 1939. 'Memorandum on inadequate reading'.

Greaves, L. B. n.d. 'The church in the Gold Coast: pacifier, but not appeaser'. Unpublished manuscript.

MSS.Afr.s.1527. *Colonial Office Correspondence and Cuttings, 1934–1939*.

MSS.Afr.s.1755. *The Development of Education in Pre-Independence Ghana (Contributions from Various Sources, 1981–2)*.

MSS.Afr.s.1985 (box 2). J. G. Griffith in *Memoirs of Gold Coast Wives, 1926–1963*.

MSS.Afr.s.2279. S. Ward. 1926–45. *Diary of Sylvia Ward*.

MSS.Brit.Emp.s.282. *Reverend C. Kingsley Williams Papers, 1927–1934*.

Wallace-Johnson, I. T. A., files on.

Other material

Abedi-Boafo, J. [1938] 1946. *And Only Mothers Know: A Thrilling Discovery in Conjugal Life*. Aburi: Mfantsiman Press.

—— 1944. *Modern Problems in Gold Coast Elementary Schools*. Mampong, Akwapim: no publisher.

Achebe, C. 1966. *A Man of the People*. Oxford: Heinemann.

—— [1972] 1975. 'What do African intellectuals read?', in C. Achebe, *Morning Yet on Creation Day*, pp. 38–41. London and Ibadan: Heinemann Educational Books.

Achimota Library Catalogue. 1935. Achimota: Achimota Press.

Achimota Review. 1937. Achimota: Achimota Press.

Ackah, C. A. 1988. *Akan Ethics: A Study of the Moral Ideas and the Moral Behaviour of the Akan Tribes*. Accra: Ghana Universities Press.

Adepoju, A., and Oppong, C. (eds.). 1994. *Gender, Work and Population in Sub-Saharan Africa*. Geneva, London and Portsmouth (NH): International Labour Office, James Currey and Heinemann.

Adi, H. 1998. *West Africans in Britain, 1900–1960: Nationalism, Pan-Africanism and Communism*. London: Lawrence and Wishart.

African Morning Post (AMP) (Accra), June 1935–September 1938; May–November 1954.

Agbodeka, F. 1972. *Ghana in the Twentieth Century*. Accra: Ghana Universities Press.

Agovi, J. E. K. 1989. 'The origin of literary theatre in colonial Ghana, 1920–1957'. Unpublished manuscript. Institute of African Studies Library, Legon: Af PN 2977.Ag72.

—— 1990. 'A duel [*sic*] sensibility: the short story in Ghana, 1944–80', in E. N. Emenyonu (ed.), *Literature and Black Aesthetics*, pp. 247–71. Ibadan: Heinemann Educational Books (Nigeria).

—— n.d. 'Theatre, law and order in pre-colonial Africa'. Unpublished manuscript. Institute of African Studies Library, Legon: Af PN 2979.Ag71.

Akyeampong, E., and Obeng, P. 1995. 'Spirituality, gender, and power in Asante history', *International Journal of African Historical Studies* 28 (3), 481–508.

Alliker Rabb, M. 1995. 'Angry beauties: (wo)manly satire and the stage', in Gill, 1995: 127–58.

Allman, J. 1993. *The Quills of the Porcupine: Asante Nationalism in an Emergent Ghana*. Wisconsin: University of Wisconsin Press.

—— and Tashjian, V. 2000. *'I Will Not Eat Stone': A Women's History of Colonial Asante*. Portsmouth, NH, Oxford and Cape Town: Heinemann, James Currey and David Philip.

Amadiume, I. 1987. *Male Daughters, Female Husbands: Gender and Sex in an African Society*. London: Zed Books.

Amarteifio, V. [1967] 1985. *Bediako the Adventurer*. Accra: Amaa Books Ltd.

Anderson, Benedict. [1985] 1991. *Imagined Communities: Reflections on the Origin and Spread of Nationalism*. London: Verso.

Angmor, C. 1996. *Contemporary Literature in Ghana, 1911–1978: A Critical Evaluation*. Accra: Woeli Publishing Services.

Anon. 1918. "'The Anglo-Fanti'' – an appreciation', *West Africa*, 28 September, 581.

Anon. 1928. 'Editorial', 'English' and 'Domestic Work', *The Teacher's Journal* 1, 3–28.

Anon. 1929a. 'CMS Niger Mission anniversary sermon', *Western Equatorial Africa Church Magazine* 34 (423), 11–15.

Anon. 1929b. 'The training of village teachers in Africa', *International Review of Missions* 18 (70), 231–49.

Anon. 1932. 'Graded library lists', *Books for Africa* 2 (3), 36–9.

Anon. 1935. 'The African teacher's library', *Books for Africa* 5 (3), 41–4.

Anon. 1936. 'Texts for translation', *Books for Africa* 6 (3), 39–40.

Anon. 1937. 'Vernacular publications', *Books for Africa* 7 (3), 45.

Anon. 1938. 'Preparation of book lists for libraries', *Books for Africa* 8 (1), 7–9.

Anon. 1939. 'A survey of literature in African languages', *Books for Africa* 9 (1), 1939, 4–12.

Anon. 1940. 'Books for the African home', *Books for Africa* 10 (3), 36.

Anon. 1941. 'Vernacular publications', *Books for Africa* 11 (2), 29.

Anon. 1951. 'A book sales experiment in Eastern Nigeria', *Books for Africa* 21 (2), 21–4.

Appadurai, A. 1996. *Modernity at Large: Cultural Dimensions of Globalization*. Minneapolis and London: University of Minneapolis Press.

—— 2000. 'Grassroots globalization and the research imagination', *Public Culture* 12 (1), 1–19.

Appiah, J. 1990. *Joe Appiah: The Autobiography of an African Patriot*. New York: Praeger.

Appiah, K. 1992. *In My Father's House: Africa in the Philosophy of Culture*. London: Methuen.

Arhin, K. 1986. 'A note on the Asante *akonkofo*: a non-literate sub-elite, 1900–1930', *Africa* 56 (1), 25–31.

Armstrong, N. 1987. *Desire and Domestic Fiction: A Political History of the Novel*. New York and Oxford: Oxford University Press.

Arnold, M. [1869] 1938. *Culture and Anarchy: An Essay in Political and Social Criticism*. London: Macmillan and Co.

Ashcroft, Bill. 2001. *Post-Colonial Transformation*. London: Routledge.

——, Griffiths, G., and Tiffin, H. 1989. *The Empire Writes Back: Theory and Practice in Post-Colonial Literatures*. London: Routledge.

Assimeng, M. 1986. *Saints and Social Structures*. Accra: Ghana Publishing Corporation.

Atiemo, A. O. 1993. *The Rise of the Charismatic Movement in the Mainline Churches in Ghana*. Accra: Ghana Universities Press.

Attoh-Ahuma, S. R. B. [1911] 1971. *The Gold Coast Nation and National Consciousness*. London: Frank Cass and Co.

Austin, F. A. 1956. 'The village school teacher', *Gold Coast Education* 1, 19–25.

Austin, G. 1993. 'Indigenous credit institutions in West Africa, c.1750–c.1960', in G. Austin and K. Sugihara (eds.), *Local Suppliers of Credit in the Third World, 1750–1960*, pp. 93–159. Basingstoke and New York: Macmillan and St Martin's Press.

Baeta, Rev. C. G. 1946. *Hints to Authors of Vernacular Books*. London: Sheldon Press.

Baku, D. K. 1987. 'An Intellectual in Nationalist Politics: The Contribution of Kobina Sekyi to the Evolution of Ghanaian National Consciousness'. Unpublished D.Phil. thesis, Sussex: University of Sussex.

Bame, K. 1985. *Come to Laugh: African Traditional Theater in Ghana*. New York: Lillian Barber Press.

Barber, K. [1981] 1997. 'Popular reactions to the petro-naira', in K. Barber (ed.), *Readings in African Popular Culture*, pp. 91–8. London, Bloomington and Oxford: International African Institute, Indiana University Press and James Currey.

—— 1987. 'Popular arts in Africa', *The African Studies Review* 30 (3), 1–78.

—— 2000. *The Generation of Plays: Yoruba Popular Life in the Theater*. Bloomington and Indianapolis: Indiana University Press.

Barnes, S. 1986. *Patrons and Power: Creating a Political Community in Metropolitan Lagos*. Manchester and London: Manchester University Press and the International African Institute.

Baron Holmes, A. B. 1972. 'Economic and Political Organizations in the Gold Coast, 1920–1945'. Unpublished Ph.D. thesis, Chicago: University of Chicago.

Bartels, F. L. 1965. *The Roots of Ghana Methodism*. Cambridge and Accra: Cambridge University Press and Methodist Book Depot.

Barton, T. 1946. 'Confidential Memo Ref. No.4276/34, 9 May, to Miss Evans, Librarian, British Council'. Private collection, E. Evans.

Baudert, S. 1931. 'Thoughts and reflections on the education of Africans', *International Review of Missions* 20 (80), 525–33.

Bhabha, H. K. 1994. *The Location of Culture*. London: Routledge.

Blay, J. Benibengor. 1944. *Emelia's Promise*. Accra: Benibengor Book Agency.

—— 1945. *After the Wedding*. Accra: Benibengor Book Agency.

—— [1947] 1971. *Be Content with Your Lot*. Aboso: Benibengor Book Agency.

—— 1969. *Alomo*. Aboso: Benibengor Book Agency.

—— 1970. *Coconut Boy*. Accra: West African Publishing Co.

Blumer, Rev. R. C. 1931. *The Aim of the Curriculum*. Achimota: Achimota College Press.

—— 1933. *The Case for Achimota*. Achimota: Achimota College Press.

Blyden, E. W. [1887] 1967. *Christianity, Islam and the Negro Race*. Edinburgh: Edinburgh University Press.

Boyce Davies, C. 1994. *Black Women, Writing and Identity: Migrations of the Subject*. London: Routledge.

Brackett, D. G. 1934. 'Books the African wants to read', *Books for Africa* 4 (2), 23–5.

Browning, J. D. (ed.). 1983. *Satire in the Eighteenth Century*. New York and London: Garland Publishing.

Buell, R. L. 1928. *The Native Problem in Africa*, vol. I. New York: Macmillan.

Butler, J. 1990. *Gender Trouble*. London: Routledge.

Cardinall, A. W. 1924. *A Gold Coast Library*. London: Francis Edwards.

Carr, K. 1901. *Miss Marie Corelli*. London: Henry J. Drane.

Casely Hayford, A. C., and Rathbone, R. 1992. 'Politics, families and freemasonry in the colonial Gold Coast', in J. F. Ade Ajayi and J. D. Y. Peel (eds.), *People and Empires in African History: Essays in Memory of Michael Crowder*, pp. 143–60. London: Longman.

Casely Hayford, J. E. 1903. *Gold Coast Native Institutions*. London: Sweet and Maxwell.

—— [1911] 1966. *Ethiopia Unbound: Studies in Race Emancipation*. London: Frank Cass.

Censor. 1912. *Don't: A Manual of Mistakes and Improprieties More or Less Prevalent in Conduct and Speech*. London, Melbourne and Toronto: Ward, Lock and Co.

de Certeau, M. 1984. *The Practice of Everyday Life*. Berkeley: University of California Press.

Chartier, R. 1995. *Forms and Meanings: Texts, Performances and Audiences from Codex to Computer*. Philadelphia: University of Pennsylvania Press.

Christian Council of the Gold Coast. 1952. 'Campaigns for literacy', *Books for Africa* 22 (3), 7–8.

Clifford, J. 1997. *Routes: Travel and Translation in the Late Twentieth Century*. Cambridge, MA: Harvard University Press.

Cobbett, W. [1830] 1980. *Advice to Young Men and (Incidentally) to Young Women in the Middle and Higher Ranks of Life in a Series of Letters Addressed to a Youth, a Bachelor, a Lover, a Husband, a Father, and a Citizen or Subject*. Oxford: Oxford University Press.

Cohen, A. 1981. *The Politics of Elite Culture: Explorations in the Dramaturgy of Power in a Modern African Society*. Berkeley: University of California Press.

Cole, C. M. 1997. '"This is actually a good interpretation of modern civilisation": popular theatre and the social imaginary in Ghana', *Africa* 67 (3), 363–88.

—— 2001. *Ghana's Concert Party Theatre*. Indiana: Indiana University Press.

Collins, J. 1994. *Highlife Time*. Accra: Anansesem Publications.

Collins, James. 1995. 'Literacy and literacies', *Annual Review of Anthropology* 24, 75–93.

Collins, J., and Richards, P. 1982. 'Popular music in West Africa: suggestions for an interpretative framework', in D. Horn and P. Tagg (eds.), *Popular Music Perspectives*, vol. I, pp. 111–41. Goteborg: International Association for the Study of Popular Music.

Colonial Office. 1935. *Memorandum on the Education of African Communities*. London: HMSO.

—— 1943. *Mass Education in African Society*. London: HMSO.

—— 1945. *Report of the Elliot Commission on Higher Education in Africa*. London: HMSO.

—— 1948a. *Education for Citizenship in Africa*. London: HMSO.

—— 1948b. *Report of the Commission of Enquiry into Disturbances in the Gold Coast, 1948*. London: HMSO.

Connell, R. W. 1987. *Gender and Power: Society, the Person and Sexual Politics*. Cambridge: Polity Press.

Corelli, M. 1895. *The Sorrows of Satan: Or the Strange Experience of One Geoffrey Tempest, Millionaire. A Romance*. London: Methuen and Co.

Cromwell, A. 1986. *An African Victorian Feminist: The Life and Times of Adelaide Smith Casely Hayford, 1868–1960*. London: Frank Cass.

Crookall, R. E. 1961. *School Libraries in West Africa*. London: University of London Press.

Cruickshank, B. 1853. *Eighteen Years on the Gold Coast of Africa*. London: Hurst and Blackett.

Cunard, N. (ed.). [1934] 1970. *Negro: An Anthology*. New York: Frederick Ungar.

Dagadu, Rev. P. K. 1951. 'Youth to-day', in *The Church in the Town*. Accra: Christian Council of the Gold Coast.

Dagenais, J. 1994. *The Ethics of Reading in Manuscript Culture: Glossing the* Libro de buen amor. Princeton, NJ: Princeton University Press.

Daily Mail (London), January 1923–June 1924.

Dako, K. 1994. 'R. E. Obeng's *Eighteenpence*: a critical review', *Journal of Black Studies* 24 (3), 344–67.

—— 1998. 'Introduction', in R. E. Obeng [1943], *Eighteenpence*, xi–xix. Accra: Sub-Saharan Publishers.

—— 1999. 'Changing gender roles in a colonial novel: R. E. Obeng's *Eighteenpence* as socio-historical source material', *Institute of African Studies Review* 15, 1. Manuscript provided by author, n.pag.

Dann, A. 1923. 'Letter to the Editor', *Western Equatorial Africa Church Magazine* 28 (343), 13–16.

Danquah, J. B. 1928. *Cases in Akan Law*. London: George Routledge and Sons.

—— 1943. *The Third Woman: A Play in Five Acts*. London: Lutterworth Press.

—— [1943] 1971. 'Foreword', in R. E. Obeng, *Eighteenpence*, pp. vii–ix. Tema: Ghana Publishing Corporation.

——— 1970. *Journey to Independence and After (J. B. Danquah's Letters), 1947–1965, Vol. I: 1947–1948.* Edited by H. K. Akyeampong. Accra: Waterville Publishing House.

Davies, M. W. (compiler). 1897. *The Marie Corelli Birthday Book.* London: Hutchinson and Co.

Davis, N. Z. 1981. 'Printing and the people: early modern France', in H. J. Graff (ed.), *Literacy and Social Development in the West: A Reader*, pp. 69–95. Cambridge: Cambridge University Press.

Denzer, L. R. 1992. 'Gender and decolonization: a study of three women in West African public life', in J. F. Ajayi and J. D. Y. Peel (eds.), *People and Empires in African History: Essays in Memory of Michael Crowder*, pp. 217–36. London and New York: Longman.

DePorte, M. 1983. 'Swift and the License of Satire', in J. D. Browning (ed.), *Satire in the Eighteenth Century*, pp. 53–69. New York and London: Garland Publishing.

Dickens, C. 1837. *The Posthumous Papers of the Pickwick Club.* London: Chapman and Hall.

Dickson, K. A. 1995. *Prohibitions: A Study in African Traditional Education.* Accra: Macmillan and Unimax.

Dixon, R. 1995. *Writing the Colonial Adventure: Race, Gender and Nation in Anglo-Australian Popular Fiction, 1875–1914.* Cambridge: Cambridge University Press.

Donkoh, W. J. 1994. 'Colonialism and Cultural Change: Some Aspects of the Impact of Modernity upon Asante'. Unpublished Ph.D. thesis, Birmingham: Centre of West African Studies, University of Birmingham.

Dougall, J. W. C. (ed.). 1931. *The Village Teacher's Guide: A Book of Guidance for African Teachers.* London: Sheldon Press.

Down, I. M. 1999. Written Interview, 5 August, UK.

Drah, F. K. 1971. 'Introduction', in J. W. de Graft Johnson, *Towards Nationhood in West Africa.* London: Frank Cass and Co.

Dussinger, J. A. 1998. 'Introduction', in S. Richardson, *Samuel Richardson's Published Commentary on Clarissa, 1747–65*, vol. III, pp. vii–xxxii. London: Pickering and Chatto.

Eagleton, T. 1982. *The Rape of Clarissa.* Minneapolis: University of Minnesota Press.

East, R. 1947. 'The preparation of African literature', in L. J. Lewis and M. Wrong (eds.), *Towards a Literate Africa*, pp. 14–23. London: Longman.

Edsman, B. M. 1979. *Lawyers in Gold Coast Politics c. 1900–1945, from Mensah Sarbah to J. B. Danquah.* Sweden: Acta Universitatis Upsaliensis.

Evans, E. 1956. *The Development of Public Library Services in the Gold Coast.* London: The Library Association.

——— 1999. Interview with Stephanie Newell, 13 July, Oxford.

—— n.d., Original typescript of 'Work with children', in *A Tropical Library Service: The Story of Ghana's Libraries*. Private collection, E. Evans.

Ezeigbo, A. 2000. Interview with Stephanie Newell, 8 March, Pietermarizburg.

Federico, A. R. 2000. *Idol of Suburbia: Marie Corelli and Late-Victorian Literary Culture*. Virginia: University Press of Virginia.

Fiawoo, F. K. [1943] 1983. *The Fifth Landing Stage: A Play in Five Acts*. Accra: Sedco Publishing.

Finnegan, R. 1981–82. 'Oral literature and writing in the South Pacific', *Pacific Quarterly* 7 (2), 22–36.

Finnegan, R. 1988. *Literacy and Orality: Studies in the Technology of Communication*. Oxford: Basil Blackwell.

Foster, P. [1965] 1998. *Education and Social Change in Ghana*. London: Routledge.

Fraser, A. 1914. 'A missionary's wife among African women', *International Review of Missions* 3 (11), 456–69.

Fraser, A. G. 1924–28. *Letters to Prayer Helpers: Achimota Letters, 1924–28*.

—— 1925. 'Aims of African education', *International Review of Missions* 14 (56), 514–22.

Fuller, R. A. 1928. *African Life Readers: Primer*. London: Ginn and Co.

Gadzekpo, A. 2001. 'Women in the West African Newspapers'. Unpublished Ph.D. thesis, Birmingham: University of Birmingham.

Garlick, P. C. 1967. 'The development of Kwahu business enterprise in Ghana since 1874 – an essay in recent oral tradition', *Journal of African History* 8 (3), 463–80.

Garriock, L. H. 1940. *Women's Work in the Home*. London: Sheldon Press.

Genette, G. 1997. *Paratexts: Thresholds of Interpretation*. Transl. J. E. Lewin. Cambridge: Cambridge University Press.

Gérard, A. S. 1981. *African Language Literatures: An Introduction to the Literary History of Sub-Saharan Africa*. Harlow: Longman.

Gill, J. E. (ed.). 1995. *Cutting Edges: Postmodern Critical Essays on Eighteenth Century Satire*. Knoxville, TN: University of Tennessee Press.

Gocking, R. 1999. *Facing Two Ways: Ghana's Coastal Communities under Colonial Rule*. Maryland, New York and Oxford: University Press of America.

Gold Coast Government. 1904a. *Report on the Education Department for the Year 1904*. Accra: Government Press.

—— 1904b. *The Questions Set at the Examinations for Junior Clerkships Civil Service Examination*. London: Government Printing Office.

—— 1906. *Report on the Education Department for the Year 1906*. Accra: Government Press.

—— 1907. *Report on the Education Department for the Year 1907*. Accra: Government Press.

—— 1913. *Report on the Education Department for the Year 1913*. Accra: Government Press.

—— 1914. *Report on the Education Department for the Year 1914*. Accra: Government Press.

—— 1915. *Education Rules Passed by the Board of Education and Approved by the Governor*. London: Waterlow and Sons for the Gold Coast Colony.

—— 1922. 'The Governor's address to the Legislative Council', *The Gold Coast Gazette* 20, 271.

—— 1923. 'The Governor's address to the Legislative Council', *The Gold Coast Gazette (Extraordinary)* 24, 385–91.

—— 1923–24. *Report on the Education Department for the Year 1923–4*. Accra: Government Press.

—— 1924–26. *Report on Achimota College*. Accra: Government Printing Department.

—— 1925. 'The Governor's address to the Legislative Council, 7 August', *The Gold Coast Gazette for the second half of 1925*, 1037–116.

—— 1927–28. *Report on the Education Department for the Year 1927–8*. Accra: Government Press.

—— 1927–29. *Report on Achimota College*. Accra: Government Printing Department.

—— 1929–30. *Report on the Education Department for the Year 1929–30*. Accra: Government Press.

—— 1929–33. *Reports on Achimota College*. Achimota: Achimota College Press.

—— 1930. *Report of the Fourth Achimota Educational Conference Held on the 15th and 16th January*. Accra: Government Printer.

—— 1930–31. *Report on the Education Department for the Year 1930–1*. Accra: Government Press.

—— 1934. *Report on Achimota College*. Achimota: Achimota College Press.

—— 1939. *Report of the Committee Appointed in 1938 by the Governor of the Gold Coast Colony to Inspect the Prince of Wales College, Achimota*. Accra: Government Printing Office.

—— 1939–40. *Report on Achimota College*. Achimota: Achimota College Press.

—— 1946. *Report on Higher Education in West Africa*. Accra: Government Printer.

Gold Coast Library Board. 1955. 'African reading', *Books for Africa* 25 (4), 72.

—— 1948. *Report of the Commission of Enquiry into Disturbances in the Gold Coast*. London: HMSO.

Gold Coast Nation (GCN) (Cape Coast), March 1912–July 1916.

Gold Coast Observer (GCO) (Cape Coast), February–November 1942.

Gold Coast Times (GCT) (Cape Coast), March 1874–February 1885; February 1929–June 1940.

Gold Diggers of 1935. Dir. Busby Berkely. USA: Warner Brothers.

Goody, J. 1987. *The Interface between the Written and the Oral*. Cambridge: Cambridge University Press.

—— 2000. *The Power of the Written Tradition*. Washington, DC, and London: Smithsonian Institution Press.

Gordon, L. [1923] 1925. *White Cargo: A Play of the Primitive*. Boston: The Four Seas Company.

Graham, C. K. 1971. *A History of Education in Ghana: From the Earliest Times to the Declaration of Independence*. London: Frank Cass and Co.

Greaves, Rev. L. B. 1932. 'A reading scheme', *Books for Africa* 2 (3), 35–9.

Guggisberg, Brig-Gen. Sir G. 1924. *The Keystone*. London: Simpkin, Marshall, Hamilton, Kent and Co.

—— 1927. 'The development of Africa' in *Selected Papers from the Transactions of the Canadian Military Institute, 1926–27*, pp. 1–15. Toronto: Bureau of Canadian Resources.

Gurrey, P. 1949. *The Teaching of English Literature in West Africa*. Accra: University College of the Gold Coast.

Guyer, J. (ed.). 1995. *Money Matters: Instability, Values and Social Payments in the Modern History of West African Communities*. Portsmouth, NH, and London: Heinemann and James Currey.

Gyekye, K. 1987. *Tradition and Modernity: Philosophical Reflections on the African Experience*. New York and Oxford: Oxford University Press.

Hackett, R. I. J. 1989. *Religion in Calabar*. Berlin: Mouton de Gruyter.

—— 1997. 'Radical Christianity and pentecostalism'. Unpublished seminar paper. Birmingham: Centre of West African Studies Seminar.

Hagan, K. O. 1968. 'The Growth of Adult Literacy and Adult Education in Ghana, 1901–1957'. Unpublished B.Litt. thesis, Oxford: University of Oxford.

Hannerz, U. 1990. 'Cosmopolitans and locals in world culture', in M. Featherstone (ed.), *Global Culture: Nationalism, Globalization and Modernity*, pp. 237–51. London: Sage.

—— 1992. *Cultural Complexity: Studies in the Social Organization of Meaning*. New York: Columbia University Press.

Harman, H. A. 1932. 'Lending libraries in Gold Coast schools', *Books for Africa* 2 (4), 53–5.

Hastings, A. 1997. *The Construction of Nationhood: Ethnicity, Religion and Nationalism*. Cambridge: Cambridge University Press.

Henry, W. 1927. *The Confessions of a Tenderfoot 'Coaster': A Trader's Chronicle of Life on the West African Coast*. London: H. F. and G. Witherby.

Hewitt, K. (ed.). 1933. 'Introduction', in *Us Women: Extracts from the Writings of Marjorie Mensah*, pp. 5–7. London: Elkin Mathews and Marrot Ltd.

Hill, R. A. (ed.). 1986. *The Marcus Garvey and Universal Negro Improvement Association Papers, Vol. V: September 1922–August 1924*. Berkeley, Los Angeles, and London: University of California Press.

Hobsbawm, E. 1987. *The Age of Empire, 1875–1914*. London: Weidenfeld and Nicolson.

Holroyd, M. 1997. *Bernard Shaw: The One-Volume Definitive Edition*. London: Chatto and Windus.

Hurston, Z. N. [1934] 1970. 'Characteristics of Negro expression', in N. Cunard (ed.), *Negro: An Anthology*, pp. 24–31. New York: Frederick Ungar.

Ikiddeh, I. 1971. 'The character of popular fiction in Ghana', in C. Heywood (ed.), *Perspectives on African Literature*, pp. 106–16. London: Heinemann.

Irele, A. 1972. 'The African publisher', in A. Irele (ed.), *Publishing in Nigeria*, pp. 501–2. Bendel State: Ethiope Publishing Corporation.

Jahoda, G. 1959. 'Love, marriage and social change', *Africa* 29, 177–89.

Jenkins, R. G. 1985. 'Gold Coast Historians and their Pursuit of the Gold Coast Pasts, 1882–1917'. Unpublished Ph.D. thesis, Birmingham: Centre of West African Studies, University of Birmingham.

—— 1990. 'Subverting "law imperialism": the journalist-historians of the Gold Coast-Ghana: 1882–1888', paper presented to the African Studies Association of the USA, 1–4 November.

Johnson, J. W. de Graft. [1928] 1971. *Towards Nationhood in West Africa: Thoughts of Young Africa Addressed to Young Britain*. London: Frank Cass.

Jones, T. J. 1922. *Education in Africa: A Study of West, South, and Equatorial Africa by the African Education Commission*. New York: Phelps-Stokes Fund.

Jones-Quartey, K. A. B. 1967. 'Kobina Sekyi: a fragment of biography', *Research Review (Institute of African Studies, University of Ghana)* 4 (1), 74–8.

—— 1974. *A Summary History of the Ghana Press, 1822–1960*. Accra-Tema: Ghana Publishing Corporation.

Jowitt, H. 1932. *Principles of Education for African Teachers*. London: Longmans, Green and Co.

—— 1934. *Suggested Methods for the African School*. London: Longmans, Green and Co.

Kay, G. B. [1972] 1992. *The Political Economy of Colonialism in Ghana: Documents and Statistics, 1900–1960*. Hampshire: Gregg Revivals.

Killingray, D. 1989. 'The role of black evangelists in the spread of Christianity in the Gold Coast, 1830–1900', *Christianity and History Newsletter* 4, 5–19.

Kimble, D. 1963. *A Political History of Ghana: The Rise of Gold Coast Nationalism, 1850–1928*. Oxford: Clarendon Press.

Kimble, H. 1956. 'A reading survey in Accra', *Universitas* 2 (3), 77–81.

Kingsley Williams, C. 1931. 'Introduction to series', in *Longmans' Simplified English Series: The Coral Island by R. M. Ballantyre*, pp. 5–6. London: Longmans, Green and Co.

—— 1933. *The Tempest*. Abridged from the Lambs' *Tales from Shakespeare*. London: Longmans, Green and Co.

—— 1937. 'Fundamental ideas' in *Achimota Review, 1927–1937*, pp. 4–7. Achimota: Achimota Press, 1937.

Kress, G. 1997. *Before Writing: Rethinking the Paths to Literacy*. London and New York: Routledge.

Lagos Times and Gold Coast Colony Advertiser (Lagos), January 1881–October 1882.

Lagos Weekly Record (LWR) (Lagos), April 1917–June 1919.

Langley, J. A. 1970. 'Modernization and its malcontents: Kobina Sekyi of Ghana and the re-statement of African political theory (1892–1956)', *Research Review (Institute of African Studies, University of Ghana)* 6 (3), 1–61.

—— [1971] 1974. 'Introduction', in K. Sekyi *The Blinkards: A Comedy and the Anglo-Fanti – A Short Story*, pp. xiii–xxix. Ibadan and Accra: Heinemann and Readwide Publishers.

—— 1973. *Pan-Africanism and Nationalism in West Africa, 1900–45: A Study in Ideology and Social Classes*. Oxford: Clarendon Press.

Larkin, B. 1997. 'Indian films and Nigerian lovers: media and the creation of parallel modernities', *Africa* 67 (3), 406–40.

Laubach, F. C. 1948. *Teaching the World to Read: A Handbook for Literacy Campaigns*. London and Redhill: Lutterworth Press.

Leavis, Q. D. [1932] 1965. *Fiction and the Reading Public*. Middlesex: Penguin Books.

Leith-Ross, S. [1939] 1965. *African Women: A Study of the Ibo of Nigeria*. London: Routledge and Kegan Paul.

Lewis, J. 2000. *Empire State-Building: War and Welfare in Kenya, 1925–52*. Oxford and Ohio: James Currey and Ohio University Press.

Lewis, L. J., and Wrong, M. (eds.). 1947. *Towards a Literate Africa*. London: Longman.

Li, A. 1995. '*Asafo* and destoolment in colonial southern Ghana, 1900–1953', *International Journal of African Historical Studies* 28 (2), 327–57.

Lindfors, B. (ed.). 1999. *Africans on Stage: Studies in Ethnological Show Business*. Bloomington and Cape Town: Indiana University Press and David Philip.

Macmillan, A. [1928] 1968. *The Red Book of West Africa*. London: Frank Cass.

Magdalen, Sister M. C. 1928. 'Education of girls in southern Nigeria', *International Review of Missions* 17 (67), 505–14.

Mann, K. 1985. *Marrying Well: Marriage, Status and Social Change Among the Educated Elite in Colonial Lagos*. Cambridge: Cambridge University Press.

Marie Corelli Calendar: A Quotation from the Works of Marie Corelli for Every Day in the Year. 1913. London: Frank Palmer.

Markley, R. 1995. '"Credit Exhausted": satire and scarcity in the 1690s', in Gill, 1995: 110–26.

Masters, B. 1978. *Now Barabbas was a Rotter: The Extraordinary Life of Marie Corelli*. London: Hamish Hamilton.

Mathetes. 1904. 'Learning a native language', *Western Equatorial Africa Diocesan Magazine* 11 (6), 100–2.

Mba, N. E. 1982. *Nigerian Women Mobilised: Women's Political Activity, 1900–1965*. Berkeley, CA: Institute of International Studies.

McCaskie, T. C. 1986. 'Accumulation, wealth and belief in Asante history, II: the twentieth century', *Africa* 56 (1), 3–23.

—— 1995. *State and Society in Pre-Colonial Asante*. Cambridge: Cambridge University Press.

Meinhof, C. 1927. 'The soul of an African language', *International Review of Missions* 16 (61), 76–84.

Mensah, M. (pseud. Mabel Dove). 1933. *Us Women: Extracts from the Writings of Marjorie Mensah*, ed. K. Hewitt. London: Elkin, Mathews and Marrot.

—— 1934. 'A woman in Jade', *Times of West Africa*, 7 November–31 December.

de Mestral, Claude. 1954. 'Christian literature for Africa', *International Review of Missions* 63 (172), 436–42.

—— 1959. *Christian Literature in Africa*. London: ICCLA.

Meyer, B. 1999. *Translating the Devil: An African Appropriation of Pietist Protestantism*. Edinburgh: Edinburgh University Press.

Miescher, S. F. 1997. 'Of documents and litigants: disputes on inheritance in Abetifi – a town of colonial Ghana', *Journal of Legal Pluralism* 39, 81–119.

—— 2000. '"My own life": writing and subjectivity in a Ghanaian teacher's diary – Boakye Yiadom (Akasease Kofi) of Abetifi, Kwawu'. Paper presented at the Social Histories of Reading in Africa conference, 8–9 July, University of Cambridge.

—— 2001a, 'The making of Presbyterian teachers: masculinities and programs of education in colonial Ghana', in L. Lindsay and S. F. Miescher (eds.), *Men and Masculinities in Modern Africa*, Portsmouth, NY: Heinemann.

—— 2001b, 'The life histories of Boakye Yiadom (Akasease Kofi of Abetifi, Kwawu): exploring the subjectivity and "voices" of a teacher-catechist in colonial Ghana', in L. White, S. F. Miescher and D. W. Cohen (eds.), *African Words, African Voices: Critical Practices in Oral History*. Indiana: Indiana University Press.

Mills, Lady D. 1924. *The Arms of the Sun*. London: Duckworth and Co.

Mirror (Lagos), November 1888.

Moore, D., and Guggisberg, Maj. F. G. 1909. *We Two in West Africa*. London: William Heinemann.

de Moraes Farias, P. F. and Barber, K. (eds.). 1990. *Self-Assertion and Brokerage: Early Cultural Nationalism in West Africa*. Birmingham: Centre of West African Studies, University of Birmingham.

Nartey, G. P. S. 1978. 'Imaginative Literature of the Dangme Peoples of South-East Ghana'. Unpublished MA thesis, Accra: University of Ghana.

Native. A. (pseud.). 1886–87. 'Marita, or the folly of love', in the *Western Echo*, January 1886–December 1887.

Ndebele, Njabulo. [1990] 2001. 'Rediscovery of the ordinary', in S. Newell (ed.), *Readings in African Popular Fiction*. Oxford, London and Indiana: James Currey, International African Institute and Indiana University Press.

Neill, H. C., and Kingsley Williams, C. 1937. 'The Teaching of English', in *Achimota Review, 1927–1937*, pp. 25–7. Achimota: Achimota Press.

Newell, S. 1996. 'From the brink of oblivion: the anxious masculinism in Nigerian market literatures', *Research in African Literatures* 27 (3), 50–67.

—— 2000. *Ghanaian Popular Fiction: 'Thrilling Discoveries in Conjugal Life' and Other Tales*. Oxford and Ohio: James Currey and Ohio University Press.

—— 2001. 'Paracolonial networks: some speculations on local readerships in colonial West Africa', *Interventions*, 3 (3), 336–54.

Ngugi wa Thiong'o. 1982. *Devil on the Cross*. Oxford: Heinemann.

Nigerian Daily Times (NDT) (Lagos), February 1930–October 1935.

Nkrumah, K. 1957. *The Autobiography of Kwame Nkrumah*. Edinburgh: Thomas Nelson and Sons.

Nkrumah, M. 1993. 'Creative Writing and the Nationalist Sentiment in Pre-Independence Ghana'. Unpublished M.Phil. thesis, Accra: University of Ghana.

Obeng, R. E. [1943] 1971. *Eighteenpence*, with Foreword by J. B. Danquah. Tema: Ghana Publishing Corporation.

—— [1943] 1998. *Eighteenpence*, introduced by K. Dako. Legon: Sub-Saharan Publishers.

—— 1952. *Tete Romafoɔ Akokoɔdurofoɔ Bi. Stories from Roman History*. Accra. Scottish Mission Book Depot.

Obiechina, E. 1973. *An African Popular Literature: A Study of Onitsha Market Pamphlets*. Cambridge: Cambridge University Press.

—— 1975. *Culture, Tradition and Society in the West African Novel*. Cambridge: Cambridge University Press.

Oduyoye, M. A. 1995. *Daughters of Anowa: African Women and Patriarchy*. New York: Orbis Books.

Ofori, H. [1958] 1968. 'The Literary Society', in F. M. Litto (ed.), *Plays from Black Africa*, pp. 295–312. New York: Hill and Wang.

—— 1999. Interview with Stephanie Newell, 13 September, Accra.

Ofosu-Appiah, L. H. 1975. *Joseph Ephraim Casely Hayford: The Man of Vision and Faith*. Accra: J. B. Danquah Memorial Lectures.

Ogali, O. A. 1956. *Veronica My Daughter*. Onitsha: Appolos Brothers Press.

Ojo, A. M. 1988a. 'Deeper Christian life ministry: a case study of the charismatic movements in western Nigeria', *Journal of Religion in Africa* 18 (2), 141–62.

—— 1988b. 'The contextual significance of the charismatic movements in independent Nigeria', *Africa* 58 (2), 175–92.

Ong, W. J. 1982. *Orality and Literacy: The Technologizing of the Word*. London: Routledge.

Opoku-Agyemang, N. J. 1995. 'Lest we forget: a critical survey of Ghanaian women's literature', *Asemka* 8, 61–84.

—— 1997. 'Recovering lost voices: the short stories of Mabel Dove-Danquah', in S. Newell (ed.), *Writing African Women: Gender, Popular Culture and Literature in West Africa*, pp. 67–80. London and New Jersey: Zed Books.

Ormsby-Gore, W. G. A. 1926. *Report by the Hon. W. G. A. Ormsby-Gore, MP, on his Visit to West Africa during the Year 1926.* London: HMSO.

Osei-Nyame, K. 1999. 'Pan-Africanist ideology and the African historical novels of self-discovery: the examples of Kobina Sekyi and J. E. Casely Hayford', *Journal of African Cultural Studies* 12 (2), 137–53.

Panford, K. 1996. 'Pan-Africanism, Africans in the diaspora and the OAU', *The Western Journal of Black Studies*, 20 (3), 140–50.

Parker, H. T. 1925. 'Introduction', in L. Gordon, *White Cargo: A Play of the Primitive*, pp. 7–11. Boston: Four Seas Company.

Peel, J. D. Y. 1968. *Aladura: A Religious Movement among the Yoruba.* London and Oxford: International African Institute and Oxford University Press.

Priebe, R. [1978] 1997. 'Popular writing in Ghana: a sociology and a rhetoric', in K. Barber (ed.), *Readings in African Popular Culture*, pp. 81–91. London, Bloomington and Oxford: International African Institute, Indiana University Press and James Currey.

—— 1986. 'The novel (Ghana)', in A. S. Gérard (ed.), *European-Language Writing in Sub-Saharan Africa*, vol. II, pp. 827–43. Budapest: Akadémiai Kiadó.

—— (ed.). 1988. *Ghanaian Literatures.* New York: Greenwood Press.

Prosser, A. R. G. 1953. 'Mass education and its relationship to formal education', *Gold Coast Education (prev. Teachers' Journal)* 1, 14–23.

Rabinowitz, P. J. 1987. *Before Reading: Narrative Conventions and the Politics of Interpretation.* Ithaca and London: Cornell University Press.

Ransom, T. 1999. *Miss Marie Corelli: Queen of Victorian Bestsellers.* Stroud: Sutton Publishing.

Rathbone, R. 1993. *Murder and Politics in Colonial Ghana.* Yale and London: Yale University Press.

—— 1995. 'The Gold Coast, the closing of the Atlantic slave trade, and Africans of the diaspora', in S. Palmié (ed.), *Slave Cultures and the Cultures of Slavery*, pp. 55–66. Knoxville, TN: University of Tennessee Press.

—— 1996. 'Defining *Akyemfo*: the construction of citizenship in Akyem Abuakwa, Ghana, 1700–1939', *Africa* 66 (4), 506–25.

Rattray, R. S. 1927–28. 'Report by the Special Commissioner for Anthropology for the year April 1927–March 1928', in *Departmental Reports*, Accra: Government Press.

Riby-Williams, K. 1999. Interview with Stephanie Newell, 25 August, Accra.

Richardson, S. [1747–48] 1985. *Clarissa, or the History of a Young Lady.* Middlesex: Viking.

Richter, J. 1929. 'Missionary work and race education in Africa', *International Review of Missions* 18 (69), 74–82.

Riley, L. 1995. 'Mary Davy's satiric novel *Familiar Letters*: refusing patriarchal inscription of women', in Gill, 1995: 206–32.

Rimmer, D. 1992. *Staying Poor: Ghana's Political Economy, 1950–1990*. Oxford: Pergamon Press.

Robertson, C. 1984. *Sharing the Same Bowl: A Socioeconomic History of Women and Class in Accra, Ghana*. Bloomington, IN: Indiana University Press.

Rushdie, S. 1991. *Imaginary Homelands: Essays and Criticism*. New York and London: Viking and Granta.

Ruskin, J. [1865] 1909. *Sesame and Lilies and the King of the Golden River*. New York and London: Macmillan.

Said, E. W. 1993. *Culture and Imperialism*. London: Vintage.

Sampson, M. J. 1937. *Gold Coast Men of Affairs (Past and Present)*. London: Arthur H. Stockwell Ltd.

Sanneh, L. 1983. *West African Christianity: The Religious Impact*. London: Hurst.

—— 1995. *Translating the Message: The Missionary Impact on Culture*. New York: Orbis Books.

Sarbah, J. M. [1898] 1968. *Fanti Customary Laws*. London: Frank Cass and Co.

—— [1906] 1968. *Fanti National Constitution*. London: Frank Cass and Co.

Sassen, S. 2000. 'Spatialities and temporalities of the global: elements for a theorization', *Public Culture* 12 (1), 215–32.

Sekyi, H. V. H. [1973] 1997. 'Foreword', in K. Sekyi, *The Blinkards: A Comedy and the Anglo-Fanti – A Short Story*, vii–xi. Ibadan and Accra: Heinemann and Readwide Publishers.

Sekyi, K. [1915] 1974. *The Blinkards*. Ibadan: Heinemann.

—— [1915 and 1918] 1997. *The Blinkards: A Comedy, and The Anglo-Fanti – A Short Story*. Ibadan and Accra: Heinemann and Readwide Publishers.

—— 1918. 'The Anglo-Fanti', *West Africa*. 25 May – 28 September.

Senanan, W. 1975. *The Genesis of the Novel in Thailand*. Bankok: T.W.P.

Senanu, K. E. 1972. 'Creative writing in Ghana', in A. W. Kayper-Mensah and H. Wolff (eds.), *Ghanaian Writing: Ghana as Seen by Her Own Writers as well as by German Authors*, pp. 13–31, Tübingen: Horst Erdmann Verlag.

Shami, S. 2000. 'Prehistories of globalization: Circassian identity in motion', *Public Culture* 12 (1), 177–204.

Showalter, E. 1991. *Sexual Anarchy: Gender and Culture at the Fin de Siècle*. London: Bloomsbury.

Sibley, J. 1930a. 'Preface' to *African Life Readers* series. London: Ginn and Co.

—— 1930b. *African Life Readers: Teachers' Manual*. London: Ginn and Co.

Sierra Leone Weekly News (SLWN) (Freetown), September 1884–January 1934.

Simensen, J. 1975a. 'Nationalism from below: the Akyem Abuakwa example', in R. Addo-Fening *et al.* (eds.), *Akyem Abuakwa and the Politics of the Inter-War Period in Ghana*, pp. 31–57. Basel and Accra: Basel Africa Bibliography and the Historical Society of Ghana.

—— 1975b. 'The *Asafo* of Kwahu, Ghana: a mass movement for local reform under colonial rule', *International Journal of African Historical Studies* 8, 383–406.

Simonton, I. V. [1912] 1928. *Hell's Playground*. London: Thornton Butterworth.

Smiles, S. [1859] 1997. *Self-Help; with Illustrations of Character and Conduct*. London: Routledge/Thoemmes Press.

Smith, E. W. 1929. *Aggrey of Africa: A Study in Black and White*. London: Student Christian Movement.

Smith, N. 1966. *The Presbyterian Church of Ghana, 1835–1960: A Younger Church in a Changing Society*. Accra: Ghana Universities Press.

Spectator (Accra), January–February 1939; January–March 1953.

Stock, B. 1993. 'Afterword', in *The Ethnography of Reading*, ed. J. Boyanrin, pp. 270–5. Berkeley, CA: University of California Press.

Stone, R. L. 1974. 'Colonial Administration and Rural Politics in South-Central Ghana, 1919–51'. Unpublished Ph.D. thesis, Cambridge: University of Cambridge.

Stratton, F. 1994. *Contemporary African Literature and the Politics of Gender*. London and New York: Routledge.

Street, B. 1984. *Literacy in Theory and Practice*. Cambridge: Cambridge University Press.

—— (ed.). 1993. *Cross-Cultural Approaches to Literacy*. Cambridge: Cambridge University Press.

Sutherland, E. 1970. *The Original Bob*. Accra: Anowuo Educational Publications.

Swanzy, H. 1958. 'A note of history', in *Voices of Ghana: Literary Contributions to the Ghana Broadcasting System, 1955–57*, pp. 11–15. Accra: Ministry of Information and Broadcasting.

Theroux, P. 1985. 'Stranger on a train: the pleasures of railways', in P. Theroux, *Sunrise with Seamonsters*, pp. 126–35. London: Hamish Hamilton.

Thomas, Rev. O. 1931, 'The teaching of reading', *Books for Africa* 1 (3), 34–5.

The Times (London), May 1924–March 1927.

The Times of West Africa (*TWA*) (Accra), March 1931–March 1935.

Twumasi, E. Y. 1971. 'Aspects of Politics in Ghana, 1929–1939'. Unpublished D.Phil. thesis, Oxford: University of Oxford.

Ugonna, N. 1966. 'Introduction' in J. E. Casely Hayford, *Ethiopia Unbound: Studies in Race Emancipation*. London: Frank Cass.

—— 1977. 'Casley Hayford: the fictive dimension of African Personality', *Ufahamu* 7 (2), 159–71.

United Society for Christian Literature (USCL). 1944. *Literacy, Laubach and the Missionary Society*. London and Redhill: Lutterworth Press.

Utchay, I. K. [1934] 1970. 'White-manning in West Africa', in N. Cunard (ed.), *Negro: An Anthology*, pp. 432–9. New York: Frederick Ungar.

Walker, A. 1956. 'Some ideas on reading', *Gold Coast Education* 1, 33–39.

Walters, J. J. [1891] 1994. *Guanya Pau: A Story of an African Princess*. London and Lincoln: University of Nebraska Press.

Walton, W. H. M., 1929, 'The secular press as an evangelistic agency', *International Review of Missions* 18 (69), 111–20.

Ward, I. C. 1941. 'African languages and literatures', *Books for Africa* 11 (4), 49–52.

Ward, W. E. F. 1937. 'Problems of class teaching', in *Achimota Review, 1927–1937*, pp. 13–24. Achimota: Achimota Press.

—— 1991. *My Africa*. Accra: Ghana Universities Press.

Watt, I. 1956. *The Rise of the Novel: Studies in Defoe, Richardson and Fielding*. London: Chatto and Windus.

Webb, R. K. 1955. *The British Working-Class Reader, 1790–1848: Literacy and Social Tension*. London: George Allen and Unwin.

West, M. 1926. *Learning to Read a Foreign Language: An Experimental Study*. London: Longmans, Green and Co.

Westermann, D. 1925. 'The place and function of the vernacular in African education', *International Review of Missions* 14 (53), 25–36.

White Cargo. 1942. Dir. Victor Saville. USA: Metro-Goldwyn-Mayer.

Wilks, I. 1993. *Forests of Gold*. Ohio: Ohio University Press.

Wilson, C. E. 1921. 'A survey of Christian literature in African languages', *International Review of Missions* 39, 376–84.

—— 1926. 'The provision of a Christian literature for Africa', *International Review of Missions* 15 (59), 506–14.

Winterbottom, J. M. 1931. *Longmans' Simplified English Series:* The Coral Island *by R. M. Ballantyre*. London: Longmans, Green and Co.

Wrong, M. 1931. 'Magazine for African villages', *Books for Africa* 1 (2), 18–23.

—— 1934. *Africa and the Making of Books: Being a Survey of Africa's Need for Literature*. London: ICCLA.

—— 1938. 'Christian literature for Africa', *International Review of Missions* 27 (107), 509–15.

Yankah, K. 1984. 'The folktale as "true" experience narrative', *Folklore Forum* 2 (17), 220–9.

Young, R. J. C. 1995. *Colonial Desire: Hybridity in Theory, Culture and Race*. London: Routledge.

Young, R. R. 1936. 'A scheme for vernaculars', *Books for Africa* 6 (4), 55–7.

—— 1945. *Teaching Adults to Read*. London: Sheldon Press.

Young, Rev. T. C. 1933. 'Developing a reading sense', *Books for Africa* 3 (1), 5–7.

Zimbardo, R. 1995. 'The semiotics of Restoration satire', in Gill, 1995: 23–42.

Zomchick, J. 1995. 'Satire and the bourgeois subject in Frances Burney's *Evelina*', in Gill, 1995: 347–66. Note: 'n.' after a page reference indicaes the number of a note on that page.

Index